TIME PAST
MEMORIES OF PROUST AND OTHERS

PAUL MORAND, JEAN COCTEAU, AND
MARIE SCHEIKÉVITCH

TRANSLATED BY
FRANÇOISE DELISLE

TIME PAST

Memories of Proust and Others

MARIE SCHEIKÉVITCH

With Illustrations

BOSTON AND NEW YORK
HOUGHTON MIFFLIN COMPANY
The Riverside Press
1935

COPYRIGHT, 1935, BY HOUGHTON MIFFLIN COMPANY

ALL RIGHTS RESERVED INCLUDING THE RIGHT TO REPRODUCE
THIS BOOK OR PARTS THEREOF IN ANY FORM

The Riverside Press
CAMBRIDGE · MASSACHUSETTS
PRINTED IN THE U.S.A.

CONTENTS

I.	GOOD-BYE TO RUSSIA	1
II.	PARIS	24
III.	MADAME ARMAN DE CAILLAVET AND ANATOLE FRANCE	67
IV.	ROUND ABOUT JULES LEMAÎTRE AND MADAME DE LOYNES	113
V.	MARCEL PROUST	154
VI.	WIDOR	217
VII.	BONI DE CASTELLANE	230
VIII.	GABRIELE D'ANNUNZIO	235
IX.	JOSEPH REINACH	242
X.	THE SALON OF MADAME DE PIERREBOURG	247
XI.	FORAIN — JACQUES-ÉMILE BLANCHE	258
XII.	LORD BALFOUR	266
XIII.	ANNA DE NOAILLES — JEAN COCTEAU	276
XIV.	PAUL VALÉRY — A POST-WAR PUBLISHER: BERNARD GRASSET — PAUL MORAND — JULIEN GREEN	286
INDEX		305

ILLUSTRATIONS

Paul Morand, Jean Cocteau, and Marie Scheikévitch
Frontispiece

Anna de Noailles	42
L'Abbé Mugnier	80
Marcel Proust	154
Forain	258
Lord Balfour	266
Paul Valéry	290

TIME PAST

« I »

GOOD-BYE TO RUSSIA

LITTLE girls have no say in the decisions of their parents.

Our father informed us one summer day at our country house that we were not going back to Moscow at the end of the holidays; we were to leave Russia for good, and he had decided to settle in Paris.

I was greatly upset by this news. Rushing off to the corner of the estate which was my very own domain, with its little garden, its tiny patch of vegetables, and its miniature grotto, I sat in my swing and began to dream. I gazed at the little alley of fuchsias we had recently planted, my brother Victor and I; I turned distracted eyes upon the great trees encompassing the lawn. To go away!... to leave one's own country, all that is familiar, the people one loves — what anguish! But with the fickleness of childhood I was at the same time mentally envisaging the attractions of the journey; I was stirred by a longing to cross a great portion of Europe and to make the acquaintance of France, that unknown land. By such unexpected prospects I was plunged, time and again, now in joy, now in despair. I dwelt sorrowfully on the incidents of our everyday life, but then my spirits would soar with hope and my mind be filled with curiosity.

Time Past

That year we had left Moscow a month earlier than usual, because our house had been chosen for the accommodation of the King of Saxony and his retinue during the festivities for the coronation of Nicholas II. From a balcony I had watched the fairylike imperial cortège as it entered the city. I had been fascinated by the beauty and splendour of the Tsar's young queen, with her glittering diadem and her snow-white dress studded with precious stones. And then, although a little girl, I had been taken to the coronation, and in the evening to the wonderful Kremlin illuminations. But upon these glowing recollections followed that of the 'Hadinka' disaster. To give the common people a share in the general rejoicings, the Government had organized festivities which had culminated in tragedy.

As mementoes of this great event, yellow and black handkerchiefs filled with sweetmeats and metal drinking-cups were being distributed to the crowd; so great became the stampede to obtain these gifts that several thousands of people were trampled to death on the badly drained grounds.

When we were back in the country, for two or three days after I saw an unbroken string of carts pass our gate, bearing the bodies of the dead covered with funeral wrappings. The contrast between so many radiant visions and this horrifying procession threw me into a state of feverish agitation.

Then I tried to picture in my mind what France would be like, the French and Paris.

A forgotten memory of the past returned: the French

Exhibition in Moscow; the crowd wandering around among the stalls which, as I was too small, I could not see properly; the unfamiliar music, the oasis of green plants, the French Punch-and-Judy show, and above all, in one of the most crowded parts of the great fair, the open-air waffle stall. The swift preparation of these frail delicacies powdered with sugar, their lovely, warm, vanilla-like smell, their novel taste, a flavour which I have never since found again, all returned to my mind.

And at twilight there had been a multi-coloured display of those illuminated fountains which Loie Fuller's brother had invented, the rainbow hues of which were later to serve as an inspiration for her famous dances. For many days I had kept among my toys a quaint bottle of eau de Cologne shaped like the Eiffel Tower, and this piece of glasswork made me long to know Paris, the city in which the real tower of iron lacework had sprung up.

One thing in this upheaval of our former life pleased me — the continual presence of my father; for up till then I had scarcely ever seen him for any length of time except during the holidays. At Moscow, engrossed by the law courts and the numerous business matters he had on his hands, he would shut himself up in one floor of our house, and appeared in my eyes a distant and all-powerful divinity. I knew that he was much sought after, continually consulted for advice, and that he often defended cases in the provinces. In his leisure moments he liked to find new treasures for his art collection, and devoted himself to music and painting. He maintained his sway over family life and over his children's lives only by occasional interventions, the secret of which escaped me. But, now that he was going to live abroad in leisure, it was he who was to take control of our destiny, the future of my elder sister, of my little brothers, and of myself.

Our Moscow house — how well I can still picture it at the end of the Pretchistenka opposite the fire-brigade station! And its courtyard, its two enclosed gardens alongside the Saint Mary's Institute, with poplar trees stretching their branches over the wall. In the spring, to my great delight, they showered down into our courtyard their long, fragrant, and somewhat sticky catkins. I would go and gather them up, and smell with keen pleasure their tiny little pointed leaves which resembled the beaks of those unseen birds whose chirpings were the first indication of warmer days, long before the buds had burst open upon the lilac bushes in our garden.

This house, like most in Moscow, was spacious and spread out over a large area. The ground floor was given over to my father. It comprised a study and a suite of rooms which contained the greater part of his collection of paintings and prints. The children were not allowed to venture in these. On the first floor was the long ballroom, sky-blue and white, and given an appearance of greater length by an arrangement of mirrors.

When I was very small, I was intrigued by the stucco medallions which decorated the padded chairs and the music stands, and was told that they were the profiles of famous musicians. Soon I could pick them all out: Handel and Gluck, who looked so much alike, Beethoven with his thick lower lip, and a youth, bewigged and pointed-nosed, whom I took for a hunchback, and who was none other than the young Mozart crammed into his collar. From the ceiling of this room hung procelain chandeliers displaying their flowers and multi-coloured birds.

Then followed several drawing-rooms and the living-rooms. On the other side of the passage were the dining-room and the children's studies, and at the end of the gallery an interior staircase led up to a smaller upper floor. The roomy basements were fitted for the household staff and the servants. In the courtyard were the stables and the coach-sheds.

It all seemed to me a veritable world....

Following the Russian family customs of those days, a swarm of devoted servants were included as a part of the family. From the janitor, tall Dinniss, moulded by twenty-five years of compulsory military service, with his Nicholas I side-whiskers, down to my 'Nanny,' they all remain inseparable in my earliest recollections. And on that day, seated in my swing, I called back to memory the lengthy days when I used to sit perched on the inner sill of the double-paned window in my nursery and watch the snow falling. I would stay there for hours, my nose stuck to the glass, comparing the spotless whiteness of the snowflakes with that of the cotton draught-excluders placed between the two layers of panes. When the cold grew severe, the outer glass was covered with fanciful designs: icy and transparent ferns, jagged moss, capricious intermingling patterns of leaves and branches. As soon as Nanny observed this fantastic forest in process of formation, she would make me come down from my perch, telling me that people go blind who look too long at these icy arabesques.

I was not yet steady on my legs and was afraid to venture out of my usual track, from the bed to the small armchair, from the chest of drawers to the window. On the floor I was acquainted with everything: the pattern of the carpet, the enormous oil stain caused by an accident with a night-light, and the twisted legs of the table. I used to drag myself as far as the white tiled brick slab of the great stove, always so hot and polished; I would put my hands on it and try to scribble over it with my pencil, but in vain — nothing would make any impression on it. Once I tried to make marks on it with a pair of scissors, but Nanny slapped me.

I was always chattering with her. She knew all the folk-tales and I never grew tired of listening to her telling them. But I never allowed her any variations in her choice of expressions, for I wished each time to renew the same pleasure. She would kiss me, telling me the while that a little light shone in my eyes.... But to speak with my parents was more difficult.

My room seemed to me enormous; however, I knew my way about it, whereas I was lost in the other rooms, except my mother's, which I entered every morning. She would kiss me and straightway have me taken back to the nursery. I should so much have liked to be able to examine at leisure all the wondrous things in her room!... For it was so fine, with one great shiny panel in which I could see reflexed the trinkets, the furniture, and Mamma herself buried in her pillows. Nanny only possessed a small broken bit of this puzzling contrivance, and she used to look at herself in it when she arranged her hair. I noticed the smallest details. I saw, forming on the surface of the cocoa, which Mamma was in no hurry to drink, the same sort of film which I had detested so much on my milk. I wanted to dip my finger into it, but Mamma was readier to look cross than Nanny.

As day succeeded day monotonously, Nanny spared me neither the rubbings with vinegar which made my calves tingle, nor the everlasting, insipid semolina puddings which sickened me; but sometimes, when drinking her tea, she would give me a little piece of her *bulka* (a sort of big round bun), or better still she would cram a slice of sausage into my mouth, whispering, 'Above all things don't you go and tell the Barina.' Morning and night I used to watch her attentively from my bed as she prostrated herself before the ikon. She kept the ikon lit up by a red night-lamp which she never failed to fill. She prayed with fervour, crossing herself the whole time and touching the floor with her forehead. Then she stood up again, as though relieved, and appeared to give it no further thought.

What fun it was in Mamma's absence to slip away into the kitchen! There I could touch almost everything.

Nikita, the porter, would come in, shaking the snow off his boots, and asking for a drink, and the cook, Vaevara, would offer him a steaming glass of tea.

One day I inquired: 'Nikita, where are the puppies?'

'Barischina, they've been drowned.'

I sobbed: 'Who allowed that?'

'The Barina said so. Everybody does it; you can't feed so many animals.'

I remained disconsolate; I could not believe it. I got the idea that only Mamma would tell me the truth. Just at that moment her chambermaid announced her return, and swiftly Nanny seized my hand and hurried me out of the kitchen. I dodged away from her in the passage and ran off to the library. Mamma was there, her head bent over a book.

'You here?'

'Mamma, Mamma, it's not true, tell me!'

'Who let you come in here? Where's Nanny?'

'The puppies haven't been drowned?'

'Were you all by yourself in your room?'

'Tell me, they're not dead?'

'When you are with Fräulein, she will be more strict with you.'

And without answering me, Mamma pressed the bell-push.

'She got away from me, Barina,' declared Nanny, rushing in, and she dragged me away in spite of my screams and protests.

One day Nanny was chatting gaily with Hélène, the dressmaker, through the half-open door of the nursery, which led into the linen-room. They had given me a piece of pink material on which I was very busy stitching with an endless piece of cotton thread. How was I to make a dress for my doll? I held out my work to them in vain; they would not listen. Footsteps were heard. It was Mamma. Hélène dashed off at full speed. Were they afraid of Mamma?

Nanny immediately bent over my performance with solicitude.

'You're not able to sew, little soul. What can you manage with such tiny fingers? Come, let me show you.'

Mamma seemed to be interested too.

I could not understand this sudden change. Why had Mamma driven away Hélène by her arrival and made Nanny so obliging? Mamma must have been keeping an eye on me from a distance. I was filled with emotion at the thought.

'Is Hélène at work?' Mamma asked.

'I've not heard her, Barina,' Nanny replied, without moving an eyelid.

Was it possible that grown-ups told lies?

Through the window I used to watch Nicholas, the coachman, harnessing the horses and then dressing himself. He could do that in the courtyard because, instead of taking anything off, he added on top of his ordinary clothes a wrap and his quilted coachman's uniform, which made him so stuffed that both his back and his chest appeared as cushions. His uniform was fastened at the shoulders by filigree buttons, and he wore a tightly drawn belt around his waist. After he had pulled on his felt boots, he encountered the greatest difficulty in clambering up to the driver's seat, where he rolled himself in a fur rug, took his gloves and cap from the outstretched hands of Nikita, the porter, and rammed the cap down over his ears. Firm and well propped up, he then sat bolt upright like a church steeple.

TIME PAST

What a business was a walk! How difficult it was to walk with the encumbrance of the many petticoats, woollen drawers, gaiters, and top boots then in fashion. The ermine bonnet covered with the Orenburg fichu was suffocating. In the street talking was not allowed. So one became all eyes. And one's arm ached, being dragged by Nanny as she walked ahead with long regular strides.

'Nanny, Nanny...'

She would not answer because she had met an acquaintance with whom she entered into a never-ending conversation. The gossips firmly held a child well muffled up. I could not even join the young boy, companion of such walks, who like myself was dragging along at the other end of the compact body formed by those gossiping women.

Out-of-doors, everything was growing whiter and whiter. In summer the roadway was well below the pavement, but in the winter with the piled up snow it was raised to the same level. I have quite an intimate knowledge of this element, the snow, which gradually invaded every corner until it ended by covering the whole city. Sometimes it fell like starlets on my muff; sometimes, before reaching the earth, it circled around like weightless doves' feathers; at one moment it was as round as hailstones; at another soft as rice in a pudding. A passing sleigh besmirched it somewhat and cut it into enormous cakelike slices. All along the broad street the granite milestones were almost completely buried. The snow fell without a break. In some places the sidewalk became so narrow on account of it that we had to walk in single file. Footprints were immediately covered up again and disappeared. The horses whinnied as they drew the sleighs. The drivers were so cold that they beat their arms violently across their chests to warm up again.

A sleigh would go by, a swift visitation, the snow creaking beneath its weight. The chestnut horse let fall golden, steaming dung, and a flock of ravenous pigeons at once swooped down upon it. Grey, white, ochre-coloured, with pinkish feet, there were vast numbers of these birds in Moscow, where they could multiply in all safety. For were they not an incarnation of the Holy Ghost?

I knew every house on the Pretchistenka. Some of them jutted out onto the pavement with unadorned façades; others were ornamented with rows of columns. In front of the house of the Governor-General stood two sentries with fixed bayonets, on guard in their sentry-boxes. They looked so patient, these poor soldiers, and all so very much alike! If Nanny had not told me that they were changed several times a day, I should have thought that they were always the same.

'Tell me, Nanny, what is that funny carriage? It is bigger than Mamma's brougham. It has six horses to pull it, and the drivers are wearing bashliks instead of caps. Why?'

'Don't you see that everyone is bowing down as it goes by? Look, inside is a holy man of God bearing the ikon lit up by a lamp: it is the Virgin.'

'The Virgin herself?'

'Poor little soul! It is the image of the Virgin. They take it to people who are ill. It heals the sick, so we must bow down to it very low.'

And Nanny crossed herself many times, bowed down, and made me kneel in the snow.

Night fell abruptly like an avalanche. Everything became lost to sight in the impenetrable woolly atmosphere. All of a sudden two reddish balls blazed forth in the sky and hovered in the dimness like the eyes of a fantastic monster.

'Good Heaven,' exclaimed Nanny, 'another fire!'

At the fire-station, lanterns of all colours were hoisted on long poles to indicate the direction of the disaster, which usually assumed the proportions of a catastrophe and gave rise to a panic.

I was afraid of fire, since it destroyed everything. Had it not, on one occasion, snapped up my little woolly cat as I was playing with it near the fireplace in the library? I well remembered how a spark fell into its curly fur, and how my father leaped forward, tore the toy from my hands, and threw it into the flames. I had sorrowfully watched those flames lick it and shrivel it up, until it became a blazing cinder and finally a little grey and formless heap. That was what fire did.

In my room, fast sinking into darkness, Nanny was holding me on her knees, while she sighed deeply and wiped her eyes with the back of her sleeve. I felt greatly moved and huddled close to her, this Nanny to whom I took all my troubles. She had to leave me to make way for the Fräulein whom I already disliked.

'Nanny, let me hug you in my arms to show you how much I love you. Oh, Nanny, your eyes are all red and your skin is full of little holes!'

'That's all right. Why are you looking at me like that?'

And then I realized that I had never looked at her before, and seeing her pockmarked face I understood why she got the nickname of 'cholera' among the servants.

'Why are you going away?'

'I can't tell you why.... You'll see. Perhaps another Nanny will come...'

'I'll throw her out of the window.'

'She won't be for you. You'll have a little brother or a little sister, I expect.'

Mad with jealousy I burst into tears and buried my face in her apron.

When she had gone, I remained unconsolable for many days.

One day Dinniss, the janitor, came rushing up to the nursery, all out of breath, to bring me some surprising news:

'Barischina, you must get yourself dressed. The Barine is asking for you. He wants to take you out for a walk.'

To go out for a walk with my father — what an unexpected treat, what a thing to be proud of! In feverish haste I allowed them to dress me in all the clothes necessary for a cold Moscow day, and there I was in the street, a little bundle wrapped in furs, my legs weighted down by gaiters and boots, trying to keep step with my father. So high did he tower above me that I was quite unable to see his face, which I loved. I know not what fancy had led him that day to grant me this delightful favour of a walk with him. He held my hand firmly in his, and I did my utmost to get along, bursting with joy, eager to meet someone who knew us so that I might still further enjoy an occasion as rare as it was great. We walked down the broad Pretchistenka flanked on both sides by private mansions, with their basement kitchens from which the copper saucepans (which was all I could see) glittered forth. Then suddenly my father stopped, and, from the ground upwards, I took stock of the person who had thus held up our walk.

High boots, large trousers, a spreading beard on his chest, and, in the middle of his face, two holes, his enormous nostrils, surmounted by bushy eyebrows; the man standing before us was of a stronger build than my father. Their conversation went on at such a height above me that I could catch only fragments. Finally I heard my father say: 'Leon Nikolayevich.' Later I understood this was our great Tolstoy. I should have recognized him by the mujik's garb he had adopted. He said: 'I have just received very distressing news.'

I gave all my attention to this grave voice.

'Tschaikovsky died last night in Saint Petersburg.'

I raised my eyes towards my father. His head was bowed and a tear shone on his cheek. Never had I seen him weep. His hand clenched mine, almost to hurt. But I noticed a veritable stream dripping from the white beard which swayed above my head. What was going to happen? It was so cold! Would all these little streams freeze and turn into icicles? Then Tolstoy's powerful hand obscured the scene — like a little yellow screen shutting away the misty sky — with the telegram he showed to my father. All this was a distraction for me.

Another day, when I came home from a walk, this same janitor was unable to suppress a sob as he bent down to pull off my snow-boots. I was thunderstruck to see this old soldier, hardened by military discipline, thus reduced to tears.

'Barischina,' he muttered, 'our Emperor Alexander III is dead!'

From every part of the house I heard the weeping of the other servants. Such grief gave one an idea of the common people's attachment to the dynasty and — a sign of the period — of their bewilderment and their utter submission to the Empire.

I felt so inwardly stirred by the sorrow all around me that I ran away and hid in the cupboard where the pelisses were hung. There I, in my turn, burst into tears. I can remember that moment very clearly. I knew that the servants were looking for me, but I deliberately remained hidden, my nose buried in a fur coat, repeating heart-brokenly: 'The Emperor is dead! Our Emperor is dead!'

Other pictures crowded upon each other. They revolved now around our country house at Petrovskoye Rasumovskoye, a house for which I had so much affection that I considered it my very own. I was born there one twentieth of July, on Saint Elijah's day, in the midst of thunder and lightning. A thunderstorm broke out almost regularly on that date, and the legend put this down to the passage of the prophet in his chariot hurling down the fire from heaven.

I especially remembered one marvellous day. A clear sunlight played upon the bushes. The lawns, bestrewed with flowers, had the appearance of many-coloured Persian carpets. Other lawns were adorned with thick-leaved plants, lobelia and camomile. Pebbles and sand of various shades formed patterns like those on Moorish or Turkish rugs. Such colourful fancies, whether in gardens or on printed cambrics, were a delight for me, child as I was. And the great cedar tree gave forth a delicious scent. On that day Marfa, the gardener's wife, had come to speak to me.

'A terrible thing happened last night while you were sound asleep, Barischina!'

'What happened?'

'I don't mind telling the Barischina, but she must promise not to give me away.'

And she whispered:

'Prince Schirinsky-Chekmatov's estate was burnt down. They brought the Princess and her little daughter in here. The child's only a month old. They're resting in the drawing-room. What a terrible misfortune! And such a fine estate too!'

'What, Marfa, did everything burn and I didn't hear a thing?'

'Hush! hush! You mustn't tell anyone what I've just told you, Barischina.'

'And were there not enough firemen to rescue everyone, Marfa?'

'Yes, thank God, everyone was saved. But not all the animals; there were so many. A whole circusful! Monkeys and bears, horses, dogs, not to mention the poultry!'

What an event in our everyday life, where nothing unexpected ever seemed to occur to disturb the customary routine! The fire might well have spread to us, because our estates ran side by side and our buildings were all made of timber.

Recovering from my amazement, I rushed off to the servants' quarters. What a commotion was there!... The servants were all jabbering at once, each giving his opinion about the fire. Nanny was holding forth louder than the rest.

'Nanny, why didn't you tell me about it when you were dressing me?'

'I didn't want to frighten you, duckie.'

'Let's go and see it, shall we?'

Dying with curiosity as she was, she asked nothing better. We slipped out by a side door into the drive. As I recall that scene, there comes back to my nostrils the smell of scorching and burning which greeted us. Of the whole estate ruins were all that remained. Some of the great trees in the park were uprooted, others lay on the ground. Near a flower-bed I caught sight of a shining object: a small silver spoon. It was impossible to go near the buildings, which were nothing but a mass of mud and cinders. We followed along the walls, and at the spot where the stables had been I was horrified to see the corpses of four horses, lying on their backs with their legs in the air. I could not bear to see any more.

TIME PAST

'You'll have to be on your best behaviour while the Prince and Princess are staying with us,' Nanny told me as she took me back. 'What would they think of a badly brought-up little girl?'

But the days went by, and still I had not caught a glimpse of our guests. Everyone was busy in the house. What could I do to get a peep at them?

Another warm morning. I got away from the path where I was supposed to remain under Nanny's vigilant eyes, and chased after a butterfly. I ran as fast as my legs could carry me. I did not care what scolding might follow. I seemed to hear drawing near a sound of galloping which answered my running steps. I recognized the sound of hoofs; they stopped at the foot of the steps in the courtyard. I put on speed and hid behind a bush through which I could watch what went on. I saw a long-maned black horse prancing. His whole body quivered with impatience; his trappings shone upon his glossy coat; his jaws were foam-flecked; and the soldier holding the bridle had difficulty in keeping the animal still. He pawed the ground, making sparks fly about. To whom did this fine animal belong? A tall young man emerged suddenly out of the main door. He was an officer wearing a round Astrakhan cap — you would have thought it made of caviar. His epaulets were pink. His tall slim body moved rhythmically. He looked so young! There was just the suggestion of a black moustache upon his radiant face. He said a few words to his orderly, and I saw him seize the horse and leap upon him with an ease and a gracefulness that thrilled me. He mastered the animal in a trice and controlled him with a firm hand. The horse made a few final gambols and then gave in, dashing off at full speed with his rider.

Behind my bush I stood with a throbbing heart.

'It's the Prince,' I told myself.

Never had I pictured to myself anyone so alluring. I hastened off to share my discovery with Nanny and to ask her many questions.

I displayed the greatest ingenuity in order to see once more this guest of ours. Could I but see him nearer, hear his voice! Alas, all my scheming failed. On one occasion only did my father summon his children to introduce them to our neighbours. In spite of my confusion, I raised my eyes to look at '*Him*': he was even more handsome than on horseback, and his voice was so deep. He smiled and stroked my hair. Boundless bliss filled my heart: I was entirely won to him, because, for this pleasant petting, it was my whole head he had encircled with his hand. From that day on his picture was always present to my mind, but I no longer dared speak of him. And then a still more astonishing favour — could he have guessed my admiration? On the day they left it was to me he brought in a box almost as big as myself, a doll which looked like him. It had smooth cheeks and sparkling eyes like his. Did he purposely choose me rather than my brothers? Did he sense the indefinable devotion I felt for him?... I longed to do something worthy so that he might notice me!

Back in town, at night in my little bed, my mind dwelt on him as on an unattainable dream. To see him again appeared as difficult as to get permission to bring up to my room one of the newborn puppies of Dianka, our reddish-brown, curly-eared bitch.

However, one day I was able, with Dinniss's help, to slip into the drawing-rooms when I knew the Prince was paying a visit. He recognized me, knew my name; as for me, I was able to look at him then without lowering my eyes. But I was quickly asked to leave. So quickly! I would so much have liked to stay a long time. The Prince drew me to him and kissed me; then, abashed and delighted, I heard him say to my parents: 'I am fond of your little Marie.'

Filled with pride, enraptured, my heart leaped within me. Heavens! What would I not have done for him!

Months went by, and spring came again. In Moscow the boulevards which run through the aristocratic district are like gardens bordered with magnificent trees. The children are taken there to play. Every day I joined my little friends and we engaged in our usual games.

One afternoon I noticed in the distance a slender silhouette striding swiftly forward.... How could I help recognizing him? He was like no one else....

I said to my friends: 'Listen, you all. You see that man over there? He is a friend of Papa's. Let's race to him and see who gets there first.'

An unconquerable energy spurred me on. I felt certain I would easily win and astonish him by my speed. The joy of surprising him and seeing him again gave me wings. I ran, I outdistanced all my friends, I drew near. I was going to touch him, but all at once, in my haste, so near to him, my foot caught in the root of a tree; I stumbled and fell at his feet with my nose in the dust. I choked with rage and humiliation. What an unmerited insult and what a disgrace that he should see me in such a condition, with my white piqué dress all creased and soiled!

The Prince stopped and set me on my feet again.

'You're not big enough to run so fast,' he said, 'and you frightened me.'

And to crown my confusion he lifted up my skirt and gave me a slap... like Papa! This action filled me with hatred for him. I had lost all prestige in my own eyes.

Why did the memory of my first love return to me with such intensity as I dreamed of our approaching departure?

I knew scarcely anything about the land we were going to live in. Every year my father had gone travelling abroad. Always, when he returned from France, he could not hide his enthusiasm. To him France represented the land of taste and freedom.

Freedom! This word was continually recurring in the conversation of the grown-ups. I could not understand this, because it seemed to me that one had merely to be 'grown-up' to be free.

While I was trying to accustom myself to the idea of leaving Russia, the preparations for our departure were being pushed ahead in Moscow. The furniture which my father had decided to send to Paris was being packed; and he went up to town every day to supervise himself the packing of the crates which contained his collection of prints and old paintings.

When the last morning arrived, I went all over our grounds, feeling that my heart was breaking. I wanted to see once more the park, the kitchen-garden, the familiar paths. I stopped by the pond to look once more at an old frog hopping about, and I felt greatly moved at the thought that she would henceforth have no daily watcher to see her dive into the limpid water. I leaned over to watch her for the last time, and it proved to be my own reflexion that I saw; that of a little girl with a long plait sweeping across her face, with a very serious countenance and one hand in the pocket of her travelling-coat. In my clenched fist I held a stone from the garden, a crystalline pebble I had decided to take with me. It is here still, in front of me on my desk, as I recall that far-off day.

Then came the heart-breaking and agitated leave-takings of friends and servants. Every one of those faces bathed in tears is still stamped in my memory. At last the train started, and I was at the window all the time. To cross Russia was a long business, and the immensity of this big country seemed to unroll itself like a long ribbon all the way to Berlin, this grey, ordered, and monotonous city with its wisely constructed rows of buildings. Where had gone the churches of Moscow with their dazzling domes and their grotesque architecture? The air grew thin in my lungs; I felt as though weighed down. Nonetheless, there were so many things to see when travelling that this discomfort gradually vanished during the subsequent journey to France and to Paris.

As soon as we had crossed the Belgian frontier, the sky

appeared lighter. The landscape seemed joyful — it was France. Was it perchance the land of fine weather?

A mellow sunshine bathed the countryside which was revealed to us as the train gaily passed through it.

'Mark well, children,' said my father, 'this splendid land which is going to be yours henceforth.'

Our dazzled eyes peered through the four windows. Here was Paris golden in the September sunshine; Paris with its coster-barrows laden with flowers and ripe grapes; Paris with its gay activity, its noises, its broad avenues frequented by people who seemed to take pleasure simply in loitering in the streets. Heaven! how big it was!...

Our carriage went through the city to the Louvre, so that we could see it. Then it followed the embankments and went up the Champs-Élysées. Our exclamations of wonder delighted our father.

'Didn't I promise to bring you to the most beautiful city in the world!' he said.

« II »

PARIS

IN PARIS we saw daily novel things and sights which amused and interested us. The streets offered us an enchanting scene and wielded a mysterious spell. Everything delighted us: the queer figures of the cab-drivers in overcoats with threefold capes and top hats of hard leather, the cries of the costermonger women, the stalls overflowing onto the pavement, the abundance of flowers, the floods of light streaming from the large cafés, the naïve tunes of the barrel-organs... And everywhere such harmony of lines, such a care for beauty, as much in the quiet streets of Passy and Auteuil, where the noise of the city died away, as in the impressive avenue of the Champs-Élysées with its thick traffic of resplendent carriages.

Paris, with its history told by its public buildings, with its modern layout, threw Moscow back into a primitive and savage past. There hovels and sumptuous dwellings alternated in discordant proximity; here palaces and parks blended the diversity of their style in surroundings of balanced and sober grandeur. The mildness of the climate made me forget the inclement winters of my childhood. The homogeneous appearance of a crowd, dressed in elegant or respectable middle-class clothes, was a contrast to the all too numerous destitute people one met in Russia shoulder to shoulder with merchants and boyars. In the autumn sun everything seemed here so comfortable and well arranged that we were soon won over to this unique city.

In the scarcely completed Rue Greuze, overlooking the Avenue Henri Martin, my father chose a flat which seemed to us, in spite of its great size, to be of very modest proportions after our quarters in Russia. We were much too excited, however, by the change in our life and too busily engaged in accustoming ourselves to new ways of living to pay much attention to this.

Moreover, Paris was celebrating the Franco-Russian alliance. There was something strangely endearing for us in these joyful celebrations in honour of Nicholas II, so we felt less as foreigners, since we had just arrived from the country the sovereigns of which were being welcomed so cordially. Remembering the illuminations at the Coronation festivities and comparing them with these, so wonderful in our eyes during these October evenings, we felt that life was opening out before us under favourable auspices.

My younger brother and I spoke French less fluently than German and English, but nevertheless we quite easily managed to make ourselves understood. The same did not apply to my youngest brother, who knew only Russian, and therefore found himself completely cut off.

What struck us as absolutely miraculous was the persistence of the fine weather, the fact that the horse-chestnut trees in the Avenue Henri Martin — trees we had not known before — bloomed for the second time that year, while their foliage seemed everlasting. In Moscow we had brief and broiling summers followed by harsh rainy autumns. There, we were accustomed, as soon as we returned from the country, to being plunged straight into a dense white winter, against which we had to defend ourselves for months at a stretch. My first conception of freedom took the form of this deliverance from the struggle against the cold. In France there were no double-paned windows needing to be blocked up; nothing was abrupt in the transition from one season to the next.

Our life was becoming organized; my father was making provision for our education. I rather dreaded the hour when I should have to face the head mistress of the school I was to attend, for I was afraid of appearing ignorant. The drive from the Trocadéro to the Rue Alphonse de Neuville seemed endless. On my way my mind pictured the strict discipline which used to rule us, my school friends and me, at our Russian school, under the exalted patronage of the Grand Duchess Serge. There, stringent rules were imposed upon us and we had to wear a uniform void of the slightest adornment. The appearance of the small house before which our carriage stopped seemed to clash so strongly with my idea of a school that I thought the cabman had made a mistake.

No preliminary tests wounded my self-esteem. The head mistress talked a while with my father, and finally remarked: 'Your daughter will go into the same class as other children of her age; she must try to keep up with them. The carriage will call for her each morning and will bring her back at five o'clock.'

How perfectly simple! No formalities or ceremonial. I felt greatly relieved, and, without any further apprehension, I fully enjoyed the remaining fortnight of the holidays.

On my first day of school life I could not get over seeing all these little girls chattering, laughing, and talking to each other freely about their holidays. They asked me many questions, for I was an object of curiosity, but they charmingly welcomed me. To arrive from Russia at that particular time was an added attraction in view of the festivities. My name, so difficult to pronounce, my hesitant speech, earned for me a host of little kindnesses and attentions. I had to tell them all I knew about my country, and when, upon being asked, I spoke a sentence in Russian, the fun and laughter knew no end.

'Come and listen to her. She's speaking an awfully difficult language, and its alphabet has got no less than thirty-six letters.'

The same day at playtime I learned something which made me thoughtful. One wild and high-spirited girl, who had at once made pals with me by pulling my pigtail, said to me: 'You know, you're very pretty! But why on earth are you dressed so frightfully?'

Her compliment delighted me; but as for my dress, I had never given it a thought, and remained taken aback by my new friend's criticism. So I began to examine my companions. There was, indeed, a great difference between the arrangement of their hair and that of my own: curls and ribbons were adornments to their young faces, whereas my hair was brushed back and plaited into thick smooth pigtails. Their frocks, trimmed with frills and pleats, were made of bright-coloured silk or wool, whereas my brown frock had no trimming whatever. I discovered that little girls in France were smart, and I made up my mind to become so.

My father never congratulated my brother or myself when we got good marks, for he would not have it we could get anything else; he made it a point of honour for us. Very quickly my young brother became the best pupil in his class at the Lycée Janson, and he kept this position all through his school life. We worked without need of encouragement or scolding, for we possessed good memories and were spurred on by pride. Mine was one day put to a harsh test. Proud of the compliments I had received for a French composition, I was bold enough to show it to my father. He read it and found it good, but upon reflexion asked me if I had not in part copied it from the encyclopaedia. I felt so humiliated that henceforth I never showed him my home work again. At school I was very happy and among my companions forgot my mother's absence. My friends often came to visit me at home, and my father, who was very hospitable, received them in Russian style. An old lady, the widow of a judge, managed the housekeeping, and her supervision continually reminded us of the presence of a stranger in our midst and robbed us of all privacy.

In Paris my father surrounded himself mainly with

artists, writers, painters, and engravers. A close friend of the Director of the Cabinet des Estampes, of the Keeper of the Records at the Comédie Française and of the directors and curators of the Bibliothèque Nationale, he wrote for the *Gazette des Beaux-Arts*, visited all the exhibitions, and added to his collection of engravings by following the sales. This collection was made up of the whole work of Rembrandt and Dürer, magnificent engravings of the seventeenth century, all the delightful marvels of the eighteenth, and most of the dainty Dutch masters.

To roam about and explore the old districts of Paris never lost its charm for my father. He often took a ride on top of the three-horse omnibus on the Trocadéro-Gare de l'Est line to watch from aloft the life of the streets. He went into all the shops for antiques on the Left Bank and on the quays, and spent much time looking through folios of drawings and prints at picture dealers'. Almost daily he came home with a new acquisition, and showed it to us, thereby giving us a lesson in art. But he himself was a painter of landscapes and portraits; for the latter his children took turns as models. He was also good at dry-point engravings and etchings, and, amongst others, made a moving engraving of Turgeniev on his death-bed.

I admired my father more than anyone else, but every time I came close to him out of a need for affection, I had to suppress my eagerness and never succeeded in breaking down the distance which he seemed to require between himself and his children. I do not know how to explain this stern attitude of his, which, in spite of his affection, demanded of us such a ceremonious deportment. Was it because of a certain shyness at showing his feelings, or the fact of being unused to looking after us? Yet he was very kind, and there was always a smile lighting up the regular and delicate features of his friendly face. But thus living in the company of a stern man we lost our childlike unconstraint; we always had to be sensible, or at any rate to appear so. The house had to be quiet, and each of us had to obey. Every day, when I came home from school, it was my duty to shut myself up in my room over my home work or extra lessons in foreign languages. When that was done, I was free to enjoy myself by reading or drawing. I acquired a great taste for reading and devoured books indiscriminately, uncontrolled and unharmed — everything that came into my hands in Russian, French, German, and English. I was sorry I could not share in the exercises, the physical training and the other games, in which my friends took part with zest, and I lived shut in upon myself and in a state of perpetual curiosity. To me everything was a source of astonishment and comparison: the French ways of life, the manners of speaking, and the differences in feeling which I was gradually discovering. But, since I was a little girl, I was equally moved by the sight of violets in mid-winter, and of flowers whose existence I had never dreamed of, like mimosa and Christmas roses, and fruits such as bananas and grapefruit.

For several months I had been asking to go to the theatre to see one of the classic plays, because several of my school friends had season tickets for the matinées at the Théâtre Français and gave enthusiastic accounts of them. Finally, one Thursday afternoon, I was taken to see a performance of *Polyeucte*, which I anticipated I should thoroughly enjoy. I knew the lines by heart and had read Corneille's tragedy through and through. How disappointed I was when I heard the actors declaiming and acting with conventional pomposity! I no longer followed the words, but started on the sly looking around to see if my neighbours were not going to jeer at the actors' way of shrieking which seemed absolutely comical, at their tremolo flourishes which jarred upon my ears, and their vocal outbursts to my mind so ridiculous. Around me my friends with season tickets appeared in a state of perfect bliss. When the actress who was playing the part of Pauline hurled out with demonic fury the famous words, '*Je vois, je sais, je crois, je suis désabusée*,' I lowered my head in utter confusion.

The lady who was in charge of me, mistaking the reason for my emotion, whispered to me: 'How beautiful, isn't it, child?'

I replied in words which she often repeated to me thereafter: 'That woman is ludicrous.... Why is she allowed to act here?'

This observation she understood in her own way, as may be gathered from her prompt answer: 'I knew you were too young to appreciate the masterpieces of our stage, poor little Marie.'

I longed to explain why I was disappointed, but an ineptitude in expressing one's feelings is one of the most painful sensations of youth. Later I came to suffer still more deeply from the everlasting misunderstanding which exists between human beings.

Surprise followed upon surprise. I was beginning to know Paris well, and used to linger, whenever I could, to gaze upon its harmonious vistas and the variety of its exquisitely changing sky. In those days the Carnival still possessed a gaiety and a liveliness obvious even to us children, who were forbidden to throw confetti. For two or three days the city was under whirling showers of many-coloured bits of paper and wildly waving streamers. The fancy-dress procession, which went along the boulevards and the main thoroughfares, caricatured characters in legends and public figures: actors, authors, the chief commissioner of the Paris police, politicians, and so on.

Politics was a novel and somewhat remote interest for a schoolgirl of my age, but one to which people were continually alluding in my presence, and it provoked discussions as much among the common people and the servants as among the sedate gentlemen in the tramcars. It was a preoccupation which seemed a part of the life of everyone, interesting the most humble people as much as the most important. Every person one met seemed to have an opinion and something to say in this matter. Were, then, affairs of State the concern of every Frenchman? In Moscow I should certainly never have heard a costermonger woman reply to a remark about the excessive price of pears: 'What can you expect, lady? They're sending prices up with their rotten politics.'

Even now, I cannot help exclaiming as I remember this

reply, even in those faroff days it was thus, though life was then relatively so cheap!... In Russia the ignorant and scared masses would never have dared thus to criticize the Government through the mouth of a common gossip. I was surprised to see that in France political questions were judged and commented upon by every citizen. They found expression in actions which every man was free to approve or condemn, and which were not veiled in mystery. At school in Russia we were not allowed to utter the slightest opinion upon any public occurrence. Here the opposite was the case. The girl in my class who had taken a liking to me informed me that she was a Bonapartist, while her parents were looking forward to the return of a king, and her brother was a convinced Republican. In order that no one should be ignorant of her opinions, she brought to school, one morning, a small statue of Napoleon and unblushingly stood it upon her desk. The Emperor was at liberty to grieve over the numerous spelling mistakes which his admirer scattered throughout her writing exercises.

Little by little friendships sprang up among the better pupils, and emulation stimulated such sympathy and affection as we felt towards each other.

One day, at playtime, I noticed in the garden tiny leaves sprouting on the trees; thus was spring arriving in Paris, unobserved and discreet. It was quite different in Russia. There the coming of spring is sudden, intoxicating, destructive. The melting of the snows, which rush away in streams, the breaking up of the ice on the river at Moscow, the Moskva-Rika, the suffocating scent of the syringas — these are the symptoms of spring. Washed clean, and as if glazed, the city — its rejuvenated golden church domes, its pink, white, and green houses — glitter with striking brilliance. Winter no longer deadens sounds; there seems to be a host of noises trying to make one forget the long silence: clatters of all sorts, the bumping and rumbling of carriages over the ill-paved streets, the clamorous cries of the costermongers selling their spring vegetables. A new vitality throbs in every living thing. In the country each tree shakes off its coating of ice, and, as a sort of hymn of deliverance, displays leaves and perfume. Swallows twitter and dart as sharp as blades across a brand-new sky. Spring thus bursts forth from the shell of winter, revealing Nature once more radiant and powerful. I was amazed at the stealthy arrival of spring in France. Could it really happen thus?

'Of course,' my friend told me; and she added ironically: 'Don't you know there is a twentieth of March chestnut tree in the Champs-Élysées? It is always in bloom by that date, and it is that tree that announces the spring.'

I burst out laughing, amused by the idea that this symbolic mission could be allotted to a tree. I went off at once to see it, and indeed discovered it, with its delicate swaying white blossoms, shivering in a somewhat biting wind.

What a disappointment it was for me, however, when I discovered that our summer holidays did not begin until the end of July! It seemed that I was being robbed of the finest days. In Russia I looked forward to going away to the country in April or May. There would still be a little snow in the ditches, but green life was piercing through this light covering everywhere, full of sap, abundant, hastening to come forth. The fields appeared covered overnight with various sorts of grass, sprinkled all over by a flutter of butterflies and insects. In the birch woods, crammed full of bluebells and lilies-of-the-valley, the scent was acrid and heady. The currant bushes bloomed at the same time as the buttercups, which appeared painted as with egg varnish. Countless species of mushrooms sprouted under the moss.

I was all the more impatient for the holidays to begin because my father had rented a villa on the Normandy coast, and I had never seen the sea. The resort chosen was Cabourg, which Marcel Proust later pictured under the name of Balbec. The writer liked it because of its long stone pier commanding the horizon, this pier along which 'budding girlhood' was soon to be seen walking.

When Russian families travelled abroad, they used to take the waters at Wiesbaden, Karlsbad, Ems, or to go to some mountain resorts in Switzerland or the Tyrol. Therefore, for most Russian children the sea remained a mystery.

The last weeks at school seemed never-ending. It was maddening to see the leaves already turning brown on the trees. In the Champs-Élysées and on the boulevards typical tourists went about sight-seeing in cabs: Cook-tourists, with spectacles, Tyrolese hats, and reading their Baedekers. They had appeared as early as the spring acacia festival.

If in the summer the Russian countryside was bursting

and overflowing with flowers, in the city the florists were uncommon and enjoyed but poor custom. On the occasion of a ball given in honour of my elder sister, my parents had been obliged to order from Nice a whole batch of fragrant blooms. I preserved, too, the memory of a precious little lilac tree which had reached us during a bitter winter from a Belgian hothouse.

But the Battle of Flowers in Paris seemed to drain the woods of posies, petals, and flowers; the elegant carriages, landaus, pony-traps overflowed with them. And in this luxurious festival the crowd was not a mere anonymous multitude; as each carriage drove by, the name of some actress or social celebrity passed from lips to lips amidst the flutter of the downy acacia blooms. However, Drags Day by far surpassed in elegance this somewhat mixed festival. The Grand Prix marked the close of the Paris season, and after that day no man of fashion showed himself in a top hat, the town emptied itself, and such people as stayed behind carefully concealed themselves behind closed shutters.

We went away. The country we crossed I never noticed. It was the sea I was anxiously watching for as I scanned the horizon. At last it appeared, pale and distant; then disappeared at a bend of the road, leaving in the air a tang of salt and spray. As a framework for the sea, I had in imagination pictured a desolate landscape, not the paltry hamlet of jerry-built cottages which we drove through from the station. The sea was only a few yards away from our villa: I ran towards it.

There it was, blue and pink, with nothing to betray its

might and its storms. The setting sun imbued it with the softness of shimmering reflexions. Yet the sea seemed to be in a hurry, as if the tides were behindhand. On the foam-fringed sand, shells, seaweed, and jellyfish seemed like wonderful gifts deposited there for me. The beam of a lighthouse described a white circle, and gradually the coast was blurred out. I looked up to the sky — already the stars were marking out the field of their celestial geometry.

It was during that stay in Normandy that I began to feel the richness of France, both in virtue of its fertile soil and of its civilization. My father, a keen guide, although so stern, took us to see all the fine cathedral cities of the district. He would not tolerate any confusion of styles; one of my remarks in front of Notre-Dame de Bayeux earned me a deserved rebuke, and so great was my mortification that I vowed never again to run the risk of such condemnation. Often one forgets the reason of a shock, but the memory of it persists. A few years ago, at Bayeux, a fleeting impression brought this incident back to my mind.

We learned to admire the paintings, the tapestries, the ancient furniture, to recognize styles of architecture and panelling. We spent also long days loafing about in the fields, on the beach, or fishing. During our excursions about the countryside, I saw everywhere monuments recording the history of the land, the successive conquests and settlements which had gone to make up its greatness and its unity. I know not if I should have experienced the same thrill had I been born French.

All the time comparisons between France and Russia forced themselves upon me, and gradually the idea took root in my mind that my own country possessed neither art nor architecture, but that in its literature, its music and dancing, was to be found the haunting expression of its character. A year before in Russia, also in the summer, how thrilled I had been when listening to the soulful singing of the soldiers! In clouds of dust, the troops marched past our estate, and at dusk the clear voice of the drum major stood out, leading a chorus of juniors. Each shade of expression had its own inflexion, and the general harmony was not spoiled by improvisation and flourishes.

In the village the accordion-player composed dizzy variations which, amplified by the bellows of his instrument, floated out under his dexterous fingers. The young men whirled around with grace and precision, or, in squatting position, red handkerchiefs in their hands, executed miracles of skilful dancing around peasant girls: light-footed dancers these, in spite of their plumpness. Wild sarabands, in a medley of colours and mirth, unfurled themselves in front of older men who sat chewing sunflower seeds. In such ways the innate and deep-rooted Russian instinct for dancing revealed itself.

Back to Paris, though still at school, I could not help marking out from the nameless crowd some personalities which forced themselves upon my notice by their appearance and who I found were people of repute. One of the first was a tall, fair youth, square-shouldered, wearing a

monocle, looking very smart in a light fawn overcoat
deliberately roomy, and always seen with two reddish-
brown basset hounds. He lived in my district, in the
Avenue d'Eylau. His name was Caran d'Ache, which in
Russian means 'pencil.' The cartoonist who had adopted
this name was really called Poiré, but he had been born
in Moscow and had lived there. He looked like his own
drawings, which were full of imagination and frank
playfulness. I sought information about him. His grandfather had served under Napoleon and had settled in
Russia. When the time came for his military service,
the young Emmanuel Poiré was sent off to Paris and
attached to the War Office. His cartoons, full of humour,
appeared in *Le Rire*, *Tout Paris*, and *La Vie Parisienne*;
they were so witty that they would have been intelligible
without words of explanation. On the occasion of a performance at the Chat Noir, a sort of revue called *L'Épopée*
about the victories of Napoleon, he had designed hundreds
of the costumes.

In my comings and goings my attention was equally
drawn to another person. I had often noticed a man
emerging from or re-entering an upholstered brougham
stationed at one end of the Rue Greuze. He was an elderly
man who wore spats and a light-coloured waistcoat seen
inside his unbuttoned fur-lined coat. His expressive
features, with the hooked nose, were flanked by grey
side-whiskers which fluttered in the wind, and he was
quite sprightly as he alighted from his carriage onto the
pavement. Then he helped his gouty Pekineses to come
down in their turn, for they were less lively than himself.

I learned that he was Monsieur de Blowitz, the chief correspondent of the London *Times*. I rushed up to examine him closely, curious to see near at hand this famous journalist who had been connected with Monsieur Thiers and all the great men of Europe. Nothing makes a greater impression upon a child than to meet someone who has known an historical personality, and for me Monsieur Thiers was as unreal, yet as unquestionable, as his fame echoed in my schoolbooks.

Finally, there was the owner of luxuriously fitted carriages, whose name it was impossible long to ignore, since I always saw him, either in a victoria, or driving his brake himself, or again riding in the Bois in an array of choice and fashionable clothes. Young, handsome, a first-rate swell, impudent, yet with the best of grace, the Comte de Castellane was the most talked-of man in Paris, the sensation of the time, and it chanced that I crossed his path almost daily.

The cinema, the various kinds of sports, the countless shows which form the amusements of youth today, were then represented by a few productions of classical plays and the circus. Therefore, imagination had to find food for dreams and poetry in reading about romantic lives, or being fired by Jules Verne's marvellous predictions, or Wells's and Kipling's fantastic stories. In those days girls did not put up photographs of Rudolph Valentino in their rooms, but had a soft place in their hearts for André Chénier, Alfred de Musset, and Lamartine. I myself often gazed at Musset's portrait, the Musset of David d'Angers's bas-relief, reproduced in Lemerre's edition, and I sought his grave at Père-Lachaise, beneath the slender willow he had asked his friends to plant there. In the square bearing his name, Lamartine seemed to pursue his meditations, his greyhound lying at his feet. Victor Hugo's fame had as yet suffered no onslaughts; his name was still full of majestic glamour; I went to see his house in the Avenue named after him. And how great was my regret that Verlaine was dead!

My father encouraged this intellectual bent of mine, because he preferred the world of ideas to that of business and placed no value on any but the liberal professions. All his sympathy went to artists. In Russia the friends of my brother and my elder sister had included the leading spirits in the theatrical movement which later led to the foundation of the Moscow Arts Theatre, and it was in my father's house that their first plays were sketched out. My father had likewise encouraged the composer Scriabin at the outset of his career, and when he came to Paris my father welcomed him as a son of his own.

In 1898, at the Salon des Artistes Français, François Sicard, a young winner of the Prix de Rome, exhibited a beautiful group of Hagar and Ishmael which attracted my father's notice. While he was admiring it, one of his friends, Monsieur Paul Boyer, Director of the School of Oriental Languages, informed him that the sculptor was a countryman of his from Touraine, and was delighted when my father gave him on the spot a commission for the young artist to do a bust of my sister. François Sicard, inspired by his model, produced a very fine piece of work; the sittings dragged on, the artist fell in love with his charming model, and thus became my brother-in-law.

At school one of my friends was the daughter of the famous lawyer Jean Cruppi, then deputy and later a cabinet minister. At his house I met a large number of people of repute, and became acquainted with the lovable Gabriel Fauré. He had a handsome face, fiery eyes, silvery hair, and from his whole person emanated that same charm which is found in his delicate compositions. Maurice Ravel arrived from Saint-Jean de Luz-Ciboure, with hollow cheeks hardly concealed by notary-like side-whiskers. Maurice Magre had beady eyes, and Léon Paul Fargue, with his firm and youthful features surmounted by a mat of hair, showed promises of a brilliant future through his unexpected rejoinders.

The Comtesse Mathieu de Noailles, however, was the person who most appeared to me as the incarnation of genius. The very first time I saw her, I was dazzled and captivated. This little woman entered the drawing-room speaking with animation and at once was the centre of attraction. She questioned in turn each of the most famous guests and no one ever answered her quickly enough. She seemed not to notice the delighted attention of her interlocutors over whom she held sway by her lively speech and witty remarks. This young woman, with a face like a white camellia and wonderful grey eyes, drew everybody to herself while she juggled with ideas and roused the company by her incredible vivacity. Her soft dovelike voice rose and fell in meandering cadences. With every shaft of her wit contagious laughter lent new youth to the most sedate. Her dynamism was such

ANNA DE NOAILLES

that it urged her on to answer herself the questions she asked. In this fashion a whole monologue poured forth with irresistible eloquence. But by then I no longer saw her, so closely did people gather around her. After making a simile which struck me as unexpected as it was humorous, this young goddess suddenly left the company amidst a bustle of admiration. And at once a dismal silence invaded the room. Never had I heard anyone express thoughts with so great a charm and in such a gifted manner.

As I drove home, my mind dwelt on her. I saw once more her small hand tidying a lock of dark hair on her forehead, or supporting a head proudly poised on a slender neck. I recalled a face into which the nose, with its delicate nostrils, gradually fused when seen from the front, though revealing on a profile view a marked upward tilt. Anna de Noailles was unlike anyone else; yet where had I heard something reminiscent of her sparkling speech? My mind sought to recapture a blending of winged and iridescent vision, and suddenly flashed back into my memory our national legend of the Fire-Bird.

I have another and very different recollection. It was during the Exhibition of 1900. Sarah Bernhardt's daughter-in-law, *née* Princess Terka Yablonowska, took me to the Thé de Ceylan tea gardens. I was very proud to go out with this beautiful young woman and keen on seeing so fashionable a place. People were so eager to taste this tea of exotic fragrance that one had almost to fight to get a small table where a boy in white uniform and queer headgear served as waiter. We had great difficulty in finding places. Scarcely were we seated when I drew Madame Bernhardt's attention to a fat man, seated floppily at an isolated table, his flabby and ravaged face bearing an expression of unspeakable sadness. When she saw him my companion rose abruptly, telling me to follow her, and went over to him.

'Dear Oscar Wilde,' she said, 'how glad I am to see you! I was talking about you to Madame Sarah a few days ago. You know how much she admires you. Will you allow us to take our tea with you?'

The man had risen from his seat when we came up. His whole features beamed into life again.

'What, Madame,' he stammered as he kissed her hand, 'will you be so kind?'

She motioned me to sit. While he spoke I scrutinized his queer face: small blue eyes, a large formless nose, deep furrows on his brow, and a gold tooth which was revealed and then disappeared following the irregular movement of the lips. He pronounced some words more distinctly than others, speaking quickly and with sudden pauses. He alluded to sufferings he had just been through, and then immediately changed the subject to mention the literary work upon which he was then engaged. This developed into a discussion about Verlaine, in the course of which there were many things I could not grasp. I understood long after, when I read *De Profundis*. Gradually, without our noticing it, everyone had left the gardens while we remained enthralled by the stories which flowed unexhaustedly from those drooping lips, often with bitter sarcasm. Wilde appeared pleased that he could talk about himself. When we got up to leave, my friend overwhelmed him with affectionate words, and I watched him go away, his back less bent, then disappear in the crowd.

'He is an extraordinary person,' Madame Bernhardt remarked. 'You will never forget having had the good fortune to see him.'

Two months later Oscar Wilde died in a hotel in the Rue des Beaux-Arts in abject poverty.

Although it was then exceptional for women to aim at a career, yet we girls found much of our time taken up by our studies, and when we went to dances, while sitting out between two waltzes, our partners, who also suffered from examination-fever, spoke to us with great enthusiasm about the lectures of Boutroux or Bergson, which we felt sure we should equally be able to follow.

When the time came for my début into society, my father decided to give a ball. Among the guests was Pierre Carolus-Duran, the painter's son, who had made the acquaintance of my brother and myself some months before. This handsome, well-dressed young man made a great impression upon me and my girl friends. I learned from him that he was a composer; that he had set *Sayama* to music, and was to have it produced at the Opéra Comique within a short time. I felt very flattered, though a little surprised, when he asked my permission to dedicate this work to me. He told me a thousand things likely to turn the head of a girl who had never been courted before.

What impressed me most was that, when we parted, he confided to me in great secrecy that he was to fight a duel on the following day, and assured me that ever since he had first met me I had always been in his thoughts, so that he had made a point of seeing me often.

On the following Friday Pierre Carolus-Duran appeared at our house, and thenceforth paid us frequent visits. When he was able to speak to me alone, he talked about his work as composer and created for us two a sort of atmosphere in which, in my imagination, I lived an ideal life. Nothing seemed to me so fascinating as to become the helpmate of an artist, and dedicate oneself to him and to his work. Everyone at home was captivated by his charm. One day he announced that his father was coming to see us. I felt greatly excited, and expected to see an old solemn-looking gentleman, for such I thought must be the President of the Société Nationale de Peinture, and a Member of the Institut. I was completely taken aback: sprightly, kindly, full of life, Carolus-Duran was even more fascinating than his son.

My father took him into his study. With great emotion Pierre Carolus-Duran told me that his fate depended upon their conversation. After a short while they called us in. Our fathers were chatting gaily and seemed to be fully in agreement. The great artist asked me in a caressing voice if I should like to become his daughter-in-law. My father was smiling — I threw myself in his arms; I was mad with joy. Day-dreaming in those days cannot be compared with what it is for the modern girl. Practically every girl then felt herself a Clara d'Ellebeuse.

My engagement was announced a few days before Varnishing Day at the Salon. The traditional lunch given by the doyen revealed to me one aspect of my future father-in-law's popularity. The big-chested and handsome man that he was made a striking figure in his grey top hat set upon silvery hair, his grey frock coat of a very individual cut, his turndown collar and white waistcoat and tie. He welcomed with a smile the painters, writers, musicians, critics, fashionable ladies, and club men who gathered together on this artistic occasion. In those times Varnishing Day was still a great attraction; society ladies set there the fashions for the coming season. Exhibitors and visitors clustered together and embarked upon eager discussions. There was not a single Parisian but knew Carolus-Duran; from all the small tables in the restaurant people greeted him, or made kindly and sometimes malicious remarks about him. If the painter on such occasions appeared in all the splendour of his fame, the outset of his career had been difficult; he liked to recall those early days.

What a pleasure it was for me to listen to him when, after my marriage, my husband and I used to spend several months with him, in his country house at Saint-Aygulf. He told me how he had come from Lille (where the house of his birth is still standing in a picturesque corner of the Place Ribour), and settled in Paris with his mother, his sister, and his father, who soon afterwards died there.

'The only thing I knew then,' he said, 'was that I wanted to become a good painter.'

When he was only three years old, he used to fill the pockets of his little dressing-gown with scraps of paper on which he scrawled all sorts of heads. His family sent him to an art school, the head of which was called Phidias Cadet de Beaupré. This somewhat presumptuous man was given to saying, 'Not only am I called Phidias, but I also happen to be a sculptor.'

He often said that Carolus would never get anywhere in painting. However, the child persevered at it. He was encouraged and guided by a worthy man named Souchon, whose pupil he proclaimed himself to be, out of gratitude, in the Salon catalogues. When his father died, Carolus and the whole family were left without means. The young painter, therefore, decided to leave France and try, with his modest accomplishments, to make his fortune in Algeria. He succeeded in getting free passage as an emigrant, and, not having the money to go by train, he saw no alternative but to walk from Paris to Marseilles.

In the Rue de l'Ancienne Comédie, as he was going to take leave of his friends in the students' quarter, he ran into one of his comrades.

'I'm going off to Africa,' he declared.

'What on earth for?'

Carolus explained his desperate position. Greatly distressed, his friend offered to rent him a little studio and to lend him the money needed to pay for it during the first months. The painter accepted, full of gratitude.

The tiny room, as dark as a cellar, was furnished with an iron bed, a table, and a few books. Carolus could not afford models, so he made portraits of all his friends.

He went to the Louvre to copy pictures and to keep himself warm. His hardships finally made him seriously ill. The same friend found him one morning in such an alarming condition that he had him removed to his own house and looked after him. When he recovered, the young painter went off to Lille to compete for the Prix Wicar. The Chevalier Wicar, a Lille painter of the time of David, had founded this scholarship to send two artists to Rome. In spite of the fact that in those days Carolus-Duran's work was deemed too realistic, his efforts were crowned with success. He sailed off to Città Vecchia on a Messageries ship with the prospect of spending four years in Italy and being able to work as he had been longing to. He was twenty-four years old and had one hundred and sixty-five francs a month at his disposal. This meant security. His whole life was later made brighter by the recollections of these years of hard work.

The students of the Wicar Foundation were lodged not far from the Piazza del Popolo, in the Via del Vantaggio, near the Via di Ripetta, which runs parallel to the Corso. Rome and the surrounding district provided every opportunity for serious studies after the great masters and the classic landscapes of its wondrous countryside. Carolus-Duran rode all over the Sabine Mountains and the Abruzzi on horseback, and stayed with the Franciscan friars at Subiaco. He had a great fondness for this little town on the Aniene, surrounded by stony hills and dominated by the castle where Popes had once dwelt. In this spot of austere grandeur Nero had established one of his summer dwellings. At a later date Saint Benedict had retired hither into a lonely grotto overlooking a sheer precipice.

Attracted by the famous monasteries and convents, dedicated to the Saint and his sister, Saint Scholastica, the painter lived there for six months in a monk's cell. He was loved for his frank, open nature, his joyfulness, and was known in the country for many miles around. He was called 'Fra Carlo,' or the 'pittore di San Francesco.' He visited Venice and Padua, settled for a year in Naples, and he told me how he had, at Sorrento, saved the life of Alvarez who was about to drown himself. Alvarez was later to become Director of the Prado in Madrid. Together with the landscape painter François Louis Français, of whom he made a fine portrait, Carolus-Duran dreamed of the future and revelled in music and poetry; he had a rich, full voice and accompanied his singing on the guitar.

Duran's first success was 'L'Assassiné,' which is now to be found in the Art Gallery at Lille. He returned to France for a while, but soon went off to Spain. There came to him the overwhelming revelation of the genius of Velasquez. His temperament was in harmony with the Spanish character. In Madrid and Toledo the influence upon his work was decisive in the development of his style.

It was later, in the Louvre, that he met Pauline Croizette, a girl of great beauty and herself a painter, whom he married. She was his model for his picture 'La Dame au Gant'; the success of this portrait marked the opening of his glorious career.

At the time I married, the life of my husband's parents was that of a long-united and devoted couple, surrounded by children and grandchildren. They preserved tender memories of the years of trial through which they had passed side by side. My mother-in-law, who admired her husband, looked after him like a mother and contrived to relieve him of all domestic worries. For many years now she had mostly stayed at home, yet understood that her husband's career imposed upon him social obligations.

My father-in-law usually left home in the morning for his studio, lunched at Foyot's, went to his club, and came home only for dinner. His eldest daughter, Marie-Anne, had married Georges Feydeau, whose sarcastic, gloomy nature, during the Sunday dinners bringing the whole family together, gave little clue to the success which his side-splitting plays were enjoying on the boulevard. Hidden in the clouds of smoke of his perpetual cigar, his biting remarks alone revealed his presence.

From time to time others came to join our intimate circle: Massenet, Henner, Widor, Jean Béraud, Monsieur and Madame Matza (*née* Alexandre Dumas), and Madame Maurice Bernhardt, Sarah Bernhardt's daughter-in-law, who presently introduced me to the great actress. In her house on the Boulevard Péreire, with its strange and sumptuous fittings, the great entrance hall on the ground floor was cluttered up with a vast quantity of furniture of every style, animal skins, odds and ends obviously collected by chance on various journeys according to fashions, and presents. Clairin's portrait of Sarah was in that room, and also enormous baskets of flowers, bearing witness to the devotion of the actress's circle of admirers. Fond though she was of luxury, she yet was not particularly attached either to jewels or to her other possessions, and lived in her house as in a theatrical setting.

As soon as Madame Sarah woke up in the morning, she began receiving a host of people, managers, authors, tradespeople of all sorts. To save time she admitted them to her bathroom, using starch to make the water opaque, so that she could carry on her conversation even in the bath. Almost every day she had friends to lunch, people like Clairin, Sardou, Reynaldo Hahn, Doctor Pozzi, Arthur Meyer, Zamacoïs, Jean Lorrain, and Eugène Morand, Paul Morand's father; and when Pierre Loti was in Paris, he never failed to turn up: she admired him and was fond of him. Each one of her friends had a nickname: Clairin was 'Jojotte,' and Doctor Pozzi 'le Docteur Dieu.' Impulsive, never blasée, young in spirit, Sarah found it great fun to relate the astonishing adventures she met with during her tours. Greedy for news and inquisitive, she would sometimes ask extremely naïve questions; she was interested in inventions, and loud in her praise of Marconi; she had a passion, too, for politics, about which she argued fiercely with extreme chauvinism.

Always in a hurry, compelled to leave her guests at table to rush off to the theatre for some rehearsal, or to supervise the stage-settings or the making of her costumes, her activities bordered on the prodigious. Scarcely was one play under way when she began studying the next.

Never weary, nothing tired her, and she was always the last person to seek rest. She had the power of dropping off to sleep for a few moments in the midst of any noise, and claimed that she was refreshed thereby. After each of these five-minute naps, Sarah always told us what she had dreamt about. To avoid interrupting her work, she dined in a little room at the theatre off a number of queer dishes of which she was fond. As she ate like a sparrow, she only pecked at the food on her plate. She really feasted on fruit. During these little dinners her table was surrounded by admirers, friends, authors, and fellow actors. Seated on a sort of throne, she presided over all, graceful in her posture, coquettish, usually dressed in white, in lissom long-sleeved dresses, girdled with stones suited to her type. Her regular and finely chiselled face, always supported upon a high collar, preserved its beauty and was crowned by a great ruffled mop of hair through which she frequently drew her expressive fingers. In her golden voice, her speech, hurried and melodious, came forth in words as unexpected and lively as were her gestures. When she began to notice that the oval of her face was not as pure as of old, she conceived the idea — anticipating the effect of modern clipped hair — before going on the stage, of making two tiny tight plaits of part of her hair over each temple and tying them securely on the top of her head, underneath her tousled hair, by which means she pulled up the muscles of her cheeks and lengthened her eyes.

Surrounded by artists, passionately fond of painting, dancing, and sculpture, she carved a few busts herself and amused herself by teasing her friends and correcting mistakes in their paintings. Sarah Bernhardt did not read much, especially towards the end of her life, and she found the stage deadly dull. Whimsical, generous to the point of folly, she would throw herself blindly into all kinds of undertakings without any practical ability; she was therefore continually exploited and always short of money. Her financial difficulties over the running of her theatre were so constant that it was a subject she avoided discussing.

However, on one occasion, she betrayed her distress in the presence of Henri Cain: how was she to get her lease renewed and to meet her obligations? But her natural optimism regaining the upper hand, she added: 'But I'm not disheartened. Nothing is lost as yet.'

In a panic, Cain dashed off to Arthur Meyer, the manager of the *Gaulois* newspaper.

'I've just been up at Sarah Bernhardt's; she's in an unbearable position. We must avert a catastrophe. Do you think it possible to launch a public subscription? You could do the trick through *Le Gaulois*, the whole of the press would fall into line, we could raise a million francs and make a good job of it.'

But Arthur Meyer, who possessed greater shrewdness, replied: 'Shouldn't we see first if Madame Sarah would agree to it?'

'Well, my dear fellow, you're one of her oldest friends, so obviously the one to go and talk it over with her.'

With great diplomacy and tact, Arthur Meyer outlined the scheme to the actress.

'Surely it wasn't you who thought of this, dear friend?' she exclaimed.

'No, it was Henri Cain.'

'I can't understand it,' Sarah went on. 'The less so the more I think about it. Did that poor chap find anything to complain about the lunch I gave him last week? I can't remember what the menu was.'

And so there was no more question of a public subscription.

Sarah Bernhardt was sometimes extremely nervous, for no doubt her untamable nerves were a part of her prodigious vitality.

One day, in New York, she was giving a dinner in her rooms at the hotel. At one point the waiters and the butler had withdrawn, and a fairly long time went by without any servants appearing. The guests were waiting for the coffee; Sarah Bernhardt rang repeatedly, but no one came. Finally she had herself carried into the passage (she had already had her leg amputated) and in her powerful and musical voice she shouted, in English, as loud as she could: 'Fire! Fire!'

The result was immediate: some fifty people rushed to her rooms.

Naturally, during the World War, Sarah Bernhardt adopted soldiers as 'godsons.' Among others there was one called Châtelain, recommended by Professor Z. He had had both legs amputated, had lost an arm, and had had his front teeth smashed; he was decorated with the *Médaille Militaire* and the *Croix de Guerre*. Sarah bought him a set of false teeth and jointed artificial legs, asking him often to lunch at the Boulevard Péreire, until the day when she was informed by the police that Châtelain had never been in the War, but had had an accident in the Saint-Gothard Pass, being suspected of having murdered a guide, and that Professor Z. had never heard of him at all.

'It is better to give and be mistaken than not to give and risk being mistaken that way,' said Sarah. And she adopted another 'godson.'

She was adored by all her servants for her generosity and kindness. Every time she went on tour she came back with new and exotic servants, about whose past she never troubled to inquire, and who went on swelling the impressive number of parasites living on her. But this way of doing things was not always without danger; one day a negro she had chosen for his picturesque appearance nearly killed one of her familiars.

Like a new Cour des Miracles, a collection of queer people always hung around her, cranks and unbalanced persons of all sorts, who followed her from town to town pestering her with fantastic requests.

At her country house at Belle-Isle where she was fond of staying, she used to play indoor games with zest, but, a bad loser, she would throw the dominoes away when the game went against her, argue endlessly and usually clear out in a huff. However, hot-tempered rather than resentful, her quarrels were short-lived.

She was always ready to spoil her friends in a thousand ways; she loved her son Maurice to the point of idolatry, and in spite of his greying hair she still looked upon him as a child, yielded to all his whims, and approved of his behaviour, though it often caused her many worries. But she was proud of his handsome appearance, his prowess as a fencer, and, blinded by motherly love, she could see no fault in him.

Sarah Bernhardt was so much the radiant centre of her own world that she might have been filled with vanity, but never did she display the least trace of it. On the contrary, she was modest; she often felt nervous, and tried to conceal this by bringing all her charm into action.

One Thursday during the War, in 1917, she invited me to lunch with her and to come to a matinée at the Français, where Colonna Romano, her pupil, was acting the part of Esther. It was at a time when the Seine was causing great fear of floods. Many people daily went to the Pont de l'Alma to measure the threatening rise of waters around the famous Zouave, for the tragedy of the floods of 1910 was still fairly fresh in memory. To this danger was added the anguish caused by the shelling of Paris and the bad news from the front. Sarah Bernhardt had not shown herself at Molière's Theatre for several years. The manager had had the stage box reserved for her and decorated with flowers. The public knew she was coming and watched for her arrival. She had already lost one leg and used to be carried about in an armchair. Feeling very nervous, she begged her granddaughters, the few friends who were present, and myself to sit at the front of the box while she concealed herself at the back, in the dark. But the audience who adored her wanted to see her. A swarm of people crowded in front of the box shouting: 'Vive Sarah! Vive Sarah!' So she had her chair pushed forward, stood up, and, filled with emotion, bestowed upon the crowd her smiles and her thanks. She had to do this several times, and when she finally sat down, to conceal her emotion she said to us: 'What's it all about? I don't understand. I think these people today mistake me for the Zouave of the stage....'

When we left the theatre, it was already dusk. In front of the Madeleine, Sarah leaned out of the window and asked: 'What is that building?'

'Why, Madame, it's the Madeleine...'

'Well, indeed! but I don't know it. I go out only at night in Paris, and all I see is the usual journey from my house to the theatre.'

The place occupied by the great actress in dramatic art was unique. Her personality stamped the parts she created with the tangible shapes which her art conjured up. Every one of her gestures, her attitudes, so exclusively belonged to her that it was impossible to imitate them; and the same applied to her impetuosity, her hurried yet harmonious delivery in that famous voice of hers. She strove to carry out her ideals with complete artistic integrity. Even though her genius was capable of various incarnations, yet she always remained herself. At the outset of her career her triumphs had been secured by the romantic acting she offered to her audiences in contrast with the prosaic tone of the period. The public was acquainted with her sumptuous mode of life, her inexhaustible kindness, her adventurous nature, and her liking for wild beasts. She allowed the legend to grow that she slept in a coffin. She indulged in fencing, went off touring in America, and was the first actress to be surrounded by extravagant publicity. It was only at the end of her life that I knew her. With her transports of passion and grace, she made an incomparable Phèdre. Her interpretation of Hamlet, full of mysterious ambiguity, will never fade from my memory. She put aside the pretentious pomp of conventional acting and reached, through sheer lyrical feeling, the intrinsic truth of her parts.

Recently, in La Musée des Arts Décoratifs, I saw once again Mucha's finical posters which in those days displayed on the walls of Paris a sugary likeness of Sarah. How far more striking she was than this, how much more alive and human!

After much suffering and hesitation I had just secured my divorce. Within the walls of my shattered home, attracted by my youth and the interest I displayed in them, there gradually gathered writers and artists, a few politicians, quite a little swarm carefully selected by myself. A longing to understand and to know, a great curiosity, urged me thus to get outside myself and forget my real loneliness. There was a great difference in atmosphere between one salon and another in those days. The confusion and cosmopolitanism of the post-War years, spreading from individuals to the realm of ideas, were as yet unknown. But I had no ambition, no husband with a career to nurse; therefore, I could quite easily mix in social circles whose opinions clashed. My friendship with certain elderly men, famous by their intellect and position, gave me occasionally the opportunity of using my influence on behalf of younger men.

By the force of circumstances those who sought my assistance grew in number. I began to feel that some meaning could be restored to my life could I only manage to make myself useful. Through a sort of atavism I had the natural Russian proclivity for being hospitable. People who frequented my house soon shared this view and enjoyed my home. At that time the Parisian smart set was restricted to a narrow circle. At a dress rehearsal it was possible to name almost every face; similarly, any event of a social and artistic character was known to everyone and discussed in the salons from all possible points of view. Great stress was laid upon behaviour. Age and experience were deemed to go together, and moral standards were stricter than nowadays. Men knew how to retain youth even after reaching maturity. Women were only just beginning to hanker after careers and ways to earn their own living. The first woman barrister was pointed out as an exception: Madame Dieulafoy, the explorer and a fellow worker with her husband, was lampooned in all the wineshops. There was not then an overabundance of dressmakers and luxury dealers, nor of places of amusement; the cinema was making a modest beginning. Society life, by contrast, was all the more intense. I wonder whether we appreciated sufficiently the security we enjoyed in those days, our chances of planning life ahead, the relaxation offered by leisure, the courtesy in social intercourse, and this taste for moderation which reigned supreme in the salons and was an added pleasure to conversation.

How charming and interesting such conversation could

prove for me! I loved to watch people's faces, to note their physical and mental reactions, and what was at first a deliberate practice became almost instinctive. I enjoyed the flow of eloquence of people who knew what they wished to say and said it pleasantly, and who could also make you regret their silence. Such people allowed their listeners time to answer and to ponder, and won you over not merely by their reputation, but by their personal charm. What a joy it was to hear thoughts expressed with taste! But for a young woman alone on her own, there were as many pitfalls as attractions in Parisian life, and it was only as a very shy, often deeply unhappy onlooker, that I showed myself in these distinguished salons.

At times I thought that the only success I might look forward to was of a subordinate nature, and that in realizing this I had already won half my battle. But at other times my thoughts wandered out of bounds, reinforced and expanded by day-dreams. In order not to fall into despair, I strove hard to forget my mistaken start in life. But the accomplished fact had left behind very painful feelings. As an onlooker I sought diversion, made deductions; sometimes I even foresaw events. I was like the jester of my own imagination, which I used in the service of others. People lived under my eyes and I looked on; few confided in me, yet many gave themselves away, or ran counter to each other, or deceived themselves. Those who were truly happy exchanged discreet smiles on the sly, such smiles as made one envious. They radiated happiness in spite of themselves, so anxious were they not to lose a single scrap of it, even when they refrained from open avowals, and their sighs were as light as larks.

Thus, one day, in a drawing-room, I watched two lovers chastely taking stock of each other, yet evidently trying to wrap up in mystery what was to remain a secret save to themselves. However, passion lurked in their eyes, and many a time the man was obliged to lower his. The woman, more collected and oblivious, allowed hers to rove in half-formulated answers to the longings they both wished to keep deeply hidden. During the general conversation they had a way of suddenly stopping in the midst of a remark, contributing nothing new. They paid tribute to the company only by their presence, not by giving themselves wholly to it. Was it to put to the test the strength of the tie uniting them that they thus lingered so long among indifferent people? Yet their impatience came to light as soon as some guest approached one of them alone, pressing for his or her opinion and forcing an explanation. Even then, with all due courtesy, each answered as if addressing but one special person in the room. At last the woman decided to go. Sheer habit made her, however, utter the usual good-byes. No doubt she was thinking that presently she would tell the man that she had had eyes and ears only for him.

The man did not follow at once. He knew that this was the correct thing to do, but the strain of the situation made him start a long discussion in which he was interested in inverse ratio to the eagerness he brought to it and the deliberateness he showed in his efforts to convince his interlocutor. The time came when he also wanted to leave, but fear that it might still be too early to conform to decency made him endeavour, in a way as clumsy as it was useless, to launch further into discussions with people whose placid answers got on his nerves.

At last he escaped. A few seconds later I left in my turn. Keeping watch on this couple had brought me to dwell on the delight of loving and being loved, the quivering life of one's whole being it brought with it, the resonance in one's heart, the need to share every joy and every grief, and the egoistic solicitude which is but a longing for more complete possession.

Outside, the night was clear, and the stars so distant that I hesitated to recognize them as stars rather than the tears at the brims of my eyes. Then it happened that in front of me, following by chance the road I had taken, a couple — my couple — seemed to glide along. They were laughing; the secrets they told each other drew them close together. The avenue being almost deserted, they felt brave and walked so closely united that the woman's arm was no longer visible locked inside the man's. He held her firmly, almost lifting her off her feet, while she tried to make herself as light as possible the better to enjoy her surrender. When I saw their faces drawing close to each other, for fear of disturbing them I turned into a side street, but this time two tears were really running down my cheeks.

In order to forget my loneliness, I accepted every invitation that came.

The welcome given to her guests by Madame Madeleine Lemaire, the well-known flower-painter, had nothing in common with that met with in drawing-rooms. As soon as one entered her studio, which stood in the yard of her house on the Rue Monceau, one felt oneself belonging to a set interested in arts at large and fine living. Her bright and lively mind had at first attracted around her a group of painters and musicians, and gradually her little gatherings had drawn in various society people who thus gained the opportunity to be on familiar terms with dramatic *artistes* and other well-known personalities. She treated all her guests alike, and the chance of hearing excellent music played by select musicians attracted the whole of the Parisian *élite* to these Tuesday gatherings in May. One could see, as one came in, that the hard-working painter had only put aside her water-colour work for a few hours, for the flower she was using as model was still to be seen in some vase or other at the back of the studio. With inexhaustible skill she painted flowers according to whatever orders came to her, and she brought infinite variety into her compositions. She turned out one dainty and airy canvas after another and maintained her success for many years.

The programmes of her musical evenings were usually very short, and each one centred around some new star: perhaps a composer producing an unpublished work, or a foreign *artiste* passing through Paris, or a society woman whose talent might even surpass that of a professional player. Madame Lemaire had a kindly word for her guests as she guided each one towards a friendly group while greeting some new arrival with a smile. Often she was greatly embarrassed to find seats for all, but with the good-humour peculiar to this salon everyone found some corner, no matter how many were present.

On one point only did Madame Lemaire show no mercy: she insisted on her audience keeping silence and paying attention. At the slightest whisper she stood up and with a vigorous protest reduced the chatterbox to submission. Any *artiste* who had the good fortune to be taken up by her to play at one of her entertainments had his reputation enhanced thereby. Madeleine Lemaire introduced him to managers likely to engage him, or to society women in a position to organize musical evenings. Generous and disinterested, she bestowed the backing of her considerable influence without expecting any return; and the friendships which she thus formed were many and lasting. Once the performance was over, she used to go from group to group with her daughter Suzette, stating her opinion with assurance and comparing her impressions with those of her guests. The fresh ring of her voice preserved its youthful charm until she was well advanced in years, and from her whole personality emanated an inimitable charm.

The success of these evenings — for instance, the Greek ball of which Parisian society was still talking several seasons after — was greater than that of any other party. How could one forget those warm nights when we listened to Reynaldo Hahn singing his compositions in his deep and captivating voice, or to the Comtesse de Guerne interpreting songs of Fauré and Mozart? Without movement, without the slightest apparent effort, the melody flowed from her lips in crystalline harmonies of such purity that one seemed to listen to the song of a fountain. With perfect technique she modulated, and you were carried away into unknown spheres. There were moments when this icelike purity was set afire by echoes of some intimate anguish, yet she always kept within the bounds of perfection. And how can one describe the singing of that other *artiste*, Madame Kinen, whose deep and noble voice possessed a volume admirably adapted to the harmonies of Gluck? And the voice of the Comtesse de Maupeou with its heartrending accents, its impetuosity, its passionate appeals, veiled over as if tears were being chased in hard metal.

« III »

MADAME ARMAN DE CAILLAVET AND ANATOLE FRANCE

THE great-grandson of Lucien Bonaparte on the side of his mother and the nephew of Princesse Mathilde, Count Joseph Primoli had a Roman patrician for his father. As he had a taste for belles-lettres, he sought out the society of *artistes* and writers, whether in his own country or abroad, and it was commonly said of him that in Paris he was the Ambassador of Italian Arts and in Rome the Ambassador of French Arts. His imposing presence was full of a nonchalant though somewhat heavy gracefulness; the fine cut of his face and his smile, which vanished into a handsome white beard, added charm to the sometimes malicious wit which he displayed with studied elegance. Scornful of official distinction, he was led by his inclinations to frequent any kind of company, where his eager interest — bordering on mania — missed no opportunity of picking up information, above all on intellectual matters. He enjoyed asking his friends embarrassing questions, thereby hitting upon their secrets, and he found great delight in bringing together people who had quarrelled, either over trifles or more irreparable matters.

Thus he invited at his home Forain, an anti-Dreyfusite, at the same time as Madame Arman de Caillavet. He was as sentimental as an old spinster and could be so moved by love stories as sometimes to play the part of Providence or Fate in the destinies of his friends, all unknown to them and often to their undoing. Having a passion for the stage, he attended all dress rehearsals and never missed the entrance examination to the School of Dramatic Art. Every spring he left Rome and his *palazzo* to come and spend a few months in Paris. His arrival was at once announced on every side, and the nickname 'Gégé,' which he allowed people to use, passed from mouth to mouth.

'Gégé has arrived... Gégé has come back...'

With exquisite politeness he lost no time in going the round of his acquaintances. There was no party, no dinner, no smart tea from which he was absent. He went everywhere with such unwearying energy that we used to pretend he had the gift of ubiquity. Then he fixed afternoons and evenings for the parties he himself gave in his flat on the Avenue du Trocadéro. He showed himself in the most exclusive salons as well as the most easygoing. Without any more ceremony he brought his friends together, treating all with equal courtesy, yet in a way to ensure decorum and order at these gatherings where guests of very different types rubbed shoulders together. Though he was not arrogant and was a man of few prejudices, yet Count Primoli was sensitive to people keeping the distance due to his birth and his distinguished ancestry. He could make this clear with one word, with Roman subtlety and a good grace entirely French.

The furnishing of his flat was not luxurious; in fact, it was entirely heterogeneous, almost comical. The two drawing-rooms, separated by a mirror which was losing its silvering, and the dining-room were encumbered with ugly furniture covered with odds and ends of no value. The famous drawing by Ingres of the Bonaparte family was one year replaced by a photograph of the same drawing. Our host liked to offer his guests pieces of modern Italian pottery bearing inscriptions which might have some relation to themselves. On the walls were hung various mementoes covered with the signatures of famous people. There was a host of photographs in little frames or in albums, for Count Primoli was fond of going about with his camera and used it a great deal. Here, too, his love of mystification drove him to take surprise photographs of people meeting in circumstances that might lead to gossip, or of persons in unexpected positions when they would certainly not have wished to be seen.

This charming old man had certainly preserved a streak of childishness in his nature, though this was generously compensated by his obliging and genuine wish to be of service. Where *artistes* were concerned, he could put aside his artful egoism. Sometimes, when carried away by his independent spirit, he grew bold and launched successful schemes. At Princesse Mathilde's house he had made friends with the Goncourt brothers and with Gustave Flaubert, had witnessed many literary events of the period, and had stored up a large number of anecdotes which he related most pleasingly. He intended to write his memoirs and kept copious notes. One day, as I was visiting him, he read me a few pages. I can remember two episodes: first, the account of his parents' marriage, and secondly, the reflexions suggested to him by his birth. I still recollect his comical description of his father's misgivings on the very steps of the church, and his subtle analysis of the parental restless temperaments. Count Primoli ascribed to the clashing personalities of his parents the burdensome heritage of his own instability. He looked at me, as he brought out this fact, trying to see me raise objections which would put his mind at rest on this matter.

Although he had given me some explanations for his ever-changing schemes, I knew that his insatiable inquisitiveness would always change his days into a medley of engagements, while his laziness would never allow him to carry out his literary ambitions. In fact, the few pages of 'Souvenirs' which were published in *La Revue de Paris*, together with a book entitled *In Stendhal's Footsteps in Rome*, are unfortunately all that survive of his dabbling in letters.

It was at Count Primoli's, in 1905, that I met Madame Arman de Caillavet. She was wearing, on that occasion, an elaborate dress and a hat from which hung bunches of grapes and vine-shoots which mingled with her henna-dyed hair. Her face, lit up by blue eyes, was vivacious, with cheeks rather full, a double chin, and powder dabbed on rather carelessly. She spoke in well-chosen words and fired out questions point-blank with unconcealed curiosity.

'I am frank. Why should not one be entirely open on

almost all subjects?' she declared. 'Nothing is unmentionable; it depends how it is expressed.'

One felt her a determined nature, combative and void of pettiness. Her whole manner revealed her as very self-assured. She knew her own intelligence, was aware of her own worth, and showed contempt towards those who seemed to her lacking in wit. Her stern judgments were delivered in ironical tones. The somewhat old-fashioned manner in which she told stories bore witness to her intercourse with an intellectual man and her literary tastes.

'I am at home every Sunday; you must come and see me,' she told me. 'Also I invite you to dinner next Wednesday. You will see Monsieur Anatole France.'

When she pronounced this distinguished name, 'Anatole France,' she brought out each syllable clearly, shut her eyes and nodded her head. Was he not, in truth, the most famous writer of the period? Was not the opportunity of meeting him a real piece of luck?

Madame Arman slipped her gloves again over chubby hands adorned with many rings; she rose, and after smiling to friends, went away with short, dignified steps.

On the following Wednesday I entered her drawing-room in the Avenue Hoche. It was dimly lit, and from the entrance hall I had already gathered, from the hubbub of voices, that a large company was within. Feeling rather overawed, I looked for the lady of the house. Clad in a light-coloured dress and displaying many jewels, she was surrounded by so many people that I had difficulty in reaching her grandfather-chair. She welcomed me graciously, made room for me by her side, and, pointing to a compact group of people pressing around Anatole France, 'He is over there,' she whispered.

I tried to catch a glimpse of the *Maître*. Unconsciously I strained my ear to catch his voice. He was standing, with head bowed. His face was unsymmetrical, his thick greyish hair encroached upon a receding brow and in the middle formed a peak from which it fell backwards, although cut short; the nose was long and crooked; one end of the thick grey moustache was turned up as in triumph, while the other drooped dejectedly. The tip of the tiny beard pointed in yet another direction. The lively eyes, from between brown lashes, shone with a malicious, mocking light, amidst a yellow, chaotic, and sullen face. Monsieur France had two voices: one rather nasal and almost cantankerous, the other very unctuous, with weighty songful notes cleverly prolonged. He did not speak with ease and kept correcting himself, looking around in a frightened way to right and left, as if he were tired to death of having to talk and make people laugh. He often stroked his beard with his shapely hand and muttered: 'Really... really...' and then burst into sudden anger, more or less feigned, and turned towards someone in the room, pretending to accuse him of the misdeeds of this or that politician. He was well aware of his lack of eloquence, for I heard him exclaim: 'When I speak, you can hear me crossing words out. When you read me, it's different.' The profusion of his ideas caused him to open parentheses which led him to others, and thus further and further away from the subject under discussion.

On that particular Sunday he dwelt on the most varied

topics; in one and the same monologue he summarized one of Jaurès's speeches and ended by describing a picture in the Art Gallery at Munich. Every now and then a new visitor greeted him and enlarged the circle around him. Clusters of people stood by the three windows and by the tea-table, where a massive silver tea-service was displayed as some unique ornament with its unlighted spirit lamp. A solitary cake, girdled with silver paper, was placed well in evidence upon the table, but none of the guests seemed to help themselves or to dare ask for anything at all.

Madame Arman rose from her armchair and went from guest to guest, keeping her eye all the time on Monsieur France.

Suddenly she called out to him: 'Monsieur, we have a fine gathering here this afternoon. Tell us that story I so enjoyed yesterday.'

He turned about sharply. 'No, Madame, I shan't do anything of the sort.'

But she insisted. 'Yes, Monsieur, you must. You tell it so well.'

He refused, with sweeping gestures of protest. However, still grumbling, he advanced a few paces towards our hostess.

'Well, here you are, Madame; since you order it, one must obey you. Although the story is very odd, it is not of general interest, and I am convinced that your charming lady visitors would much prefer to go on being flirted with.'

He was leaning against the mantelpiece, all eyes focussed on him. Addressing himself to Monsieur Calmann-Lévy, his publisher, he began:

'You see, my friend, it's a very old story. I discovered it, or rather rediscovered it, in a book I bought from a dealer on the quays. I really don't know why Madame Arman wants me to relate it; there's nothing very funny about the story, and I can't make head or tail of it.'

'Come, Monsieur,' Madame Arman expostulated, 'everybody knows...'

He cut her short.

'No, definitely not, giving it thought, the more I feel you really want me on the mat, the more I am convinced that this particular story is not worth repeating. So I shan't tell it. I can't help it; you shouldn't have provoked me.'

He thrust his hands in his pockets and walked a little way off with Calmann-Lévy, and I heard him laugh and say in a whisper: 'Really, really, no, not that one!'

Madame Arman was a woman of determination. If she felt sympathy for anyone, she would show it by entreating her distinguished friend to take an interest in her protégés, to invite them to see him, and to carry out the promises, which he made all the more recklessly, since once the petitioners had gone he thought no more of them. At heart Madame Arman was convinced that she had a function to fulfil, and she spent her time as much in telling Anatole France what to do as in making him collaborate in some work which she deemed worthy of his reputation. She was bold in spirit and decisive in her actions. If one of her favourites deceived her by his behaviour, his conversation, or his writings, she disposed of him with an alacrity doubled by a streak of cruelty and a complete indifference as to what might be said. Had she not flown in the face of public opinion and won recognition for her liaison with France? Its duration and Anatole France's reputation gave it the seal of legitimacy, consecrated her choice, and placed this intimacy on a par with other famous friendships.

Madame Arman had possessed literary leanings before she came to know Monsieur France, but his daily visits had fashioned her to his own bookish conception of an Egeria worthy of the name. Although she was fond of speaking about ideas they had discussed together in private, yet Madame Arman had views of her own, very definite and often contrary to his. In short, she was the downright man in this partnership. She was well aware that a whimsical element was a part of Monsieur Anatole's nature; that he was so touchy, so perpetually rebellious, yet so listless as to need her constant management. It was certainly by her undauntable insistence that she prevailed over his apathy and compelled him to set to work.

In a room of the second floor of her house, she had set two desks back to back, one at which Anatole France sat writing, while at the other she classified his notes and documents. With her practical instinct she took charge of his dealings with publishers. Monsieur France's makeup was so full of contradictions! By taste and inclination he loved all that was refined, rare, inaccessible, yet he hated with almost equal vigour those who had helped to create this world in which he lived, and in which certain restraints he had to place upon himself exasperated him. In her struggle against what she called his laziness, Madame Arman had forced upon him social duties and habits he found it difficult to put up with; yet, though he may not have realized it, the incense she burnt at his altar was absolutely necessary to the great man. Thus, raised on a pinnacle, he despised almost everyone; prone to speak with a lack of interest which verged upon the contemptuous, his cultured mind yet made him delight in whatever bore the stamp of distinction and his rebellious temperament knocked over conventions, using his critical faculty as a means of wreaking vengeance. Deeply convinced that folly led the world, he only grew tender over its weaknesses; but, though indulgent to its vices, he showed no mercy towards errors of taste. His own literary traditions made him deliciously conventional, and he derived a voluptuous pleasure from following in the footsteps of his intellectual forbears; nevertheless, he was a creature of impulse and at moments felt deep revolt against his servitude. He then put aside all discipline and abandoned himself to his inclinations. He had, however, so long been subjected to constraint that he very soon fell back into the groove of his daily life and work.

On the occasion of my first visit at the Avenue Hoche, towards the close of the afternoon a queer person came in noisily; the closely cropped hair, the large eyes, the flat nose with a wart on the tip, the toothless mouth — every feature of this man's beaming countenance was pregnant with frank good-heartedness. He was a strapping fellow, and his broad figure was clothed in a jacket rather too short; a loose bow-tie of enormous dimensions, blue with white spots, projected from his turndown collar. He seemed to be in merry spirits, and spoke in a thunderous voice. His booming laugh rang out as he went from guest to guest shaking their hands warmly. After a time I found myself face to face with him.

'I see that I must introduce myself,' he said. 'I am, Madame' — and his eyes twinkled mockingly — 'I am The Master' — pausing a moment to stress the word — 'of the house. Tell me, France,' he bawled, 'is this another of your fair admirers?'

Madame Arman came to my rescue, but her husband's somewhat brusque manners had not displeased me, and his perfect naturalness added cordiality to the somewhat formal atmosphere of the salon. None the less, I could detect behind his outspoken behaviour a certain element of malice and the secret desire to play his part. I learned later that this was also how his wife judged him.

If Monsieur Arman was the *enfant terrible* of the house, Monsieur France was the spoilt child. Madame Arman always contrived to keep the incense burning to his fame. She could not brook hearing in a salon any writer extolled but her own. She was addicted to violent sarcasm in this matter and was not afraid of her remarks being repeated.

She was fond of attracting foreign writers to her house. Monsieur Arman was present at all these gatherings and always with bantering good-humour. One evening, at dinner, when Anatole France claimed not to care about public opinion, Monsieur Arman banged his fist upon the table. Everyone gave a start.

Rejoicing in the effect he had produced, he shouted: 'I don't agree! No, I don't at all agree!'

He looked all around at the silent guests and proceeded: 'You do, in the first instance, expect from the public, and quite justly, the admiration which your works inspire.'

He flattered France, but sometimes he took the liberty of poking fun at him. One evening he told us how, as a collaborator on *Le Figaro* on the subject of yachting, he once had to write up the English regattas. As he had influenza at the time, he resorted to Anatole France.

'My friend, you are a distinguished writer. Do my little paper for me.' France acceded to his request. 'However,' Monsieur Arman went on, 'judge of my surprise when *Le Figaro* sent the text back to me full of corrections. I who had imagined it would be my best article! France had certainly filled it with a thousand elegant things — clouds, blue waves, and God knows what besides. The sub-editor did not appreciate it. He had, without knowing it, "blocked-out" Anatole France.'

However, one daily collaboration made Anatole France and Monsieur Arman close partners: this was the arrangement of the menu. They were both equally fond of their food. Very often the Wednesday dinners would include dishes made from recipes discovered in eighteenth-century cookery books. The guests were informed of this at the beginning of the meal, and Monsieur Arman would await the arrival of the masterpiece with religious anxiety. Generally the dish would turn out to be very complicated and seasoned with various spices. Madame Arman's cooking was always rather heavy. Stuffed pike, pheasant *à l'allemande, céleri à la portugaise, cassoulet toulousain, fricassée* of chicken with red pepper, were served. Our hostess made no use of Madame Aubernon's bell, yet could guide the conversation skilfully and make each guest pull his full weight. She would provoke them, put them on their mettle, and lavish encouraging words when they hesitated to come out of their shells.

Guests of distinction were announced, just as the dishes were. Often it would be some politician, and Madame Arman would whisper his name, and add, 'He will give explanations of his behaviour.'

For certain festive occasions lectures were arranged. The Abbé Moreux, the astronomer, gave us a lecture when he first came to live in Paris; and Guglielmo Ferrero's eloquence earned him a great success. In these discussions there would participate Aristide Briand, the Abbé Mugnier, Joseph Reinach, Loie Fuller, Count Primoli, and Adrien Hébrard; it was a treat to hear the latter in conversation with Madame Arman (whom he called the Récamier of the Avenue Hoche) or with Anatole France, so affable when he liked, and whose learning was so worthy of admiration.

When France wished to captivate, his charm was inimitable; if, for instance, he described a Greek statue, his hands, in tender gestures, seemed to caress its shape.

Brimming with emotion Madame Arman would then say softly: 'Oh, you are so charming, Monsieur.'

And, turning to me: 'You see, little one, there is only one man who counts, it is Monsieur France.'

Madame Arman always showed friendly feelings towards

Time Past

me. I liked her frank, fearless nature, and her zest for life which kept her young in spirit. She paid no heed to the passing years, but, like an intrepid traveller, was interested in everything and always ready to go out for a walk or to visit some exhibition.

She hated sentimentality, but she had an excellent heart. I had many opportunities of becoming aware of this.

Here are two of her letters I choose amidst many others:

Caillavet Estate
nr. Laugoisan (Gironde)
Capian, November 1, 1908

Dear Little Friend,

It is only yesterday I learned, after being away for a short while, of the sudden aggravation in your father's illness. I feel very grieved and send you words of deep sympathy. This is a trial which renders your uncertain life even more bitter, but your friends must surround you with more solicitude and attention than ever. I know that this does not suffice, but until better days do come... and at your age it is so legitimate to hope. Keep me informed, and though I dare not predict an amelioration for which your letter gives little hope, yet do not doubt that my best wishes go out to you and that it is always with the most sincere sympathy I think of you in all your troubles.

Most affectionately
L. Arman de Caillavet

L'ABBÉ MUGNIER

Madame de Caillavet and Anatole France

Château de Caillavet
October 18

Dear Little Friend,

I delayed replying to your charming letter, for I had here so much to do, the whole house to rearrange. Having had the misfortune to do away with one piece of furniture, all the others, as in a sort of catching disease, suddenly appeared impossible to keep. Thus one contrives to disturb one's life for lack of a contented mind, for I was really quite peaceful amidst my old furniture; all I needed to do was not to look at it.

And you, little dreamer, what has become of you since we said good-bye one evening in September? What have the days brought you? Alas, it is really little they do bring, these days which follow upon each other, monotonous and deceptive! At your age, reckoned to be the spring of life, one should have a right to look forward to flowers, lovely walks, handsome distractions. This is what Madame X, always so silly and grandiloquent, calls the right to happiness. But in fact life does not care a hang about this, and to make fun of us it seems to put into us longings and dreams. They are lucky who get hold of something, and even then one has to admit that whatever falls to one's share does so only by chance. Still, I can give you praise for being an artist, for loving beautiful things, and I congratulate you upon being yourself beautiful and attractive. That already is something like the fragrance of incense burning for you and intoxicating you, for want of something better.... And who knows if that something better will not come? Nothing more likely.

The autumn is very beautiful. It is a season I have always liked, even before my years came to be in perfect harmony with it. Every human being, so we are told, has an age and a season which best suits the secret age of his spirit. I believe I have reached that age.

Tell me all that goes through your mind; you know that it

always interests me; explain to me what is for you the colour of the sky and if, when you walk, you see the skyline as pink, or black, or simply uncertain. And believe that I am always happy to receive your news.

Affectionately
L. ARMAN DE CAILLAVET

Monsieur France sends his kindest regards.

In 1907, the new review *Les Lettres*, the contributors to which were nearly all frequent visitors at the Avenue Hoche, organized a dinner in honour of Anatole France and Georg Brandes at the Touring Club's châlet. So one bright June evening saw a large foregathering around Madame Arman: René Béhaine, René Boylesve, P. L. Couchaud, André Doderet, Robert Dreyfus, Monsieur and Madame Fernand Gregh, Charles Muller, François Porché, Jérôme and Jean Tharaud, Marcelle Tinayre and others. After the toast by Fernand Gregh, Georg Brandes rose and read a long and elaborate speech, ending with greeting to the young generation of France.

Then Anatole France spoke. He had prepared nothing.

'Some thirty years ago,' he began, 'I read a sonnet written on the fly-leaf of a book which bore the insignia of Charles IX. It was attributed to Charles IX himself, first because it was not a very good sonnet, and also because the handwriting resembled this king's signatures. In this sonnet the king, addressing a lady, says: "I love you, I love deeply, but I cannot tell you of my love. Venus was born in the sea-foam and her first admirers were the fish, dumb animals. I am like these subjects of the newborn Venus."'

Then, harping on a familiar theme: 'As for myself, I say to my friends who have treated me with such kindness that I love them very much, and that precisely for that reason I cannot tell it to them in fine phrases. I am not good at expressing myself except with my pen, when I can scratch things out on paper. You cannot see my corrections because I tear up the paper. But when I speak, things to scratch out become unbearable to me and far more to those who have to listen.'

With mock humility he expressed his thanks to Georg Brandes, and then added: 'Monsieur Brandes has shown that real history is the history of literature. He has shown that belles-lettres — that is to say, the history of the human mind as it manifests itself in its finest creations — make real history, and that literary facts, if we take the word "literary" in its broadest and most exalted sense, are the most important facts for humanity, those which give rise to other facts.'

From this stenographic text it is, indeed, clear that Nature had not endowed Anatole France with the gift of eloquence. But this is the advice he proffered to the review: 'When a review is young, when a review is at the age of love-making, it must love mightily, and it must hate as mightily as it loves, because love which is not completed by hate is not really love at all. You have achieved nothing by simply loving beauty; it is further essential for you to store up for ugliness, for old antiquated ugliness, a hatred that is ever new.'

Madame Arman was smiling from beneath her tiny curls, now grown white.

'Tonight,' she said, 'I can see the incarnation of beauty in those two handsome foreign women Monsieur Brandes has brought with him.'

She went up to Madame Victor de Goloubeff and her sister.

'It would be a great pleasure to see you at my Sunday gatherings,' she said; 'your beauty would lend them distinction.'

The appearance of each new book by France was awaited with curiosity in every quarter. At the Avenue Hoche the matter was discussed, long ahead, in an atmosphere of mystery. Sometimes intimate acquaintances had the good luck to be present at the reading of some passages from the unpublished work. One night France read to us the opening pages of his *Penguin Island*. Madame Arman gave the signal for applause. When the master came to the passage which describes the toilet of the female penguin, she began to cough mischievously and threw knowing glances at all the ladies present. After the reading we fell to discussing the implications, while Anatole France fenced off compliments. He declared that it was fun to turn his own period into parables so as to lend it a savour which otherwise it would lack. One fair and enthusiastic admirer kept on repeating, 'It's better than Voltaire.' Nothing could more easily win the heart of the lady of the house.

About 1905 the famous artist Steinlen had helped to decorate the Taverne de Paris, a restaurant in the Avenue de Clichy, now pulled down. To show us his frescoes,

Madame de Caillavet and Anatole France

Steinlen invited Madame de Caillavet, Anatole France, and myself to lunch at the Taverne.

He took us to one end of the room, where his paintings were displayed with those of Abel Faivre and several others in one of those settings in the 1900 style which are now quite rightly held to be the acme of bad taste. Madame Arman praised him highly. When we had settled down, our host pointed to an additional place.

'I have invited one of my friends,' he said, 'the legal champion of the Nord strikers, Aristide Briand.'

Soon after arrived a fairly tall man, slightly round-shouldered, hollow in the chest, untidy in his dress, but full of supple ease. His head was striking, with thick hair, and captivating eyes; he spoke in serious, persuasive tones. Anatole France bombarded him with questions. He answered them ingeniously and was patently striving to speak sincerely. His slender, elegant hands seemed by their sober gestures to add weight to the meaning of his words. On hearing his explanations, everything seemed plausible; one scheme followed upon another according to the trend of his musings, and his mind looked into the future and based its arguments upon facts which he presented with great felicity. His ability to give a clear account of a complicated situation inspired confidence. He adorned his talk with little tales from life, thus enlivening his account without making it ponderous. His voice was deep and possessed a very individual ring; he spoke in serious tones, stressing certain words and phrases. From time to time he would let slip a biting remark, yet he betrayed no partisan spirit; on the contrary, a philosophic attitude which he had acquired through experiences which had not embittered him, but had only given him a gentle and kindly irony.

As the conversation went on, Aristide Briand ingeniously deflected it to the subject of nature. Here he betrayed his poetic temperament. With genuine feeling he explained to us how fond he was of angling. I have seldom heard so fine a description of the awakening of the countryside around the angler who sits silently watching every ripple on the water. He detailed the various sensations that such waiting produces, without seeming to attach any importance to the matter except as an exact account of the facts. Stroke by stroke he conjured up a whole landscape, the weather of the morning, and the musings of the angler's mind, ending in the concentrated attention he fixes upon the end of his line. As he spoke, his eyes followed the convolutions of the blue smoke from his cigarettes — for he drew fresh cigarettes mechanically from his pocket.

The defender of Broutchoux, Falempin, and Couane, strikers in the Nord, looked like a countryman with placid habits and an idyllic soul. There was something so enjoyable in his manner of telling stories that the people at the near-by tables had ceased their conversations. But of this he was quite unaware, as he sat lost in his musings, far away from the present.

The impression I got from this meeting was of a profoundly humane personality with an attentive mind ready to take up and consider every suggestion.

After that lunch with Steinlen, I often accompanied

Madame Arman and Anatole France during their walks. They liked to go to dealers in antiques, and a book they had found or any curio often started France on long stories. Sometimes they were recollections of his childhood (a few of which are found in *Le Petit Pierre*); at other times they were of things he had read. He launched directly upon his subject, as if he supposed his audience possessed an erudition equal to his, and kept on referring to various authors whose arguments he commented on. He gave the impression that he was carrying on aloud a discussion with himself, the data of which remained mysterious for those who listened, while, either through absent-mindedness or contempt, he neglected to explain them.

I noticed also that when one arrived at the Villa Saïd, France seemed to adapt his conscious remarks to one as to a stream of intimate thoughts he had been brooding over. Thus, greeting you with a friendly gesture, he went on with his private monologue in your presence. If you could make sense of what he said, all the better; otherwise, you had to seek compensation in the numerous digressions he was sure to embark upon. Later, I came to realize that Marcel Proust had likewise this faculty of being able to pursue, in front of any chance stranger, the development of thoughts which had inwardly occupied him.

One Sunday morning, in 1908, I arrived early at Anatole France's, for at dinner on the preceding Friday in the Avenue Hoche he had promised to show me some books. As I was introduced into his study by the old Joséphine, the 'hot-tempered' as he liked to call her, I found him walking up and down. In front of him was seated, huddled in an armchair, a man with unkempt hair and beard framing a wan face. His puny body disappeared in clothes far too big; he spoke with difficulty, seemed embarrassed and made uncertain gestures.

France turned towards me: 'Do you know, Madame, whom you see here, the most famous mathematician of our time? — Monsieur Poincaré, here is a young lady I introduce to you.' I was keenly interested. Anatole France went on: 'And guess, fair lady, what this great man has come to ask me. That I vote for him at the Academy! He lives so lost in the most lofty intellectual speculations that he is completely ignorant I no longer show myself at the illustrious Assembly on the quays — but if I ever go...' Henry Poincaré seemed to curl up deeper into his armchair. He muttered something quite unintelligible. I felt paralyzed by his shyness, his inability to express himself.

Then, with a suddenness which showed his alert mind, France called upon him to speak: 'It is now your turn to tell me something: is it true that Paul Painlevé is as learned as he is rumoured to be?'

At once the little man pulled himself up as if electrified: 'He is prodigious,' he began; 'his daring has often surprised me; with his lucid and powerful will he has forged ahead on the most improbable hypotheses and brought forth a series of studies and experiments which already make of his work a perfect achievement. His name will live in posterity, and should he die tomorrow you can be sure that he has produced one of the most lofty achievements of French science.'

Madame de Caillavet and Anatole France

For several months, at the beginning of 1909, we had begun to feel a certain uneasiness in the atmosphere of the Caillavets' salon. A journey which Monsieur France proposed to take to lecture in Argentina had been once or twice alluded to. Little by little this idea began to take shape, and Madame Arman appeared at times favourable to it, and at others distinctly hostile. All at once the news was confirmed.

Our gatherings during that period were marred by the discord which divided the writer and his Egeria. But France cracked jokes, and thereupon Madame Arman tried to look upon this journey as a very short absence, and endeavoured to console herself with the idea that France's fame would be increased a hundredfold thereby.

France went away. People still continued to meet in the Avenue Hoche; but with every new week that went by, our hostess's uneasiness grew worse and she began to complain of the lack of news. Soon she could no longer hide her anxiety, and broke into a torrent of abuse against this 'uncivilized' country, as she called it, where Monsieur France had gone to speak words of wisdom.

'A country of monkeys and parrots,' she said, 'at the other end of the world, where, when one looks up to the stars, it is not the Great Bear one sees, but the Southern Cross.'

Extravagant rumours were heard everywhere in Paris. For a while Madame Arman closed her door on her friends, then, calling a few of her familiars through the telephone, she asked them to come. She had at last received news and wanted to impart it. The letter she produced from her handbag was only from her valet François, whom she had lent to Monsieur France; but she seemed peaceful once more, finding comfort in the details received. We saw her reborn to life from that instant. Never before had I so well understood how deeply attached she was to the reputation and the person of the famous writer.

After her guests had left her, she kept me with her; we dined together, and she took pleasure in opening her heart to me with delightful unconstraint.

'He is such a child,' she explained; 'if you only knew how weak and naïve he is, so easy to dupe!'

Very much moved, she enumerated all the reasons she had for admiring him. She wanted to strengthen her idol, to show me that he was beyond suspicion.

After this talk, I felt my affection for my old friend greater than ever. About that time I went to London for a few days. There, a letter from a friend left me no longer in doubt as to Monsieur France's fickle behaviour. Here is an extract from it:

> Perhaps you have been told about the prodigious adventure of Anatole France whose return is expected any day in Paris.... I hope you will be present to hear the latest confession and the supreme lies concerning this journey far more anacreontic than literary, for the literary part of it met with poor success, while the amorous adventure is flourishing. Our illustrious friend, who set out as a Sainte-Beuve, ends as a Baron Hulot. You know that the heroine is an old actress, Mademoiselle Brindeau, who is almost as old as the Récamier of the Avenue Hoche. Here is indeed a story from my personal stock of anecdotes: We were dining, some fifteen years ago, at Jules Simon's home, a few friends together among

whom were Alexandre Dumas, Doctor Germain Sée, and myself. When making our way home after dinner, chatting together the three of us, the famous doctor gave Dumas and myself advice concerning the wisdom of people who, having reached the unbelievable age he referred to as 'almost centenarian,' had yet preserved vitality in all their bodily functions. You may guess that this advice (and your audacious shrewdness will understand the full import of it) heartened his two listeners. A week later Alexandre Dumas stopped me on the boulevard and said to me: 'You know, dear friend, all that advice is wasted. Doctor Sée is just ruining himself, and for... Mademoiselle Brindeau!...'

I was in Paris again when France came back. The very next day, just by luck, I met the couple at Versailles. Madame Arman was agitated and sad; France shamefaced and in a bad temper. They invited me to come with them in the park; I felt that Madame Arman longed for the nearness of a friend, a witness to those days when there was no discord between them, and that my passive presence might help to the reconciliation she was in haste to secure. Or perhaps she was also seeking someone who might explain to the outside world that nothing was changed in their relations. We wandered about the gardens; contrary to his habit, Monsieur France scarcely spoke; his companion, on the other hand, asked him a thousand questions and tried to relate to him all that had happened during his absence. She had made up her mind to appear unconcerned, but I guessed how weary she was; however, it was part of her nature to be brave. Her self-esteem demanded it.

At the beginning of September, on the seventh to be

exact, she asked me to go with her and Anatole France to lunch at Madeleine Lemaire's at Réveillon, in Seine-et-Marne. We went by motor-car. The details of that journey are for ever engraved in my memory. Madame Arman seemed more agitated than even at Versailles; her impatience to recapture the unfaithful man pierced through every one of her remarks. She enjoyed a bitter satisfaction in pointing out to him his defection, and on the road, drawing his attention to a landscape he did not admire sufficiently to her taste, she exclaimed, as an echo of deeper feelings, 'Ah! Monsieur, you have lost all sense of beauty!'

And a little further on, 'Monsieur, you have no pride.' Her remarks irritated him.

Then she conjured up for my benefit memories of their first meeting.

'It was at Madame Aubernon's. Monsieur France was very shy; no one knew him; he had scarcely published anything as yet.'

At this recollection he seemed to grow more tender. He spoke of his youth, the lessons he gave, the frugal meals he used to take in the suburbs we were just crossing. Very much moved, she whispered: 'You were so pathetic, Monsieur. Give me your hand.' And brusquely, grumpily, he held forth a hand which he just as hurriedly withdrew, and relapsed into renewed silence.

To create a diversion, she questioned me about my life: 'And with you, is there anything new?'

As I replied in the negative: 'What can you expect, little one? Men are such a poor lot, nowadays. But at least there was one worth his salt, and he still exists.'

She was smiling at France, but he did not seem at all to relish this compliment.

Somewhere about Coulommiers, the chauffeur not knowing the way, we lost our direction. It was past two o'clock when the car stopped in front of Madeleine Lemaire's mansion. The return journey was tragic. Shortage of petrol caused us to stop in the Vincennes woods. Madame Arman, who could no longer hide her distress, disappeared in a dark path. For a long time she wandered about alone, having forbidden anyone to follow her in these woods where night was falling. She later came back, walking slowly, a little quieter, and proposed we should dine at Marguery's. It was the last time I was alone with Anatole France and Madame Arman face to face.

As she had resolved to fight to the end, Madame Arman used to say: 'What is really needed, don't you see, is for Monsieur France to come and have a rest at Capian,[1] and pull himself together. You will see, Monsieur, what good the country will do you. You will like the grape-gathering and will become yourself again.'

Her voice sounded more assured. She felt she was once more at the helm; for he agreed, as if caught in fault.

I was at home a few days later when, during the morning, the doorbell rang several times in haste. It was Madame Arman come to see me without any warning, greatly to my surprise, for she never did this. I found her prostrate in an armchair.

[1] Madame Arman's country house in Gironde.

'Little one,' she said hurriedly, 'I am so unhappy, I wish I were dead.'

Her face was drawn, her hat, set askew, let escape a few streaks of white hair. I put my arms around her and protested.

'Yes,' she went on, 'I would like to die, and Professor X refuses to give me poison. I know that you also had once a longing to disappear. I felt I had to see you.'

I tried to appease her, to reason with her. I managed to make her look upon their forthcoming departure for Gironde as the end of her troubles. Big tears shone in her eyes. There came back to me a saying of hers she had so often repeated; so I told her: 'You used to say, Madame, that the kingdom of Man is upon Earth, and now you wish to desert it.'

She sighed; her emotion made me realize how deeply she was hurt.

'How could he lower himself to that extent?' she whispered. 'Such conduct is not worthy of him. In another man, it might be admitted, but in Monsieur France, the greatest mind of our time, it is a shame!'

I proposed, as the weather was admirable, to go for a little stroll. We walked up the Avenue Hoche; I felt very sad, but was far from realizing I was seeing my old friend for the last time. She walked with some trouble, stopping now and again to get her breath. Steeped in her grief, the world all around her no longer existed. I feel sure that when illness came to her, she opposed no resistance, having exhausted beforehand all her strength: Madame Arman died of love.

She found, however, the courage to set off for Gironde. I wrote to her several times during her stay there which lasted two or three months. Each time she herself answered except during the dangerous part of her illness when she asked Monsieur France to do so.

'I am asked,' he wrote, 'by our friend, to thank you warmly for your affectionate remembrance of her, and to tell you that she is much better and will soon be able to come back to Paris. It is a great pleasure for me to deliver this message, since it is to you, and therefore offers me the opportunity of sending you my friendly greetings. I have quite a longing to see once again your bright face.'

Madame Arman must have returned to Paris at the end of the year. Her health remained shaky and the news one received from the Avenue Hoche was far from reassuring. Several times Monsieur France came to tell me how she was. He did not appear to foresee a fatal issue.

Two days before that sad event he had a little note delivered to me:

> I would have come to see you yesterday, but I have to keep indoors on account of a troublesome lumbago. But it would give me a great pleasure to see you this afternoon on your way home from the studio. Alas, I cannot yet give you very good news of our friend.

Madame Arman passed away on Wednesday, the twelfth of January, 1910. The next day I went to the Villa Saïd. I was received by the old maid, Joséphine: 'Go up, Madame. Monsieur France is in a terrible state; he does nothing but cry.'

He was walking up and down the room, sobbing.

Time Past

'Ah! Madame,' he exclaimed, 'it is a dead man you come to see! I am more dead than she is. How could she forsake me thus? It is desertion. I was far from foreseeing such a misfortune. She had my interests so much at heart, let alone my fame. She was intelligent, had prodigious ability, foresight and ingenuity. And do you know how I left her? "I must go, Madame, for I have lumbago." Not one tender word, or affectionate remark. Well, it is true, I had lumbago, but not as bad as all that. I could have stayed near her, and I did not see her again except in death. She had found again her beauty as when at forty, full round cheeks and a peaceful face.'

Copious tears came with each sentence.

'And that snow, last evening, it was my friend's shroud. Besides, all things will now bring her back to me: in every street and every town, everywhere her memory will follow me.'

He stopped in front of a small piece of furniture which he pushed away with his foot.

'It was she chose it. And then I have such remorse, but if I made her suffer, it was out of weakness, not wickedness. She would have liked me to surrender myself to her as she did to me. She knew no self-abnegation.'

He stopped abruptly.

'Do you know what she did to me? She deceived me.'

Witnessing my astonishment, he went on:

'Yes, she deceived me regarding her age: she was sixty-nine. Could you ever have believed this? What will now become of me? She was a society woman, but without pettiness; there ought to be another word to apply to her.'

For a long while he thus spoke of her. He was completely broken with grief. Now and again he threw himself on a chair, then got up again and went on walking up and down the room. Over his clothes he wore a dressing-gown, a scarf was round his neck and a skull-cap on his head.

I got up to go.

'Do stay,' he said to me; 'lunch with me. I can't be left alone. I must also learn to give orders; it was she always did so here. Joséphine is so hot-tempered.'

The day before the funeral he came to have lunch with me. Very depressed, he wept without restraint. 'To-morrow,' he said, 'I shall have to behave myself. But near you I can weep.'

At the Church Saint Philippe du Roule, during the ceremony, he preserved a set face and a courageous attitude. He kept apart from the family. While all eyes watched him, he remained tense, his neck buried between his shoulders, and his eyes fixed in space, though his face was all of a tremor. He did not weep; and his hands, deep in his pockets, squeezed no other hand. At the end of the service he made off by himself to go to the cemetery.

During the fortnight that followed, the people of Paris lived through an anxious time. The Seine was rising daily more and more; then came the floods during which the town looked like a besieged city. These were gloomy days streaked with rain and snow.

One morning Monsieur France came for me to go and lunch at La Pérousse. The wildness of the weather suited his sorrowful state. The ground floor of the restaurant was flooded; we had to go to the first floor. The swift current of the Seine was ochre in colour.

During the meal Monsieur France told me about a journey he had made with Madame Arman in 1908, in Sicily and Greece.

'She had a very inquisitive mind; it was marvellous to follow her, for she wanted to visit everything. Look, these floods make me think of the first eruption of Vesuvius in which perished Pliny the Elder. It was in 79. On the other side of the Naples Bay, his young nephew, a cad, did not even bestir himself to see what on earth could be this mountain on fire. It is true that in those days the volcano crater was covered up with vines. Still, less callous than he was, we shall go after lunch, if you do not mind, to see what has become of my print-seller in the Rue de Seine, where I am told punts have to be used to go about.'

Very often, after Madame Arman's death, Monsieur France came to lunch at my home. He always spoke of her, praised all her qualities and said that his remorse was so heavy to bear that he preferred not to remain alone. My son, quite a little boy at the time, was very much impressed by the old man's tears. He knew how much I admired him.

One day he asked me: 'Is it true that Monsieur France is so learned that he knows everything?'

I assured him that it was, and added: 'He will come to lunch tomorrow. If there is something important you want to know, he will certainly be willing to tell you.'

When France arrived, the little one ran to him: 'My mamma says that you know everything, sir.'

France interrupted him: 'That is to say I know all the unimportant things; but come, what is it you want?'

'Is it true, sir, that Cain killed Abel?'

'I think I can tell you it is pretty certain he did, but that is a long time ago,' answered France with a smile.

'But, sir, what I can't understand,' went on my son, 'is how he could have thought of killing him, since there were not as yet any dead people, and Adam and Eve lived quite alone with their children.'

France replied: 'Indeed, perfectly true, child, and I am delighted at your way of reasoning, but I am going to tell you what most likely did happen. Cain could not have conceived the notion of killing his brother, as you have so truly remarked, but he was violent, brutal, and it was out of clumsiness he killed Abel and we may add — is this not true, Madame? — that on that day evil was born. You have asked me there a very clever question, and I congratulate you upon it.'

A few days later he brought to my son, as a reward, a handsome picture book.

Anatole France told me once that, when he was a youth, his parents gave him very little pocket money, though his ambitions were great. For instance, he longed to get a good seat at the Opéra Italien. To fulfil this whim he had to economize for weeks to save the money needed for such an expense. After many privations he managed it. Ensconced in a stall seat, provided with opera glasses he had borrowed from one of his mother's friends, he was waiting for the curtain to rise. The theatre was overfull; above him and everywhere he saw resplendent women who all appeared beautiful to him. He looked at them through his glasses, much interested in the expression on faces. Darkness fell over the room.

Suddenly he felt a big hand landing on his shoulder. He looked back. A venerable old man behind him whispered with much authority: 'Young man, give me your seat. I am Monsieur Ingres.'

Much upset, Anatole France had to comply.

'Don't you see,' he added, 'such was the magic of fame of those days that not for a moment did I think I had any right to protest, yet, God only knows what bitter disappointment it cost me to surrender a stall acquired at such a sacrifice!'

'Madame,' he told me one day, coming to see me, 'you are kind to welcome the old man that I am. If you hear it said that I go into society, don't you believe it; people deceive you, for I see no one. I shun all human gatherings, where I no longer fit, but I have a proposal to make to you: Would you like to come and spend the day with me at Saint-Quentin, the day after tomorrow? We could go and look at the La Tours.'

I was delighted to accept. We took an early train, lunched in that town of which I keep only a grey shadowy recollection. But to visit a museum with Anatole France — what a treat this was! In front of each pastel he had a story to tell. The caretaker, having guessed who his visitor was, followed in our wake. Anatole France engaged him in talk, and the old fellow, very proud to have the care of such treasures, told us that the museum had just been enlarged through the bequest of several portraits which, unfortunately, had suffered through being moved a number of times. It was just about that time that Monsieur France was planning to write an essay on Prud'hon and his friend Constance Mayer. I have always felt that somehow he much preferred things to people; but when he was in a good mood this preference could become so charming.

During the return journey it was very cold in the train, and he insisted that I should cover my knees with his overcoat which he took off. I protested, but he said: 'Don't go and overtire yourself, and see that you don't get ill.'

And a little later, with much sadness: 'Do you think that this earth feels habitable to me? But if you don't mind being bored, let me come to lunch with you on Friday. You are the very best of all divine things; it is an atheist tells you so.'

Then, with a sigh: 'Madame Arman never would abdicate, and sometimes this irritated me, but life without her has lost all interest for me. It was she knew how to make it lively; in Paris or when travelling she was indefatigable.'

Here is a fragment from one of Anatole France's letters which I received in London:

> Your little card came to smile upon me in my old and mournful hutch. It found me in such a listless state that I

have scarcely any feelings left and no way of expression. Words, even those the most familiar in former days, have become quite strange to me; yet I must come to life a little to tell you that I have kept the most delightful recollection of our trip to Saint-Quentin and think tenderly of you. I have made notes of all I have been able to find concerning Prud'hon's stay at Rome; what I have still to do is to search in Rome itself for the traces of this poor Burgundian state pensioner.

But I have received at this very moment a prospectus of the World Exhibition to be held in the Piazza Armi, on the banks of the Tiber. It will be frightful and awkward. Yet I do not lose the hope of visiting Rome and Naples with you, and I cherish the fancy, although I have no handsome genie to help me to travel to dreamland. What I need is reality, the trees, the sky, the sea, and yourself, dear Madame, for perfect concord. Please have all the Prud'hons photographed for me; it will be a great help.

I brought back for Monsieur France photographs of all the Prud'hons which were in London.

When he had finished the sketch on Madame Jarre's portrait, he sent me a note:

I request you to come and see Madame Jarre who has arrived. Should you like me also to take you to see Stettiner who has two pastels which he says are Nattier's, and very charming, much in La Tour's style? I have another proposal to make to you. Should you like to meet Rémy de Gourmont, who knows that he owes you his appointment on *Le Temps*? I shall act as matchmaker and make you meet at my house. Love me a little bit. I kiss your nails, which are marvellous jewels.

I was unable to reply at once, so Monsieur France despatched his old Joséphine with the following note:

You have not told me if you would like to meet Rémy de Gourmont. He comes to see me tomorrow about eleven o'clock. I should very much like to know if you are also coming, because in that case I shall make him wait, and if not, I shall not make him hope in vain.

So, on that Sunday, I made the acquaintance of Rémy de Gourmont and I saw him several times at the Villa Saïd. I had passed on to Monsieur Hébrard, Gourmont's wish to write for *Le Temps*, and his article on Verlaine had just appeared. However, he was not successful as a contributor to *Le Temps*.

On Sunday mornings Monsieur France not only received his friends, but sometimes politicians arrived unannounced to claim his support. I have often seen the writer much embarrassed when the perilous honour was offered him to preside at some meeting. He sought all possible reasons to refuse, then, quite at his wits' ends, I have heard him simply propose to suppress the presiding officer. He tangled himself up in his long explanations and did not know how to show the door to these people. As soon as they had left he would sigh: 'Madame Arman used to save me all this.'

Every day he missed her more keenly.

But one day I found him full of smiles.

'Imagine,' he told me, 'that I am pressed by a person who pretends to have "tender feelings" for me. Such things no longer befit my years. Not that I fear being beguiled, but, think of it, she wants to tell me of these tender feelings! You who have loved Madame Arman, who returned your affection, can you conceive of anything further from my thoughts? This young woman puts me in mind of the horses on a merry-go-round at the fair. I know that the piebald horse will always appear in his turn.'

Some little while after this he told me that François, Madame de Caillavet's valet, had sent him Emma, the second housemaid, and that he had engaged her as his housekeeper.

'She remains so grateful to her mistress,' he told me; 'with her I shall be able to speak of Madame de Caillavet.'

At that time, France was once more working; he was collecting material for a book he had long planned and which was to be *Les Dieux ont Soif*. Every day I received little notes from him.

> *Very dear Madame,* Was it not agreed I should see you before you leave Paris? Should you like to lunch at the Villa Saïd? If so, on what day? I have completed a fair half, or rather an ugly half, of my novel, and feel stupid after so much work. Nevertheless, although as blind as a mole, I kiss your hand in affectionate deference, in memory of those days when I used to belong to this race of humans of which you are an adornment.

A few days later came another note:

> *Dear Madame,* I have just received a wire telling me that Rodin and his great friend, Madame de Choiseul, will come to lunch with me tomorrow, Saturday, at twelve-forty-five. Come, dear lady, come, dear friend, bring your graciousness and your radiance into my forsaken home. I kiss your hands.

That lunch proved most amusing. A long discussion concerning art started between France and Rodin. The latter hardly gave time to our host to put in a word; France gesticulated in despair, rose from the table every second, fetching either a small statue or some fragments of sculpture. But Rodin found fault with every sculpture shown to him: 'All you show me,' he exclaimed, 'may be authentic fragments; yet, if I picture in my mind the work to which they belong, I feel certain it is bastard work. You must not believe, my friend, that fragments which show some beauty stand for a beautiful complete work. I know quite well that I have myself been accused of sometimes showing of a piece of sculpture only some part I deemed important. There was justification in my choice — while fragments one purchases are often very deceptive.'

Compact in figure, with a most powerful face, Rodin brushed his hand over his flowing beard. It seemed to me that he pretended to be deafer than he really was whenever he did not want to hear. His strong hand, with the square fingers, often rested flat upon the table; he looked like a god escaped from a Roman fountain. His friend chatted without cease, but I could not make out anything in what she said. She was got up like a wardrobe dealer; her spacious hips, at coffee time, brushed against the tray and the coffee-set was smashed to smithereens.

Monsieur France had some trouble to hide his annoyance, and, although he tried to renew the talk, I felt he longed for but one thing: to see his visitors go. I rose first from the table. He escorted me as far as the front door: 'This woman is the most vulgar creature I have ever received; but I shan't be caught again. She bored me stiff, and I set great value upon my coffee cups!'

In London, where I spent a few days, I went to the Wallace Collection, selected a model of cups similar to those Monsieur France had lost, and had the complete set of a dozen cups reproduced. 'Dear Madame and friend,' he wrote to me, 'I am overwhelmed by your kindness: such handsome cups and offered by such beautiful hands! You will be the first to drink from them.'

Monsieur France was always sad.

'If you do not mind, dear Madame, I shall dine with you today. It will chase away my black thoughts.'

'Next Monday,' he explained as he arrived, 'I must hunt in the Louvres attics for a Tiarini, Joseph begging Mary to forgive him for having thought her unfaithful. It is a great compliment to this cuckold and to the Bologna school that I should go hunting for them in these attics. But Couchaud has, for the last six months, moved heaven and earth to have this Tiarini shown me. In truth,' he added, 'this will amuse me even more than lunching with goddesses, who are often but goddesses from Hades. For I should do nothing to escape them, since I am so weary of the light of day. By the way, do you know that the young woman I told you about still pursues me?'

I found this mixture of weariness and a longing to tell me of his good fortunes most comical. Monsieur France was my father's age, and I looked upon him as a very old gentleman — one knows little pity when one is scarcely more than twenty. During two and a half years I saw a good deal of the famous author. I went with him to Prouté's, to Honoré Champion's, and another bookseller in the Rue des Beaux Arts. Sometimes we went for a walk as far as Versailles.

> Oh! divine friend, a bandage around my head and my stomach turned sour with cocaine, it is only thus I could appear in front of you. I have been operated upon, and will not be fit to show myself before Monday. I kiss your hands.

He varied everlastingly his polite formulas:

> *Dear Lady and Friend,* It is with your delightful enamel pencil I write to you to convey first of all my tender homage. I shall make use of it to note my dreams, though I have only sad and painful ones. I wish you a happy New Year. The world smiles at your beauty. I kiss with affectionate respect your sprained white wrist. Come to lunch with me either Saturday or Monday. No one will be there but yourself and your old friend.

One afternoon we went to the theatre to see Lucien Guitry act the part of Crainquebille. Monsieur France much admired this great actor. After the play we went to Guitry's dressing-room. The actor was extremely witty; his conversation was lively, he related most things with a minimum of words and unexpected expressions. France paid him a thousand compliments and congratulated him on the taste with which he had arranged his dressing-room.

> *Dear Madame and Friend,* I shall come to fetch you today, Wednesday, at twelve-thirty. I kiss your hands.
> A. F.

I have had great worries, and Emma, the little housekeeper of my small establishment, has just been operated upon (and, I must say, successfully).

That day I found Monsieur France rather agitated. He asked me to go with him, Rue Henner, where Emma had been operated upon.

In entering the patient's room, I found her propped up on pink cushions, dressed in a dainty pink silk bed-jacket, her hair with a Marcel wave, and on her bed Anatole France's precious books displayed with flattering inscriptions. She showed them to me with justified pride. I had never set eyes on Emma since the days when she was in her mistress's service, Avenue Hoche. The change I noticed in her way of talking and dressing led me to guess the part she played in Anatole France's life. However, she was quite humble in her talk when she recalled Madame Arman's memory; rather ill at ease to hear Monsieur France paying her compliments, she tried to divert the conversation from herself. He, on the contrary, kept referring to the qualities he had found in her; I felt greatly embarrassed listening to his talk. My mind went back to Madame Arman and the contempt she would have felt in seeing that her illustrious friend was once more on the wrong track. I suppose Emma noticed my coolness, for from that day it became evident that Monsieur France's attitude towards me changed a great deal. I refused, when he once came to ask me, to go and 'eat a chop with Emma,' as he put it. Little by little she managed to frighten away all of Madame de Caillavet's friends. Monsieur France became nervous, suspicious, and took everything in bad part.

Dear Madame, I was rather aware I am unsociable; your letter leaves me in no doubt on this point. I will not impose my presence upon you at Lemaître's, at Madame H. Adam's, nor in Italy. Have no fear that I shall intrude on you, and believe, dear Madame, that I remain ever your most respectful and devoted

A. FRANCE

P.S. I read your letter over again, dear Madame. I should never have thought that, at my age, one could receive such an unkind one.

Certainly we no longer seemed to understand each other. As long as Monsieur France had led what life suited him without wishing to make me a party to it, I had been delighted to see him as often as he liked; but to go and 'eat a chop with Emma' did not appeal to me. Besides, I felt less and less respect for the writer's disposition. His political views were also alien to mine. Something about him, bordering on caddishness, which had become apparent to me, was above all what drew me away from him.

I also disliked his way of running down people, of reviling the most spontaneous and natural feelings in others. Had he not once said to a young girl, in my presence, when she told him of her affection for her elder brother, 'I should guess, dear lady, that your love for your brother is somewhat incestuous?' The young Argentine looked at me, turned her back on Monsieur France, and would never see him again. 'Keep some good-will towards me, for it is so precious to me, and may I see you again happy and radiant,' he wrote to me on the next day.

But when a disagreement has arisen between two people, it is all the more difficult to clear it up when each party keeps the causes of it secret. I attempted no explanation with Monsieur France. What could I have told him?

In the bundle of his letters I have preserved, I have several notes dating from that period. Sometimes he reproaches me with my neglect of him, at other times he cancels his lunch with me, which he had himself arranged.

Two more months went by. One afternoon, in the Avenue de l'Opéra, I heard hurried steps behind me and Monsieur France's voice saying, 'Don't hasten so, Madame.' I stopped. Monsieur France was near me, his coat collar raised, himself looking glum.

'How light you are! Your feet seem hardly to touch the earth,' he told me. 'Just walk a few steps with me, I wanted to speak to you of Prud'hon. You never told me that your old friend, Madame Hippolyte Adam, has in her possession two fine drawings of his? I should like to see them. Could you bring us to meet?'

'Nothing more easy, *cher maître*, mention a day, and I feel sure Madame Adam will come at my invitation.'

'I know,' he went on, 'that you no longer love me; one day I shall tell you of a drama in which I have been the unwilling hero and which will make you understand my present mood.'

'Dear Monsieur France,' I replied, 'I assure you that your "goddesses from Hades," as you call them, do not at all interest me. I am waiting for *Les Dieux ont Soif*, and, as you have been kind enough to tell me I played a minute part in bringing you to collect the material and write this book, very beautiful I have no doubt, I feel very happy in the small share I have in it.'

'I will make you a present of the manuscript,' he told me; 'it belongs to you by right. You make me feel better. I will see you on Thursday. Madame Arman was quite right in being fond of you.'

Madame Adam and I had been waiting for a good half-hour, Monsieur France had not appeared. Sometimes he was late, but never as much as that. Had he forgotten? We sat at table. At the end of the meal the doorbell rang, and here is the note which was handed to me:

> *Madame,* Allow me not to come to lunch with you today. I fear I might meet some one of the numerous persons in the eyes of whom you have made me appear ridiculous.
> Yours respectfully
> A. F.

I was flabbergasted and — I confess it — furious.

The 'goddesses from Hades' no more went in fear of meeting me. I had no longer any desire to see Monsieur France.

Then came the War, his hurried flight from Paris, his offer to enlist, and his life at La Béchellerie.

Through various friends he sent me several invitations to spend a few days in his retreat. I did not accept. He lived surrounded by admirers, being made much of, and enjoying the idea that his life was drawing to an end in the peaceful atmosphere of philosophy.

Time Past

For me, the France I admired I retrace in only a few of his pages, and among them, those of *Les Dieux ont Soif* preserve a peculiar flavour.

I did not attend the patriarch's funeral.

« IV »

ROUND ABOUT JULES LEMAÎTRE AND MADAME DE LOYNES

ONE of the most pleasant salons in Paris was that of Monsieur and Madame de Saint-Marceaux. An excellent musician, the sculptor's wife arranged musical evenings, and twice a week, on Sundays and Fridays, invited to dinner a select gathering of writers, painters, and musicians. At one of these dinners I was seated by the side of Jules Lemaître. I had already met him in various salons, above all at Madame Bulteau's, where he was a constant visitor. However, I had never had a long conversation with him.

The Friday dinners and musical evenings were unique occasions to which Madame de Saint-Marceaux admitted no one, even of princely or royal birth, who was not of great personal distinction. People who were exclusively in the fashion, no matter what their rank or popularity, were rigorously excluded. The 'Fridays' at the Boulevard Malesherbes were arranged in this way: first came the dinner for about fifteen people specially selected; then after dinner, artists, writers, or amateurs, invited once and for all, came dressed just as they liked, in evening suits or uniforms or town suits, the women in evening dresses or town frocks.

The frequenters of that house, above all the privileged

ones of the Friday, always fully enjoyed those evenings, thanks to the intelligence, the authority, and the kindness of heart which made Madame de Saint-Marceaux an exceptional hostess. On the evening mentioned there were as guests: Madame Alexandre Dumas, Forain, Adrien Hébrard, the painter Jean Béraud, Doctor Babinski, Boldini, the barrister Aubépin, and the sculptor's two stepsons. After dinner came a few familiars.

The conversation was always animated, but with a pleasant restraint in conformity with the strict disposition of our hostess who allowed no deviation from tradition. Yet she was attracted by all artistic endeavour and tolerant enough to pay attention to innovations on those lines. It was at her house that Isadora Duncan made her first appearance when she danced draped in scanty veils, which performance was in those days an indication of a certain daring in a fashionable hostess. The famous dancer's reputation was launched from the Boulevard Malesherbes.

On that Friday, when I sat next to Jules Lemaître, he was specially full of life. He related with humour the sitting of the Academy on the previous day. He never missed these sessions at the Quai Conti, where his erudition, without pedantry, often brought gaiety to the literary debates. He came back from them with a wealth of observations which, related in a pleasant tone, yet betrayed his mischievous and caustic wit.

Jean Cocteau's genius at finding words is undeniable. One day, in an improvisation, he compared Jules Lemaître's pink face, with its fluffy hair and silvery beard, to a superb strawberry delicately placed, in January, upon cotton-wool. Jules Lemaître's refined and small features expressed great affability. In the pools under his glasses, his small deep-sunken eyes appeared like two forget-me-nots; he had prominent cheek-bones which now and again were suddenly flushed. His voice, without being powerful, was clear-toned and melodious. He possessed eloquence and charm, the latter discreet and kindly. He had a horror of all exaggeration. His indulgence towards love affairs, the passionate interest they aroused in him, lent a sort of hesitation to his speech when he referred to such matters, above all near a young woman, so much were tenderness and shyness always at war within him. He claimed to be of an age which he in fact never reached, and at that time, in 1909, he was fifty-seven, which in our days is still young.

As often happened to me, I had arrived at Madame de Saint-Marceaux's accompanied by Adrien Hébrard, the editor of *Le Temps*, whom I familiarly used to call my 'Nanny.' That expression, known to some intimate friends, delighted Jules Lemaître. At the end of the meal he asked me if I should not like to have him as a governess. I seized the opportunity and replied that, indeed, since I wished to become more acquainted with the subtleties of the French language, nothing would please me more than to benefit by his advice.

I went to all his lectures, admired him greatly, but would never have dared to invite him to my house. He forestalled me, and thus began an acquaintance which soon changed into friendship. Once a week I lunched at his home, Rue d'Artois, generally on the Wednesday; on other mornings he came to my place.

Later, Jean Cocteau and Anna de Noailles, though the latter less often, came to join these love-feasts of the Wednesday. Jules Lemaître developed a real affection for Jean Cocteau, whom he sometimes called 'your fiancé,' or again 'Ariel,' and the varied talents of this young prodigy delighted him. He used to quote as an example of his simplicity and grace certain verses from the dance of Sophocles.

Soon there was established between us four a habit which lasted until the War: Anna de Noailles, Jules Lemaître, Jean Cocteau, and I went to dine together on the evening of every fourteenth of July at the Quatre Sergents de la Rochelle, and we adopted for our group the nickname of 'The Four Sergeants.' We always sat at a table on the pavement outside the restaurant, the better to share in the public rejoicing. My companions' liveliness and wit were inexhaustible. For nothing on earth would we have missed this treat, which was our fête amidst the general festivities, and we refused vigorously to let any new person join our group. In order not to be recognized by the public, we always went in the most inconspicuous clothes. We made the carriage put us down in a street near-by, and arrived at the restaurant arm in arm, just like the dwellers in the district. After the meal, we accepted all invitations which came to us to dance with perfect strangers, and to the tune of violins and cornets threw ourselves into the fray. This treat was for us an everlasting subject of jokes, and we jealously kept our secret.

In 1913, Edmond Rostand, who daily saw Anna de Noailles, was exceptionally invited by her to join us. When Jules Lemaître, Jean Cocteau, and I arrived at the meeting-place, Rue Scheffer, Anna de Noailles was already seated in Rostand's sumptuous car, upholstered in grey felt. The poet himself was wearing the wide cape with velvet collar and the felt hat with wide brims so much associated with his legendary appearance. We, who always wanted to pass unnoticed, at once realized that this time our fourteenth of July would be spoiled.

Edmond Rostand's fragile health imposed on him all sorts of precautions; therefore, he had the car driven to the very door of the restaurant, refused to dine on the pavement, and obliged us to find accommodation in a dining-hall on the first floor where only a balcony looked on the dancing. Lost in that banquet hall, where prevailed a cork smell from Burgundy bottles and a stale atmosphere of cigars, we felt quite severed from the festivities. After the meal Rostand took Anna de Noailles on the balcony. The mirth from the street was rising up to them. In the dense crowd couples whirled around. They looked on for a while, and Rostand, moved in spite of himself by the proximity of this noisy crowd which brought back to his mind memories of enthusiastic receptions at the theatre, remarked sententiously: 'To think that this Parisian crowd will always be ignorant that two poets are tonight gazing upon it: Anna de Noailles and Edmond Rostand.'

Time Past

One might have imagined that the author of *Cyrano* was quite accustomed to fame! Not at all. Sensitive, and at heart really modest, his shyness and the constant care he took of his delicate health caused him to be distrustful and misanthropic. When we came down from our perch, this outburst of vainglory was already over, but he had no wish to pursue the evening in accordance with our usual rites. Anna de Noailles decided that we had better all go to my home, which we did. There, feeling secure, Rostand begged me to go to the corner café and get bottles of beer, which drink he intended to have in spite of his strict diet; such was his only concession to the popular spirit of festivity.

I was very fond of the luncheons *tête-à-tête* with Jules Lemaître, during which he spoke of himself and confided in me.

'My father,' he told me, 'was a schoolmaster at Travers. I was myself sent to the Jesuits' Secondary School at Orléans. It is said that the lord bishop, Monseigneur Dupanloup, noticed me; this is no doubt an exaggeration, but it was reported to me by affectionate parents. I was sent to Paris to the Jesuits' Secondary School of Notre-Dame des Champs, and in the following year I was admitted at the École Normale.'

'I know that you proved there one of the most brilliant pupils.'

'But nobody is perfect, for I had been expelled from Notre-Dame des Champs for having smoked and drawn one of my teachers with a hog's head.'

Little by little he related his life.

'As a teacher at Havre, I taught the top classical form, and had among my pupils Jules Tellier and Hugues le Roux, with whom you are going to lunch this very morning.'

'Havre,' he sighed; 'what memories does it not bring back! I was so young... I fell desperately in love with a young girl, Mademoiselle Medgé, but I was very shy and never dared declare myself.... She became Madame Engel. Like everyone else, I used to write poetry in those days. She was my inspiration for "Musica," "A Meeting," "The Blue Shawl."'

'I had often wondered, as I read your first volume of poems for whom they had been written:

> '"Her charm, forgotten, seemed, for good and all,
> Until, perchance, her presence graced the ball."'

'That's quite correct,' he said; 'you are a little hussy. "To a Young Girl" was dedicated to Madame Engel's daughter, twenty years after my first love:

> '"Such eyes as yours, though dark clear sparkling,
> — Precocious to distil delight —
> Your charming mother, long before you,
> When but a maid displayed as bright."'

'Likewise, "To a Grandfather" was addressed to Monsieur Medgé.'

After Havre, which he left in 1880, Jules Lemaître was appointed to a post as professor in Algiers. During the summer holidays of that year, Madame Menard de Franc, one of his parents' friends, introduced him to Pauline Deschalais, an orphan girl of eighteen, brought up at the convent of Sainte-Foy at Neuilly. Gentle, pretty, there was about her a poetical grace which delighted Jules Lemaître's sensitive heart, and he asked her hand. The poem 'The Convent,' and still more 'The Grape Harvest,' both of which were written for his fiancée, give an idea of what he felt.

> 'There over heads angelic,
> O'er brows pale and refined,
> The sound of chants is breathing,
> As over flowers the wind.'

They were married in 1881 in the chapel of the convent where Pauline had been brought up. A few months later Jules Lemaître took his wife to Algiers.

The young professor had already a brilliant academic reputation, but the pupil from the Augustine Nuns found in him only an inexperienced and somewhat clumsy lover. Scarcely four months after they settled in Algeria, she preferred an officer garrisoned in the town: drama and rupture. Jules Lemaître was distracted, for he worshipped his wife; he forgave her, but applied for a post in another town. He was appointed at Besançon, then at Grenoble, where his daughter Madeleine was born. Madame Jules Lemaître died in giving her birth. This sudden and cruel conclusion plunged the husband into despair. Fate went on pursuing him: three months later the little girl died in her turn. Leaving behind him two graves, Jules Lemaître came to Paris, where he settled for good.

As early as 1879 he was a contributor to *La Revue Bleue*, *La Revue Hebdomadaire*, and *La Revue des Deux Mondes*. An article on Bersot, his head at the École Normale, attracted attention. He had already published *Serenius* as well as his first poems, and submitted his two doctorate theses in the Sorbonne, the Latin one on Corneille, the French on Dancourt. However, his real fame dates from 1885, when he succeeded J. J. Weiss on the staff of *Les Débats* and wrote for *La Revue Bleue* an article on Renan, with which he was not satisfied, but which created a great stir. Following Yung's advice, he paid a visit to Renan, who received him with kindness and greatly encouraged him. Thus the philosopher once more proved the truth of his reputation for good-will and friendliness.

Then came the time when Lemaître fell under the ascendancy of the person who most influenced his life, the Comtesse de Loynes. It was at a fancy-dress ball at Arsène Houssaye's that he first met her. She was forty-seven, he thirty-two. She was wearing the costume of the Margaret of *Faust*, of mauve satin adorned with black velvet. A black velvet mask covered her face. The youthful tone of her voice and her conversation charmed Jules Lemaître. He fell deeply in love with the stranger in mauve. On her side Madame de Loynes noticed him. She was clever enough to guess, in the shy and unobtrusive provincial, rather clumsy, and so badly dressed, a born writer and an admirer who was going to bring a new interest into her life. She fixed a rendezvous with him, in her box at the Théâtre Français. But, cautious and malicious, she took with her a friend to whom she had confided her secret. Sheltering behind a pillar, the two ladies awaited the writer's arrival. When he appeared, inelegant, nervous, and short-sighted, walking with small, hesitant steps,

Madame de Loynes's companion could not help exclaiming: 'Oh! but he is awful!'

'You are mistaken. I like him very much, and you will see that he will go far.'

None but Madame de Loynes could have judged with such insight. Had she not known how to gather around her most of the famous men of her time, over whom she held sway in queenly fashion?

The Comtesse de Loynes, *née* Detourbet, from a family living in Rheims where her father was a Government contractor, had been a spoilt child on account of her delicate health. On the day of her first Communion, which she made under her godfather, the Archbishop of Rheims, she felt so poorly that her candle had to be taken from her, as it proved too heavy for her fragile frame. This delicate health, which she retained for many long years, was one of her seductions, and from quite an early age her charm affected people around her. It won her the affection of a little playmate, a little girl who worshipped her, but who died when ten years old. Jeanne Detourbet was broken with grief over this death, and, long after, the relation she made of it to Jules Lemaître inspired him with the story of 'Myrrha,' which is in the volume of his short stories. When the time came for completing her education, Jeanne Detourbet's parents entrusted her to an uncle, Charles Didier, who took her to Paris. This uncle, who was blind, was so in a double sense, and lived under the spell of the young girl who made him do just what she pleased. He was very friendly with the Dennerys to whom he introduced his niece. That was in 1857.

Dennery was the first to put her in touch with people, gave her Sainte-Beuve as teacher and launched her into society. She was at once much sought after and had a salon, Place Vendôme. Her early admirers were Girardin, Flaubert, Prince Napoleon, Doctor Bravais whom Alphonse Daudet had portrayed in his *Nabob*, and many others.

Mademoiselle Detourbet had slightly modified the spelling of her name, and on her visiting cards it was Madame de Tourbey who invited her friends. Slender, well-built, of medium height, though she was not beautiful as to features, there was something harmonious in her person, with her dark reddish hair, her deep green eyes and her sparkling teeth. She was graceful of carriage, had beautiful hands, wore dresses from La Ferrière, Worth, Doucet, besides princess gowns with trains, the work of her maid, and always in light shades, white, mauve, or sky-blue; Madame de Tourbey hated black.

. Her health remained delicate; she had often to keep to her bedroom. She read a great deal, knitted, avoided paying calls, and drove in the Bois in a brougham upholstered in white satin, a gift from the Prince Napoleon. Her friends had frequent occasion to be anxious about her. After pneumonia, her doctor advised she should spend a few months in good air, in preference on a height.

The 'Nabob' Bravais put at her disposal his country mansion of Belleau in the neighbourhood of Paris. Therapeutic methods still left much to be desired in those days. But when Madame de Tourbey arrived, she was surprised to find the avenue which led from the entrance gate to the house, some two kilometres long, covered with rose petals. This delightful attention was typical of the famous doctor.

Concerning Bravais's originality there were many stories. He was at the time much in demand among people of mark, who held him in esteem and protected him. Here is one of these stories:

In that same mansion at Belleau he was one day entertaining Ismaïl Pasha, Viceroy of Egypt.

During lunch this latter said to him with a laugh: 'I should not mind buying your mansion, Bravais.'

'If Your Highness offers me two millions...'

This price was so grossly exaggerated that it was comical.

Without batting an eyelash, Ismaïl Pasha replied: 'The two millions are yours and the mansion is mine.'

The day went by; there was no more question of what Doctor Bravais looked upon as a piece of banter.

But when he took the Prince to the station: 'I have not forgotten our bargain, my dear Bravais,' said Ismaïl Pasha. 'Here is a cheque for two millions, but keep the mansion; I give it to you.'

In those days manners were more gallant and medicine more empiric, which did not prevent Doctor Bravais from earning fortunes and yet dying in want.

Another time Madame de Tourbey was in still greater danger. Her lungs very much affected, she was despaired of by the doctors. Prince Napoleon brought her a young medical man with whom he had previously had the following conversation:

'If you save this person, Doctor, I will look after your future. I shall have you appointed consulting physician at a medical spa and your fortune will be made.'

'Do you allow me entire freedom in this case, Prince?'

'Certainly.'

After he had examined the patient, the doctor thought the matter out and declared: 'I will not leave the patient; I shall arrange for melted tar to stream down the walls of her room and I shall condemn Madame de Tourbey to complete silence.'

This plan was carried out. To keep his patient cheerful, the doctor played cards with her, but whenever Madame de Tourbey attempted to speak, she straightway lost. This strange cure proved successful, and the young doctor saw his future assured.

Numerous men sought Madame de Tourbey in marriage, among them Ernest Baroche, the Minister's son, whom she had known for several years. Baroche was the intimate friend of the Comte de Loynes, who also felt very much drawn to the beautiful young woman. But the war of 1870 played havoc with all plans of marriage. Ernest Baroche was killed in the battle of Le Bourget. His love and concern for Madame de Tourbey had been such that not only did he bequeath to her all his fortune, but he had previously made her promise, in case the Comte de Loynes should be the one to survive, that she would marry him. She was in London, as a guest to the French Ambassador, when the Comte de Loynes came to remind her of this promise.

The family De Loynes did not approve of the match,

and at no time became acquainted with the new countess. The couple were married in Paris, in 1871, at the chapel of the Visitandines.

The Comte de Loynes was handsome, but rather spineless. He entertained dreams of managing a sugar refinery which he possessed at Meaux. He launched into various business schemes: all turned out disastrously. Since he lacked experience and had no great liking for work he began to squander his wife's fortune. Other reasons contributed to make their married life unhappy.

Madame de Loynes, taking no notice of her husband, went on receiving people daily from five to seven. All Parisians of repute showed themselves in the Rue de l'Arcade. About that time her familiars were Taine, Renan, the Houssayes, François Magnard, editor of *Le Figaro*, the historian Albert Vandal, François Coppée, Paul Déroulède, and so on. She tried to have a little private talk with each person and contrived to give to each the impression that she was passionately interested in his future. She had a gift for listening, and her conversation was eloquent and varied, thanks to her memory and the diversity of her social contacts. Madame de Loynes did not specially appreciate mere witticisms, yet she had a quick mind and was brisk at repartee. Faithful in her friendships, she was a woman worth consulting, more so since she was always eager to help and cared not if she compromised her reputation; thus, when Prince Napoleon was ordered into exile and came to bid her good-bye, she did not hesitate to return his call at Pragins. She was indeed so faithful to her old friends that she sacrificed everything to them. When Arthur Meyer was treated by all who frequented the house, from Jules Lemaître himself to Léon Daudet, with the aversion he so well deserved, Madame de Loynes still continued to see him every day from half-past four to five, all by himself, for no one would have liked to meet him. No sooner was Madame de Loynes dead than Arthur Meyer thanked her for this faithfulness and friendship by publishing a most venomous book about her.

She often discovered and knew how to bring out new gifts in her friends. It was she who gave Jules Lemaître the idea of writing plays and became his collaborator. Madame de Loynes followed all the details with great intelligence, discussed the plays, supervised the rehearsals, and frequently insisted on alterations. She was not very sensitive to music and entirely unaffected by painting; her house, lacking in rarities and valuable furniture, did not reflect the dawning influence of the Goncourts.

Her married life was short-lived, since, following friends' advice, she soon separated from her husband. The number of intellectual men attracted by her charm increased more and more, for she was so full of attentions and greatly spoilt her friends. Here are some of her gracious ways as explained to me by Jules Lemaître:

Her table had the reputation of being the best in Paris. For the menus, masterpieces of culinary art, she spared herself no trouble, sending for specialities to the very towns of their origin, and for the setting of the table she insisted on faultless waiting, choice flowers, and a number of guests never exceeding ten. She also demanded punctuality; dinner was served at seven-thirty, and ill-luck to the guests who came late; they had to take their seats and forgo the preceding course. Among those unfortunate was often the witty Grosclaude, but he was easily forgiven on account of his ready wit and his sharp intelligence, even if his puns and cock-and-bull stories were not entirely shrewd or circumspect. Grosclaude was an ardent pioneer of French colonial policy, and later, in another realm, with his gifts as diplomat, played the part of an *Éminence Grise*.

One day, Grosclaude offered Madame de Loynes a very pretty little bell, such as Madame Aubernon had the habit of using at her table among her guests. But Madame de Loynes tried it only two or three times, then discarded it; her authority was enough to ensure silence from others when she wished to give a chance to a brilliant talker; and never did she allow general conversation.

Here is the menu of the dinner she gave in Anatole France's honour on January 12, 1893, when he was made Chevalier de la Légion d'Honneur. The small parchment card was decorated with the badge of the Legion.

Potage cultivateur
Rognons de coq à la Villeroy
Truite saumonée cardinal
Filet de boeuf Trianon
Poularde à la Néva
Bécasses sur canapé
Salade suédoise
Artichauts vénitiens
Paniers de mandarines
Fruits glacés
Desserts

LEMAÎTRE AND MADAME DE LOYNES

Madame de Loynes had ample ground to be proud of Jules Lemaître's career: in everything he met with success; he acquired a name as a dramatist, and his gift and reputation as a writer were undeniable. His daily Morning Bulletin in *Le Temps* was always awaited and appreciated. In 1898, he heroically — for nothing could be more drastically and unpleasantly contrary to all his habits and tastes — agreed to become president of the Ligue de la Patrie Française. During several years this peaceful and discreet intellectual man endured the torture of speaking at meetings, just for the love of France, addressing crowds north and south, east and west, and sometimes being received with stones and jeers. From this he came to be a royalist and joined the Action Française. He was elected to the Académie Française in 1897, as a successor to Victor Duruy. He could have entered it in 1895, but when he realized what a pleasure it would give Henry Houssaye to become an academician, he withdrew in his favour. The Comtesse de Loynes, who shared Jules Lemaître's affection for Henry Houssaye, added to the happiness of the new member by offering him a sumptuous dinner. On the table, amidst flowers, was set at the place of honour an academician's hat adorned with a huge ostrich feather.

Jules Lemaître had himself illustrated the menu cards. One depicted the Comtesse de Loynes offering the palm to Henry Houssaye; on another Jules Lemaître bowing as his friend went by; a third showed Henry Houssaye gazing at his own bust.

Time Past

Consommé aux laîtues
Crissens au parmesan
Petites truites des Ardennes
Jambon du Rhin, sauce au vin du Rhin
Carré de mouton à la bretonne
Poularde truffée
Pâté de Pouvillon
Asperges en branches
Claque d'académicien glacé

I give this menu to show that the golden age of the culinary art is extinct; we no longer know such feasts!

To celebrate the return of Brazza to France, Madame de Loynes gave a dinner followed by a reception in her new dwelling, Avenue des Champs-Élysées. The explorer had that very day broken his arm on leaving the Chamber of Deputies. Having been hastily attended by a surgeon, he did not fail his hostess, though he was in pain and wore his arm in a sling. Madame de Loynes appointed a valet to look specially after him, during the dinner. At dessert three servants were needed to bring upon the table a ship made of sugar icing and named 'Brazzaville.' This masterpiece was the work of Joséphine, the famous confectioner.

Jules Lemaître gave me a comical account of a party at his friend's house which was an utter failure on account of Madame de Thèbes. The famous pythoness behaved in an odious way; she predicted misfortunes to everyone, notably to Paul Deschanel, who, she predicted, would die a bloody death. This prospect made him furious, and the guests begged Madame de Loynes never to ask this Cassandra again.

The Comtesse, eclectic as she was, invited just as easily Mata-Hari to come and dance with her musicians, as Monsieur and Madame Curie to give a lecture on radium.

Madame de Loynes's salon lasted until her death. She knew how to find new friends when old ones had disappeared, and in spite of a certain fulness of figure, she preserved her daintiness. As I write, I look at one of her last photographs. She is in a garden with a poodle at her side, her face is still charming and her figure shows still a fine bearing. There are several extant portraits of her: a pastel by Alphonse Muraton, an oil painting by Amaury Duval, dating from her youth. This painter gives her dark hair, to make her appear like Rachel with whom she had indeed a likeness, and whose wild genius was just then having such a marked influence on art and fashion. I have in my possession two letters which Amaury Duval wrote to his model at the time he painted her portrait. Here they are:

1862

That I should forgive you, Madame? I would rather paint a halo around your head on your portrait because of all your kindness to me and the encouragement you give me. If I could only reward you for all this by a good portrait, but I have great fears! Nevertheless, get well again quick, I have almost the right to say for both our sakes, and I shall be ready when you are: every day at the usual time I shall be at my post, without need to remind me (with the exception of Saturdays).

Believe, dear Madame, that I am always yours sincerely
AMAURY DUVAL

Time Past

1862

Dear Madame,

What a long time it is since I saw you! It is hardly my fault; I am so overwhelmed with callers that I am worn out. ... I have to run away.... Then your portrait is bringing me trouble with smart ladies who threaten my life to have theirs ... so I don't know which way to turn, but I do not nurse the delusion it is my painting attracts them, but the hope that they will appear as pretty as you. Let them try, and truly I shall run away; I am tired, sad; you must admit I am not meant to paint portraits. Our first sittings come back to my mind, and I shudder at the recollection. Here is the address of the frame-maker for your portrait; he is a clever and conscientious man: Crozat, 30 Rue Bergère.

Your portrait is quite finished, but not dry yet. I shall sign it tomorrow. I have a proposal to make: would you mind if it is exhibited on March the first at the Italiens with my 'Venus'? I am told the show will be important. But it is as you like; I leave you to decide. I wanted to come and discuss all this with you today; but in such weather! I am furious to have to tell you only by letter of the friendly and grateful feelings of your devoted painter

AMAURY DUVAL

This portrait is now in the Louvre. Madame de Loynes left it in her will to Jules Lemaître. The first time I lunched at the Rue d'Artois, when I entered the studio which served the writer as study and library, my eyes were attracted to this portrait of a diaphanous young woman, whose hair is carefully smoothed down on each side of her face, and who is lost in thought, her forehead resting on her hand. Dressed in a black taffeta dress, she is truly ravishing. I am not fond of Amaury Duval's painting, but the personality of his model captivated me.

In one of the corners of the frame Jules Lemaître had fixed a bunch of Parma violets. All that I knew of his Egeria was now coupled with that face. I was thinking thus when he came in. Straightway he started to speak about her; he was still so shaken by her recent death that his emotions moved at random among his recollections. He told me in turn of her qualities, her tyranny, her influence, and even how he had tried to introduce some of her culinary recipes into his bachelor home.

'I have prepared for you, after her fashion, a dish I hope you will appreciate. It is lamb with tomatoes, hearts of artichokes, mushrooms, and all sorts of delicious little things.'

Jules Lemaître's dwelling was perfectly fitted to his needs. It comprised one huge studio, so lofty of ceiling that, to provide living-room accommodation, it had been possible to build in two further floors to its height; on the first was a drawing-room, dining-room, and another small room. At the very top were the bedrooms. The dining-room looked on a narrow garden where three handsome trees proved a great joy to Lemaître. When the weather allowed it, we had our meal in the garden.

During lunch, Lemaître, his elbows resting on the table, asked me questions. I felt his curiosity somewhat malicious, but I also guessed his sympathy. He was so simple that he gave one confidence, though he did not forget the object of my visit. He inquired how I was getting on with my studies, questioned me as to my tastes in books, gave me a summary of his, then treated me to a first inspection of his library, promising to let me little by little explore it further. Ever since my youth I had written little things just for myself. I kept a journal, took numerous notes, had scribbled a novel, some short stories... Jules Lemaître insisted on seeing my modest efforts, promising his advice as to literary style, and chose a day to come for this purpose.

I was at this time very devoted to Anatole France whose gifts had dazzled me, but I quickly became much fonder of Jules Lemaître, and later I even regretted the affection I had shown to Anatole France, who only deserved my admiration. The opposite of France, Jules Lemaître was always in a good temper. When he had worries or difficulties, he simply said: 'Forgive me, little one. I shan't be very entertaining today, I feel sad.'

On certain days he was in capital form and very brilliant; on others he was somewhat melancholy and romantic; but always he was genuine. His speech no more ran to extravagance than his thoughts. He never bored you with an empty compliment as did France, but his remarks were judicious and not lacking in irony.

'This white collar suits your pretty face,' he would say to me. 'Your hat matches your hair, but take it off.' 'Now is the springtime. Are you not in love?' 'First of all, have you worked well? I am going to be very severe today.' 'Always aim at perfection. Try to express your thoughts with as few words as possible.' 'Never be grandiloquent. Avoid adjectives and adverbs. After lunch I shall read you some Racine and some Molière.' 'I understand nothing in Stéphane Mallarmé; can you explain him to me?'

Later, Jean Cocteau set at this job in earnest, but all in vain; we had to give it up.

Here is the portrait Jules Lemaître gives of himself in this connexion:

> Being but a native of Touraine, descendant of a race noted for its common-sense, moderation, and humour, after twenty years of conformity to classical habits and the inborn need of lucidity in style, I am too badly prepared to understand their gospel. I have read their verses and have not seen in them as much substance as even the turkey of our childhood fables was able to detect, for if this fowl had very poor sight, he yet managed to see something. I have not been able to resign myself to words which, strung together according to the rules of syntax, appear to make sense and yet have none, holding the mind maliciously suspended in the void, as in a fallacious riddle or a charade based on no word at all.[1]

Little by little I began to feel attached to Jules Lemaître as would a niece to an uncle. He liked to alter my surname in all sorts of funny ways by means of Russian diminutives: he called me Machinka, Machinskaia, Marishka. Here are some of the letters he wrote to me:

Dear Machinka,

I am grateful that you think of me a little, and your note gives me great pleasure. I was saying last Saturday to Jean Cocteau, 'You must come to lunch with Machinka.' — 'But she is in London.' — 'That's wrong of her.' Therefore, Jean Cocteau will come alone tomorrow and we shall speak ill of you.

I have seen of late neither Tochè [2] nor Madame de Noailles,

---

[1] Jules Lemaître, *Les Contemporains*, 4th series.
[2] Nickname given to Madame Bulteau. (*Author's note.*)

nor anybody. I am not doing much; only some stories just by the way. And you? Are you writing what you have promised me to do? I shall be so happy when you come back.

My very fondest homage.

JULES LEMAÎTRE

June, 1913

Dear Machinka, That little note of yours I found at Venice has greatly touched me. I have very fond thoughts of you. I might tell you that it would have been most pleasant to be here with you thirty years ago, but it comes to my mind that you would only just have been born, and that I should not have known what to do with you. So I must withdraw that wish. Tell Jean Cocteau that I am too lazy to write to him, but that I try, I also, to see 'Venice' as would a child! The results are deplorable.

I kiss you with all due respect, dear Machinka.

JULES LEMAÎTRE

Travers

Dear Machinka,

I have just spent a fortnight in Royon, where I found the climate not too cold. I shall be at Travers until the end of the month; then I am going for a trip of a fortnight in a car; then again Travers until the end of September, so I think. Such are my plans. I think of you with tender respect (it is appalling, Machinka, how much we respect you!). Have you worked a little, in spite of the illness of your small niece?

Most affectionately yours

JULES LEMAÎTRE

Anatole France and Jules Lemaître had been at one time fairly close friends, but a disagreement between them went back, I believe, as far as 1893. *Les Rois*, a novel by Jules Lemaître, had appeared in serial form in *Le Temps*. France in his review of the book, the rough draft of which was, so it appeared, Madame de Caillavet's work, while bestowing flowers on Jules Lemaître, slightly made fun of his pedagogical forbears, his virtuous simple-mindedness, and 'the steadfastness of his scepticism.' Jules Lemaître, although writing plays which would not have been out of place on the stage of the Théâtre Libre, was nevertheless only a Parisian of recent date; he felt deeply hurt by these touches of irony. In the following year the publication of *Le Lys Rouge* gave him the chance to reply. He had guessed, like everyone else, Madame de Caillavet's influence on France's mitigated praises of his book, and since it was known that the heroine of *Le Lys Rouge* was in some ways the picture of Madame de Caillavet, he did not fail to point his epigrams at her.

Madame de Caillavet and Madame de Loynes did not move in the same circles. Rivals as they were already through their salons, they chose this quarrel to set their great men against each other. The Dreyfus scandal made the barrier between the two ladies impassable, and they both did their very best to aggravate this antagonism which lasted as long as their lives.

Madame de Caillavet, always sarcastic, neglected no occasion of making fun of all she heard about Madame de Loynes's salon. The latter died first, in 1908. I heard Madame de Caillavet describe her rival's funeral and quote, so as to give it life, a saying of Adrien Hébrard to the grieving Jules Lemaître, 'My friend, you will meet her again in a better demi-monde.'

Scarcely two years later Anatole France was shedding tears even more bitter at Madame de Caillavet's funeral.

I used to see in turn the two widowers, who certainly did not lack feminine attention calculated to make them forget their grief and cast off their yoke, and one evening I discussed their quarrel with Adrien Hébrard.

'Don't you think,' I asked, 'that I could bring about a reconciliation between them? It seems to me they are quite willing. We might see them start upon a new *Dialogue of the Dead.*'

That plan appealed to my Nanny. 'Try it, child,' he told me; 'try it.'

I first approached Jules Lemaître and found him quite disposed to see Anatole France again, all the more so since he had always deplored their estrangement. He at once suggested he should invite Anatole France to lunch at his house, and the very next day I received the following note:

> If next Friday or on Saturday, seventeenth, or any day in the following week, Anatole France and you could come to have lunch with me in my garden, it would give me great pleasure to have you both.
>
> Affectionately yours
> JULES LEMAÎTRE

I went at once to show this note at the Villa Saïd. Anatole France was delighted that Jules Lemaître had taken the initiative; he valued his former friend's intelligence and very much wanted to meet him again to see if he would still, as of old, find pleasure in a talk with him. They vied with each other in politeness, for France, on his side, wanted the first meeting to be at the Villa Saïd. But busy as they both were, it took me nearly a month amid a hundred difficulties before we had fixed on a day. At one moment the lunch was to be at France's home, the next at Jules Lemaître's, or then again at mine.

Here are some of the letters which I received in turn:

Dear Madame and Friend,
    I would willingly go to Jules Lemaître's for lunch on Monday next with you. The gods who are never very fond of me have deprived me of the Saturday.
    I kiss your hands.
ANATOLE FRANCE

Travers
    Tell Anatole France that I sincerely thank him and would have been very happy to lunch at his home with you. But I am now with my mother who is slowly passing away, and the doctor tells me I must not leave her. I cannot, therefore, quite tell when I shall be back in Paris. I am bitterly disappointed, but send you affectionate regards.
JULES LEMAÎTRE

    Best of greetings, Madame. I am just leaving for the country, so very much regret I cannot yet go to lunch at our friend Lemaître's.
ANATOLE FRANCE

    Next Thursday suits me perfectly, at twelve-thirty at my home. Tell France he is a darling. And so you are. And try to bring Tochè.
Affectionately
JULES LEMAÎTRE

The meeting took place at last on a Thursday of January, 1911, when I took Anatole France to lunch, Rue d'Artois. I had the habit, about that time, when I was not too lazy, to note in my diary events and conversations which appeared to me interesting. I find at the date of that Thursday the details of the meeting.

Anatole France came for me. He was in splendid form. His healthy constitution was evidenced by his way of walking and moving; his lively eyes were sparkling. He rubbed his elegant hands together in precise gestures which denoted that he was full of joy. He teased me:

'You are going to be present at a sort of first night. I have never been at Jules Lemaître's home, at least not for a very long time. Gougy, the bookseller, tells me that his collection of books is now a most handsome one; Gougy himself helped with it. I shall be most interested in it. He has, so I am told, some of Molière's original editions. I feel sure he must also have little books of the eighteenth century, containing rather licentious illustrations which he is fond of showing to pretty ladies when they come to visit him. Beware, Madame!... Upon my word, I shall myself find pleasure in looking at them.'

They threw themselves into each other's arms. Just as of old people pacified the Minotaur by means of a sacrifice, Jules Lemaître handed over to France, as a gift, a volume of Parny, once in the possession of Sainte-Beuve, and adorned with an engraving by Prud'hon, a proof before letters. This delicate attention touched Anatole France at a most sensitive spot; he was then preparing to write an essay on the painter and his friend Constance Mayer.

The conversation branched off on Sainte-Beuve. Both granted him the highest intellectual qualities and a sincere pessimism which marked him out from the artificial and affected melancholy of the other romantics. On questions of literature they were both as unconventional as learned. Pleased with themselves, they showed indulgence towards Sainte-Beuve and forgave him all his indiscretions regarding Adèle Hugo, on the ground that, when told about the *Livre d'Amour*, she had agreed to its being published when all three should be dead: Hugo, Sainte-Beuve, and herself. France related story upon story, in a delightfully charming fashion. As Jules Lemaître congratulated him upon this, he replied that he could at last express himself with complete sincerity.

Our host listened to him, his quite evident pleasure showing now and again, but in all his answers he showed himself so humble and modest that France remarked it somewhat embarrassed him, making him feel the disadvantage of being a few years older.

Anatole France kept walking up and down the studio, examining with great interest every curio. The conversation passed on to Napoleon, then Robespierre and fixed itself on Joan of Arc just as France had stopped, in a corner on the right, in front of the plaster cast which Maurice Barrès had given to Jules Lemaître.

'Don't you see, my friend,' explained France, 'although this present has come to you from Maurice Barrès and you believe it to represent Joan, this small head can never have been hers? How could they have placed, in the fifteenth century or the sixteenth, any statue of Joan of

Arc on a cathedral? This must be either a Saint Maurice or a Saint George.'[1]

Lemaître then brought the conversation to Anatole France's *Joan of Arc*.

'My book is a failure,' said the latter. 'I ought to have drawn a picture of the reign of Charles VII instead of relating the story of that child, for the more documents I unearthed about my heroine, the more she dwindled and disappeared. It is certain that the authentic information we possess about her is very scanty and that she is submerged under the mass of facts belonging to the history of her time. Do you know that Orléans was delivered without her help? When I read her answers at the trial, I noticed that they were of two kinds: the proverbs she uttered as would any true peasant and which for this very reason preserved some clumsiness and sounded enigmatic, and her direct answers which reveal a simple soul and a brain not very developed. Her age was not even quite clear in the chronicles of the time, and her contemporaries seemed so little impressed by her that such an important man as Jacques Gélu, and one enjoying much consideration, could call her *Puce* as banter upon the word *Pucelle*.'

Lemaître appeared convinced by those arguments. France, once on this subject, called forth Bossuet's evidence, and pointed to the oblivion in which Joan of Arc fell during the following centuries.

[1] This head was never on a cathedral, and has never indeed been said to have been. It belonged to a monument consecrated to Joan of Arc on a square in Orléans, and was erected by Charles VII after the war of rehabilitation. (*Author's note*.)

'It is Napoleon,' he exclaimed, 'who rehabilitated the worship of Joan because she incarnated the idea of Coronation.'

Thereupon we went into the dining-room. France fell to and did justice to the lunch. Jules Lemaître had taken pains to arrange a succulent meal and he gave us to drink some of his cheering Touraine wine. They vied with each other in enjoyment of the meal and exchanged cooking recipes, growing animated like two boys released from school. In spite of myself, I compared one with the other.

After the coffee, Jules Lemaître showed us his books. I do not know why, but at that moment I had the impression that his scepticism, more affected than real, was becoming an obsession. The reflexions of France, as he talked to me when we left, perhaps bore upon this. It was already past three; Jules Lemaître, as was his habit when he felt shy, removed his eyeglasses, wiped his eyes and his kindly gaze lost all precision.

'I am going, my friend,' he said, 'to ask you a question; just reply yes or no. It is today Thursday. Should you like to come to the Académie with me? I am just going.'

'No,' replied France. 'I mean, I do not refuse to go back sometime, and I even promise you to do so only with you. But understand my position. If I go today, I shall lead people to believe I am going to take an active part in the next election, and this I do not wish to imply in any way. As I have not been at the recent sessions, I should appear as one who comes to veto the decisions without following the debates, and if I openly favoured a candidate, I should do him great harm, since for one vote I should bring him I should cause him to lose several. So don't mention it; I promise you I shall go back to the Académie, but not today.'

We left our host.

'Lemaître is charming, very charming,' muttered Anatole France as he tenderly hugged the small volume which once upon a time had belonged to Sainte-Beuve. 'There is only one thing which shocks me about him; that is to find him so tolerant. He has cut down so much of his real opinions that they appear like garments too short in which he himself does not feel comfortable. He has just told us that he will, next year, give a course of lectures on Chateaubriand and that the prospect bores him. If it feels like an imposition from his schoolmaster, why do it? He is free, after all, but there you are!...'

Here pierced the secret jealousy which he could not help feeling for Jules Lemaître's powers of attracting.

'He is eloquent, he will charm his audience, it will be a great success—it means something to please the ladies — while in my case, I catch fire.... I must have the real thing.... I have wicked passions. But hush!... your chaste ears would not put up with the tale of where I spent the evening yesterday. I went to a simple meeting...'

I copy here the lines with which I ended the entry in my diary for the day: 'It seems to me that their friendship is more a form of mutual tolerance, which is equivalent to a medium sort of admiration. They will never be near on fundamental matters, it is only on superficial things they are alike. But each, on his own line, will push on to the extreme limits of his capacity.'

After the loss of Madame de Loynes, Jules Lemaître ended by arranging for himself a very comfortable life. He made friends again with some of his stage interpreters, Lucien Guitry and his wife, Madame Worms-Barretta, and others. He dined regularly every Friday at Madame de Saint-Marceaux's and lunched on Saturday at Madame Bulteau's. He was an intimate friend of the Daudet family, and godfather to the little Philippe, to whom he bequeathed his library. He also preserved a keen interest in L'Action Française, which the Comtesse de Loynes had always supported and which profited by money she had left in her will to Madame Léon Daudet to be used for propaganda. He had also looked up a few of the old friends whom Madame de Loynes's tyrannical affection had frightened away. One day he made me understand, in very discreet fashion, that his old friend's jealousy had, in latter times, made him suffer a little. However, his nature was so kindly and affectionate that he was quite game for submitting to new influences.

He told me that he had formed the habit, from the very beginning of his liaison with the Comtesse de Loynes, of writing her a daily letter, always illustrated. These witty drawings were of great delicacy and depicted the events of their lives. The Comtesse had complained one day about his lack of will power, and had predicted: 'When I am dead, my friend, you will end your life in vile and low haunts, a pipe to your lips as you sit in front of empty beer-glasses.'

Time Past

At once he had sent her a drawing so picturing himself. Here is a little poem dedicated to Madame de Loynes which I think has never been in print before:

> *Je n'ai jamais jeté la fleur*
> *Que l'amitié m'avait donnée,*
> *Petite fleur même fanée,*
> *Sans que ce fut à contre-coeur.*
>
> *Je n'ai jamais contre un meilleur*
> *Changé le meuble de l'année,*
> *L'objet usé de la journée,*
> *Sans en avoir presque douleur.*
>
> *Je n'ai jamais, qu'à faible haleine*
> *Et d'un accent serré de peine,*
> *Laissé tomber le mot: 'Adieu.'*
>
> *Malade du mal de la terre*
> *Tout bas soupirant après l'ère*
> *Où ce mot doit se perdre en Dieu.*

Jules Lemaître did not consider himself a great poet, but he liked to quote his monosyllabic poem:

LA LOIRE

Diable!
Que
De
Sable!

Oh!
Quelle
Belle
Eau!

Gloire
Et
La
Loire.

By way of compensation it was with joy that he recalled his first play on the stage, his successes as a dramatist, and the part which Madame de Loynes could justly claim in all this. Not only had she been his inspiration and his collaborator, but her advice as to the choice of interpreters had contributed to his triumph. He had dedicated his first three plays to her: *Révoltée*, *Le Député Leveau*, and *Le Mariage Blanc*. *La Massière*, acted at the Renaissance Theatre by Guitry, Marthe Brandès, and Judic, created a great stir. I seem to remember that Cécile Sorel acted in *Flipote* in 1893.

Sarah Bernhardt created, with Guitry and de Max, *Les Rois*, which Lemaître had adapted from his novel published that same year. After the Comtesse de Loynes's death, the Opéra-Comique gave *Le Mariage de Télémaque*.

Lemaître devoted the greatest care to the preparation of his courses of lectures, always searching for information, and, contrary to France's habit, did not keep his friends informed of the progress of his work. He never tried upon them the striking sentences meant for his audience. Only now and again, if he felt some satisfaction over a happy rendering he had hit upon, he drew attention to it: 'Truly, after giving it thought, I have made a nice little discovery. If you don't quite grasp it, that does not matter; I shall carefully emphasize it when publishing a volume of my lectures.'

Jules Lemaître was very much loved, and in the salons he frequented his lack of selfishness, his spontaneity veiled by an irony more apparent than real, won him devoted friends. Being himself kindly and affectionate, he preserved the freshness of feeling and the hunger for loving which marked him in youth. It was a true friendship that bound him to Madame Bulteau to whom he offered as a token of esteem most of his manuscripts.

About this matter he said to me: 'But to you also I must give some of my manuscripts. I have put aside for you three tales and one Morning Bulletin.'

Here is the Morning Bulletin in which he makes fun of the banning of François Coppée's one-act play *Le Pater*. As for the tales, *L'Aventure de Rosario, Un Amour, Molière à Chambord*, I had them made into a small volume bound in white vellum.

MORNING BULLETIN

After eight days of influenza:

A morning paper gave yesterday the full text of *Le Pater*, the one-act play which has been banned by the authorities.

Having now read it, we inquire with more confidence than previously: What mysterious danger did the authorities fear? The public knows quite well that the Communards killed priests and that the regular army shot Communards. The public knows that the Commune has been a fair felon and is not ignorant of the fact that repression, necessary and just, must have been somewhat implacable and summary, since there are crises during which justice has no leisure to be tactful and exactly discriminating. But that is the point, people will say; it is better not to recall such things. And why not? It seems to me, on the contrary, excellent that they should not be forgotten. *Intelligite et erudimini*.

Did the authorities fear a too energetic reprobation of the rebellion of 1871? Such fear would be strange.... Or was it the hissing from the Communards they dreaded? If so, how cowardly!

The most probable reaction would have been that nothing at all would have happened. I should have understood the Censor's apprehension should the play have been given at a popular theatre. But in such a place as the Comédie Française, in this most solemn of all institutions, a theatre in which the proletariat, if ever they come, do so with a feeling of deference, at heart already very bourgeois!... Oh! there was no need to make all that fuss!

I really believe that the Government had some innocent Machiavellian purpose in all this. They wanted to renew the trick which had succeeded so well with *La Conspiration de Général Mallet*. This is the way a new venture in censorship sets out: When there is a possibility of a play creating some disturbance, the authorities first ban it. Then, when the public has vigorously protested, when it has loudly proclaimed, 'Indeed, indeed, are we thus to be treated as children?' the ban is simply lifted. For the authorities are then quite confident that the passionate reaction they feared has exhausted itself and that the public will show itself all the more cool-headed for having been thought riotous....

But truly, was it so necessary, just for *Le Pater*, to beat so much about the bush?

I also preserve with great care one of Jules Lemaître's exercise books when he was a child: beautifully written and adorning with round-hand and slanting Script mottoes and obvious truisms: '*Beauty is good to look upon*' — '*If Man knew how to limit his desires he would live always contented*' — '*Develop early habits of tidiness and diligence.*'

On each page appeared the carefully written signature: 'Jules Lemaître, born at Travers, April 27th, 1853.' The fly-leaf of the book bears the date 1862. He was nine years old.

In his way of talking, spontaneous and sincere, he would bring forth the correct word to dispute wrong impressions or statements. One evening, as we were dining at Anna de Noailles's, with Adrien Hébrard, the essayest René Gillouin, and a few other friends, I was discussing with Gillouin the different parts played by religion and literature in Protestant compared with Catholic countries. Lemaître came close to us.

'And you, dear friend,' I asked him, 'what do you think about this subject, you who pretend to be an atheist?'

With a slight start as of shocked decency he replied: 'Oh! Machinka, not atheist, simply impious!'

René Gillouin was thereupon reminded of what had happened to him that very evening with the editor of *Le Temps* to whom he had explained the sort of uneasiness he felt, in connection with a recent book by Romain Rolland, in contact with an author so evidently enamoured of virility.

'You are right,' replied Hébrard, 'he is ambi-sexual.'

The curve of destiny nearly brought Lemaître back to a marriage, the outcome of the romantic adventure of his youth. His disposition of mind caused him to remain attached to the past.

'Even if one dreams of the future, it is on the past one builds, as best one can. In fact the future is only darkness and terror.'[1]

He had always kept in touch with the woman who had first inspired him with love, and since she was by then a widow, he often saw her. They had both preserved

[1] Jules Lemaître, *Old Books*. (*Author's note.*)

'memories of the past' and a fair dose of sentimentality which drew them together in long talks. During these friendly conversations Madame Engel retained her discreet charm as of old. She was building up with her old friend plans for their future — when someone came to mar their happiness.

The woman who then gained hold of Lemaître's life was nothing idyllic. By nature entirely different from Madame Engel, she took the initiative in guiding his existence and turned it entirely topsy-turvy. The hurricane which thus caught him up proved of such violence as to break him. In turn shaken by passion and despair, he lived in a perpetual state of torment and confided to me that he was unhappy, torn by remorse and conscious of his weakness. His health became altered, and each time I saw him he complained of fits of oppression and other ailments.

One summer day I was waiting for him for lunch, when he arrived more weary than usual. I heard him complain to my old Joséphine in the hall when she inquired about his health. She tried to take a cumbersome and heavy object which escaped from his hand and fell, rolling on the floor with a metallic din. I hurried to greet him. Perspiration showed all over his forehead.

'Ah! Machinka, I am worn out, done for: this walking-stick is really too heavy.'

I picked up with both hands the strange object which was still on the floor. It was a stick of solid bronze, adorned with queer sculptures.

'But, indeed, dear friend, why go about with Hercules' club?'

'Well, little one, what can I do? It is a present... and *she* simply makes scenes if I don't take it with me.'

A few days later I lunched at his place and said to the devoted person who ruled over his home: 'How can you let Monsieur Lemaître go out with that cumbersome present?'

'A present!' she exclaimed; 'he very well, indeed, paid for it with his own pennies, and the bronze alone cost him three thousand francs.... If it only depended on me, the stick would soon have been thrown away, but...'

She quickly disappeared and came back to place under my nose the bill duly receipted.

Every year, on April 27, his birthday, I brought flowers to Jules Lemaître. When he was sixty, so that he might live double the time, I gave him one hundred and twenty tulips of all shades. In 1914 he was sixty-one. I went to offer him a basket of spring flowers, but for the first time he was not at home.

Dear Machinka, Goddess of the snows and bestower of roses, could you make me very happy by coming to lunch in my garden next Monday at twelve-fifteen, with Jean Cocteau?
With much love, but respectful homage
JULES LEMAÎTRE

And later:

Monday 27-4-14
Dear Machinka, What a marvellous basket of flowers! You have tried to console me because I am sixty-one. Many thanks, snow-white friend. I am very upset that I missed you

when you called, radiant and so fragrant, but I shall come to see you tomorrow or the next day after my lunch.

A heart full of love.

JULES LEMAÎTRE

All the friends of Jules Lemaître could see his health ebbing daily. He told many, as he did me, that he was not happy. One of the last occasions when I saw him was at a party given by Madame Adolphe Brisson at La Roseraie de l'Haÿ. He seemed to me very shaky and it hurt one to look at him.

It was already too late when he pulled himself together and started for his home in Touraine. He thought highly of his native air. That was at the end of July, 1914. He had just had another attack, rather slight this time, of angina pectoris. His niece and his housekeeper did not reveal to him the seriousness of the European events.

On August the second, the tocsin rang. The patient was resting in the garden unaware of the declaration of war. Arriving in a car, unexpected visitors burst upon him: 'We come to take you with us; it is war, war!...'

Jules Lemaître was not strong enough for such news. It was the final blow. It killed him.

He is now resting in the small cemetery at Travers between his parents' graves.

« V »

MARCEL PROUST

It was in 1905 that I saw Marcel Proust for the first time, at one of Madeleine Lemaire's musical evenings. Proust has himself, in his *Salons*, drawn a picture of those evenings, where the elegance and distinction of the audience were on a par with the music offered. The guests were so numerous that many of them could find room only in the inner courtyard, where indeed it was pleasant to go, for these musical evenings, being held in the spring and sometimes even in the early summer, the weather invited to a migration under the lilacs in bloom.

One evening, at the other end of the studio, I noticed in a group of people a very pale young man with admirable eyes. Over his whole person was imprinted a graceful weariness; his hands, long and exquisite, moved in pleasingly harmonious gestures. Now and again one folded itself back under his chin to support it, or else was placed in front of his mouth to hide his laughter, the sparkling eyes alone betraying his mirth. He was a voluble talker. His eyes continually wandered about without appearing to fix their attention anywhere, but they were so penetrating that it was evident one was confronting a pitiless observer.

MARCEL PROUST

MARCEL PROUST

Marcel Proust's voice had several ranges of tone, and from being almost confidential could swell out ringingly, or at other moments fade away into whispers. He expressed himself by means of allusions; an extreme politeness and a longing to show himself affectionate breathed through all his remarks. He compelled attention from his hearers, and rewarded them always by flashes of wit which flared up at the very moment he appeared most modest and detached, as if having lost all interest in what he was saying. This affectation was very charming. I noticed also the care he took to express himself with precision, coming back over details, choosing unexpected comparisons, quoting writers, and now and again interspersing his discourse with a stanza of verse. His conversation displayed a rich eloquence, a wide and original culture; to each person he approached he no doubt said unusual things, for the interest he aroused was most noticeable.

When he listened to music, his eyes, so precisely observant when he talked, at once looked far away: he no longer moved; his head, slightly thrown back, appeared overburdened by the mass of black hair framing it with darkness. He could bend his limbs about and intermingle them with the ease of a child; his wrists were double-jointed; his legs coiled around each other as do tropical creepers.

I discussed him with several of his friends, who told me many different things, but all agreed on one point: he was like no one else. It must in truth be stated that numerous were those who did not believe in his genius. I read his essay on Ruskin and his first book, *Les Plaisirs et Les Jours*, and felt a keen interest in the minuteness of his analyses, the compactness of his details converging to the same effect, and the subjectivity with which he surveyed various positions. But I was greatly surprised to hear that he had taken up Ruskin's work in order to translate it, though he hardly knew English. Ruskin's style is rich, supple, daring in striking similes. Proust took scrupulous care over this work. Our friends, Madeleine and Léon Yeatman, saw much of him about this time; at every moment he rushed to them to verify a detail and make sure he allowed no mistake to slip into his translation.

They told me that one evening there came a ring at their door. It was Proust's valet inquiring:

'Monsieur sent me to ask what became of Shelley's heart.'

Another time, as my friends were coming home from a dinner in town, they found Proust installed in the concierge's lodge to open the front door when required.

'The concierge is ill,' he explained, 'and as her husband needed to go out to fetch her something, I told him I would take his place while I waited for you. So you see, I am at my post.'

Marcel Proust's kindness was a real thing, a spontaneous gesture directed towards those he could help.

When, in 1900, Ruskin passed away at eighty-one, at Brantwood, near the lake of Coniston, Proust, brooding over the author he so much admired, re-read the page where Ruskin speaks of a little man whose statue is to be found on one of the façades of Rouen Cathedral. He wished at once to go to Rouen. One fine morning, therefore, he took an early train accompanied by Monsieur and Madame Yeatman, and spent the whole day visiting the Cathedral and other churches in the town. He wanted to find, among the countless sculptures adorning the Portail des Libraires, the small statue which did not measure more than ten centimetres in height. It was Madeleine Yeatman spotted it, greatly to Proust's joy, for he despaired of ever discovering among all these stone denizens the little fellow who had inspired Ruskin with that fine page quoted in *En Mémoire des Églises Assassinés*. The sacristan who escorted the visitors assured them he had known Ruskin. Proust was delighted and asked numerous questions to which the man replied as far as his memory would help; it seemed to our friends he rather piled it on, in view of Proust's evident interest. At the end of the visit Proust asked his companions if twenty francs were a sufficient tip, a considerable sum in those days. They assured him it was. All three left the Cathedral, but Marcel suddenly broke away to go back, and joining his companions a few moments later: 'I have added another louis,' he explained. 'Think of it, a man who has known Ruskin certainly deserves that!'

One should read, in *Pastiches et Mélanges*, the prodigious description Proust elaborated about this page of Ruskin, inspired by the beauty of Rouen Cathedral and the pathetic, crumbling statuette.

Rumours were in these days everywhere heard that Proust was inaccessible; that he loved solitude; lived by night and slept by day, surrounded by devoted friends few of whom were admitted to his room of which the walls were lined with cork. Although I appreciated his remarkable gifts, he was still for me a mere acquaintance. But during the year 1911, Reynaldo Hahn spoke to me about him during one of the weekly luncheons at Madame Caroline Reboux's, meals we had nicknamed 'luncheons Thermidor' on account of the succulent lobster which was usually served. Young men of letters gathered around Paul Reboux's mother; she allowed each guest to bring, when his turn came, a friend of his own choice. The 'coming' young men of the period were very appreciative of their hostess's welcome, for she possessed rare qualities and very good taste. It was at her home that Reynaldo told me, with an air of mystery, that Proust was busy over a book which would create a great stir. He proposed to make me better acquainted with Proust and begged me to help the fortune of the book. I was on very friendly terms with Adrien Hébrard, editor of *Le Temps*, he explained, and the support of that newspaper would be of supreme importance.

I had not long to wait for this meeting, which I had not solicited but had long desired: Proust came to see me. However, whether out of diffidence or because he wished to ascertain during that first visit how far I was worthy of being told about something which already was of prime interest in his life, each time the conversation seemed to approach the subject of his book, by some skilful manoeuvre he avoided speaking about it. I felt greatly embarrassed by the compliments with which his talk was permeated; he kept on overwhelming me with them.

They appeared so exaggerated that, in order to change the subject, I, in my turn, diverted the talk and spoke about Russian literature. Proust immediately pricked up his ears. I told him how seldom I traced the peculiar atmosphere of our writers in the translations I looked into; how shocked I was at the arbitrary cutting of the text, as for instance the suppression of all the end part of *War and Peace*, and how far the French were still from knowing our rich literature. I quoted Turgeniev, Tolstoy, Dostoievsky, but when I named Gontcharoff I realized Proust did not know him. So I took pleasure in introducing him to Oblomoff, the hero of the novel bearing that name, who has become the prototype of the nonchalant Russian. I also summed up the plot of *Obriff* (The Abyss), another famous novel by Gontcharoff, in which Vera, the heroine, is as striking a figure as Natacha in *War and Peace*, or the young girl of Turgeniev's *First Love*. Proust's interest being awakened, I was obliged to make more precise the sketches I traced of these characters, and I became aware of his wish to understand these authors, and of his longing to ascertain how far his sensitiveness bore any relation to theirs.

He explained to me his devotion to Dostoievsky, but he enlarged even more on his reasons for liking Russian music, being certain of the influence it had had on modern French music. This was the time when, under Serge de Diaghilev, the Russian Ballets proved to be the great event of the spring season. We agreed to go together to see them.

It was a queer sensation I retained from this first visit,

Time Past

where, without telling each other anything of our personal lives, we both had the feeling (Marcel confirmed this later) of perfectly understanding and knowing each other. When he was about to leave, I ventured to say I had read all he had so far published; he looked at me with mistrust, sat down again, and craftily put me a few posers. I understood that I was to pass a sort of exam, and fortunately I managed it, for it was with a kindly smile and the promise to come again that he followed me in the hall. Nevertheless, on the doorstep, he assumed once more that decorous behaviour which had so paralyzed me when he first arrived.

Marcel Proust's alternation between friendliness and remoteness, like warm and then icy water he seemed in turn to shower over his friends, rendered intercourse with him peculiar: sensitiveness, imagination were perhaps at war with a longing to preserve his freedom. The next day I received from him marvellous roses.

That same year I saw him several times, but it was only during the summer of 1912 that our acquaintance took an affectionate character. I was then at Houlgate spending a holiday with friends, among whom was Calmette, and we often went to the Cabourg Casino. One September evening I was surprised to see Marcel Proust wandering about, lost and staggering under the lights, and wearing, in spite of the heat, a heavy overcoat unfastened so as to reveal a loose dinner-jacket and under it several woolly waistcoats. He had then a beard, which made his face longer than it really was, giving it the appearance of an El Greco. He carried an extraordinary straw hat in his hand; altogether his presence in such a place seemed very weird. Mine was just as strange for another reason. I cheerfully went up to him, for he had not yet noticed me, and took him to Calmette, the editor of *Le Figaro*, who had been the first to welcome Proust's articles in his newspaper and whose obligingness was proverbial. And indeed Calmette, although in much of a hurry to get to the baccarat room, anticipated Proust's request for the publication of *Pastiches*.

'Yes, it is settled,' he explained. 'I spoke about it to Francis Chevassu for the supplement.'

I spent the whole evening with Proust. He was surprised at having met me so near the gambling rooms, for I was not playing, and he tried to find out what I came for in this place, where I parted from my friends on the threshold which promised pleasure. Taking advantage of his position as a man by choice unattached, he brought me to confess that, although I pretended to show reluctance for society life, and thought little of it, I yet filled my time with futile occupations, to take my mind off sorrow by means of daily distraction; just as a wounded person fears any motion causing pain, I tried to avoid certain thoughts, and though I knew this way of existing could scarcely be called living, while thus engaged life nevertheless flew by. He urged me to tell him more.

Everywhere, legal or illegal love-making whispered close to me, brushing against me and hurting, leaving, like the foam of the sea as it withdraws, a raging and bitter track. These kisses given to others, these love-words passing beyond me, these hands clasping, everything created a disturbing atmosphere from which emerged a yearning for love. I went through life like the third horse to a troika, driven tandem ahead of the pair, and galloping at the edge of the road, looking elsewhere.

Marcel Proust listened to me, evidently satisfied at having conquered my reticence; as for myself, feeling his sensitiveness attuned to my mood, I was not dissatisfied. Thus then became established between us an atmosphere of trust often renewed during subsequent talks which later he recalled as 'the brilliant and vivid memories of Cabourg.' Indeed, I spent long evenings with him at the Casino: he no longer suggested we should go to a theatre or walk into the gambling rooms, convinced as he was that I infinitely preferred his conversation. It was so varied, so different from the talks at our first meetings! He now realized that his work interested me, so he spoke about it, though never by openly starting the subject. He pronounced the name of 'Swann' in a most suave way, *Suane*, as a sort of secret slipping through his lips. He told me of the guiding themes of his book, in part already conceived and written; he opened parentheses to explain its composition, stopped suddenly to dwell on an important detail — all this with digressions, and comparisons derived from the lives of people we both knew. I had the impression of viewing the back of a tapestry, the design and meaning of which I should not understand until the author turned its right side to me.

There was a curious contrast between his deliberate modesty concerning himself — I would even say humility — and his sarcasms, his pitiless remarks when he portrayed some of our contemporaries; his delineation then became sharp-edged, though he at once wanted to soften it by more kindly remarks, sometimes even of an excessive indulgence. On the following day, when he recalled what he had said previously, he made me promise to forget it, gave me other pictures rather blurred over, yet far more cruel in this veiled form.

These nightly outings allowed him to find contact again with the external world. We were continually interrupted by the servants of the hotel who came to deliver messages to Proust, to tell him that his orders had been attended to, or that appointments solicited or refused had been arranged or cancelled. A mail always reached him at that late hour, though there were no more deliveries; Proust threw a rapid glance at the envelopes and thrust them into his overcoat pockets; already bursting with boxes of medicines and newspapers unopened.

Nothing escaped him: as he talked, he took note of the people moving about us; sometimes he asked me questions.

'Have you noticed that couple walking by a moment ago? Can you imagine the life of two such people? The woman appeared much put out by her friend's losses at the gambling table; I suppose that on the terrace she is going to reproach him; shall we go and watch them?'

We went out, in a night abloom with stars. Marcel, while listening to the lovers' discussion, explained to me why he never left his room before that late hour, the delights of which he enjoyed as with a miser's joy. But at the least breeze I would notice that he looked chilly and make him go home. His bad health was no secret for me; he had explained to me the care he had to take of himself, the fumigations to which he was compelled because of his asthma, his regret not to be able to stand the scent of flowers. His frailty was evident from his wasted face, the dark rings around his eyes lending them intensity, and his thin body to which layers upon layers of clothes did not manage to give substance. His hair, very close-set, was unusually thick, with stray bits getting tangled on his forehead and the nape of his neck. Although cut rather short, it added size to his head, in contrast to his limbs, his delicate hands, and his feet which did not appear meant for walking.

His presence in the Casino never went unnoticed; the servants' politeness, as they showed eagerness to serve him, his appearance so different from that of a reveller, his ease of manner, were indications that he had purposely chosen this place as a centre of observation, and that he felt at home in it; all this helped to attract attention. I noticed that people turned back to look at us, all the more so on account of the gusto with which Marcel now and again imitated certain persons and lent to our conversation a twist opposed to reality. No one has ever, orally, made up pastiches with such perfection and fun. So also his *Pastiches*, which *Le Figaro* was about to publish, remain masterpieces in that style, on account of his thorough knowledge of the authors he imitated; these sketches would by themselves vouch for Proust's gifts. When he conjured up any person he wanted to describe to me and whom I did not know, he adopted that person's gestures, tricks, and voice; I then saw appearing in front of me an old lady famous under the Second Empire, or else the very type of the military man of that same period.

Proust did not display the stunning manner of a Jean Cocteau, who also had a genius for imitating people, nor that exclusively belonging to Chaliapine, but a deep understanding which portrayed at the same time character and external appearance, and brought forth member after member to conjure up a whole society. The very theme of the narrative was a compact succession of observations reaching beyond the person portrayed to evoke his caste, his origins. Marcel had a passion for this game; he enjoyed it as a scientific nature-study, perpetually adding here and there a detail the better to depict an external feature, or searching deeper into a trait of the mental make-up. No longer was he then the Marcel who stammered confused excuses, accused himself of failings of which he was not guilty, or searched sadly for misdeeds he reproached himself with. No, he was now a Marcel sure of himself, and conscious of his prodigious gifts. He displayed them in your honour with a generosity of which he enjoyed the rebound.

Such was his way of ascertaining what documentary treasures he had accumulated; on the top of this, at the same moment, his listener became for him a new subject to study — suddenly he scanned your features with devilish malice: Had you fully understood the meaning of his tale? Straightway, he managed to put you more precisely to the test. With the wariness of a thief, he questioned you and judged you. Sometimes he laid traps, pretending he had forgotten a fact or a name. His scorn burst out if his interlocutors had erred through boasting, or when, pretending they knew, had confused matters and been grossly mistaken. He used to tell stories specially concerned with the ignorance of society people, and the self-possession with which they go right off the track amidst their errors. His eyes, so particularly mobile, flashed with malice; he had great difficulty in veiling his laughter which suddenly burst forth, pitiless, in strident notes.

This gift of analysis was a source of great joy for him, but also of many torments. Often, indeed, he attributed to his fellow creatures powers of acuteness greater than they possessed, and tortured himself by inferring from these all sorts of grievances people were far from entertaining against him. He even foretold disapproval which had never occurred to the persons to whom he attributed motives of behaviour which were solely the fruit of his own perspicacity. His subtlety and susceptibility were so great that the misunderstandings which, temporarily, separated him from most of his friends, had their origin in his imagination which created sentimental complications such as he himself enjoyed and had a gift to draw.

Proust's memory, always active, was another faculty which increased his chances of suffering; having for long concentrated it on the study of classical authors and the behaviour of his contemporaries, he used it on his own behalf, and kept with meticulous exactness the count of what he considered due to him. Misunderstandings usually arose simply from the fact that, on account of his health, he did not live under normal conditions, so that information which reached him through several friends, even the most obliging, was often distorted. His despondent moods made him dread any withdrawal of affection on the part of his friends. He resorted to subterfuges to test friendships he deeply valued. In one special case he borrowed a fair sum of money simply to win the evidence that this loan, readily granted, was a proof that nothing was altered in the feelings of one of his friends towards him. But, since he always wanted to make his position clear, when he wrote to thank his friend for the loan, he explained his motives.

When he came back from Cabourg, Proust set out to find a publisher. The people who formed the little group awaiting the advent of his book knew the difficulties he was about to meet. He himself realized that the length of the book was one of the objections. Yet he revealed nothing at first regarding the details of his negotiations. One day, however, he gave me a few indications, making me promise not to say a word to anyone; I was therefore all the more surprised to learn almost at once, from four different persons, how far the matter had progressed. This was one characteristic of Marcel's secrets: they were 'partially' entrusted to several people....

During the winter and spring of 1913, Marcel Proust frequently came to see me. We often dined at a restaurant, and several times went again to the Russian Ballets in the company of Jean Cocteau. Marcel's presence in a theatre as smart as the Champs-Élysées always created a stir, for after a few marked successes in society he had often withdrawn for long to keep at his work. He was an unusual apparition, for those who did not know him, this in part on account of his clothes about which he was indifferent, though he always carried out the rites of dressing with refinement, elegance, and care, but also because of his complexion which was due to the hothouse plant life of his cork-lined rooms, and because of his voice, in turn sonorous, gentle in its modulations, or dropping to church-like whispers.

'Who is that? Who on earth can it be?' To such questions answered the merry eagerness of his friends who had sometimes been very long without seeing him: 'What luck! Here's Marcel!'

One evening at a supper at Larue's, Maurice Rostand, a great admirer of Proust's work, came to join us after leaving the theatre.

It was delightful for Marcel to see himself thus surrounded by a group of enthusiastic young men, keen on his 'message,' to whom he read, in privacy, parts of his books. These adepts, reserved towards each other, were so all the more since not one of them had any notion how far his information extended. They were the first to acclaim the importance of *Swann*.

Marcel was full of friendly attentions for me. On my side I was attached to him through affection and admiration; we were continually giving each other flowers. Here is a letter of his dating from that period; it contained precious slips of proof:

> To thank you for the marvellous lilacs (which make me more happy than old Silvestre Bonnard when he received from the Comtesse de Trépof *La Légende Dorée du Clerc*

Toutouillé with the *Life of Saint Doctrovée*), I artlessly imitate the Notre-Dame tumbler and gather for you a few proofs from my book (which *no one* but you has seen), to send them to you as *lilacs* 'invisible but penetrating' in fragrance. I have hesitated a long while before sending these extracts clumsily cut out and glued on paper. They are so much like what you know about me, and consequently so different from the main body of the book, giving an entirely false idea of it, that it is almost painful for me thus to slander my work beforehand. But perhaps you will read them and understand the uneasiness I felt, though above all the sweet joy superseding it at the knowledge that the first hands into which come proofs of my book are to be yours. Also, it seems to me that my lilacs forestalled yours whose perfume will for ever permeate the sadness of my summer evenings. As for the adorable things you say to me, I dare not thank you for them, for I dare not believe in them nor see in them more than the compassion of a great heart. I was telling you the other evening, remembering the way life wounded you, that when I saw you from the distance bleeding as from the big bunch of red roses on your bosom, you put me in mind of a dove stabbed through the heart. But you are also a carrier and providential dove, and then again the dove, inspiration of our other poet friends: 'The Visible Holy Spirit.'

Your most respectful and grateful admirer

MARCEL PROUST

P.S. I now cannot put my hand on the slip where there is mention of lilac trees beaten by the rain under the *cooing* of distant thunder. So that the last sentence in my letter will have no meaning for you, since you will not understand why it is associated with rain.

Marcel completed his work on the proof-sheets, and his corrections are evidence of the material his rare outings furnished him with. He incorporated such material in his text, adding and developing endlessly.

Swann's Way was at last to appear in November. Marcel was busy with the publicity campaign. Friends — Lucien Daudet in *Le Figaro*, Maurice Rostand in *Comoedia*, Jacques Émile Blanche, Jean Cocteau, and several others — wrote articles, all enthusiastic and remarkable. Lucien Daudet's article was of a keenness and insight to do credit to his judgment. I did my share by proposing to Adrien Hébrard that an interview with Marcel Proust should appear in *Le Temps*, and this duly happened on November 12, 1913, the interviewer being Élie Joseph Bois.

This interview is interesting for several reasons: to begin with, it is the first document in which Marcel Proust explains himself freely concerning his work, and gives precious indications to it, as a whole. The very date of the interview enables us to put a stop to discussions which have arisen regarding the way Proust composed his books, and to doubts which have been expressed concerning the existence of a central scheme.

But apart from its historical importance, this interview bears the stamp of a critical mind of the first order, and Élie Joseph Bois is among those who have at once understood what constituted the main interest of the book and have not hesitated to proclaim its originality and its worth.

I have been careful in adding to my personal recollections on this matter by having a recent talk with Monsieur Bois, now editor of *Le Petit Parisien*. This is what he told me.

Monsieur Hébrard summoned him: 'Go and see Marcel Proust. He has just written a book to which my attention has been drawn by a person whom I wish to oblige. Go and interview him, but I warn you that Proust is a very peculiar being. I choose you among my collaborators because I believe you will be able to understand him. Make an appointment at once.'

And thus it was done. When Bois arrived at the Boulevard Haussmann, one afternoon at three o'clock, he was introduced into the young author's study, a dim room lined with cork. In the light of a small lamp, Proust, in his brown dressing-gown, was impressive to anyone who had never seen him before, especially from the brilliance of his eyes which grew more and more animated as he talked about his book.

Bois took notes for long hours, and it was quite late in the evening when he left Proust, carrying away with him a copy of *Du Côté de chez Swann*. This conversation, during which the author's intentions and the genesis of his books had been so minutely explained, aroused in Bois genuine enthusiasm. He felt obliged to read the book at once and spent the whole night in that occupation. In spite of the density of Proust's style, Bois had read the whole book without fatigue when the morning came, and had even read over again the opening part, which he admired most. Using his notes, he traced the main outlines of his article and took it to Proust to make quite sure he had really grasped his meaning. Céleste brought it back to him with a letter containing copious annotations. Proust, although liking it, feared it might appear as but a duplicate of another article due to appear in *Le Figaro*. But it was Bois's interview that commanded attention, and it still carries weight.

Then *Le Temps*, which usually does not publish that sort of article, on November twenty-first gave in its bulletin, 'People and things that matter in the World of Letters,' long extracts from *Du Côté de chez Swann*. An important thing was, however, to secure as soon as possible an article from the famous critic Paul Souday. Adrien Hébrard had the habit of allowing entire freedom to his collaborators; nevertheless, he promised to approach Paul Souday and ask him to make haste. So, less than a month later, on December 10, 1913, the literary page of *Le Temps* was devoted to an analysis of *Swann*. My recollection of it is still clear: Souday, though recognizing the worth of the book, was very critical of its composition and development. He had not yet discovered Proust, and his admiration came only much later.

Marcel, in order to thank me, sent loads of roses, carnations, orchids, lilies, all sorts of flowers in fabulous quantity, with this letter:

Madame,

When last year Reynaldo got me caught in the gear wheels of *Le Temps*, I absolutely opposed the idea that you should be mixed in this business and should exert yourself on my behalf. It was painful to me to tarnish by utilitarian motives my brilliant and vivid memories of Cabourg. But I was, indeed, gripped fast by the wheels, so that what I feared has come to pass. Well! I not only don't regret it, but now that to my respectful sympathy is added gratitude, I am fonder of you than ever. I send you a few flowers to stave off a longing

I feel for acting concretely in accordance with my thoughts and for bestowing some gift upon a person at the very moment she engages my fancy and emotions. Accept them (it gives me such pleasure to think they are going to be taken to you, and you will read my name and know they come from me as you arrange them in your home), accept them in homage from your deeply and respectfully grateful

MARCEL PROUST

I have not told you how much, in itself, and purely for utilitarian reasons, what you have done for me pleases me. My publisher will be delighted; as for me it brought me great joy. When you see Reynaldo tell him, please, that I am sending my card, or perhaps 'my works,' to Monsieur Hébrard.

Du Côté de chez Swann is, in our days, more accessible and appears in all its significance now the whole work is known and universally admired. When it was first issued, its beauty did not so easily strike the reader who thought he could judge of the whole composition by that one volume. Yet its serious and novel character could not pass unnoticed. If the printing had been better, and if the frivolity most people bring to reading was not so injurious to *Swann*, its success might have been more striking. Its qualities called for the future. Nevertheless, its author was in despair at seeing himself appreciated only by a few restricted sets who praised the book to the skies. The length of the work was in itself a fact which upset certain distinguished personages who later became Proust's fervent admirers; for instance, René Boylesve who, after a hasty reading, told me that Proust's style seemed to him so opposed to French traditions that he had the impression of reading a foreign writer. The long elaborations and digressions had put him off; he maintained that they disturbed the balance of the whole composition. It was in vain I endeavoured to bring him to change his opinion; I did not even succeed in making him take up again the partly read book.

'I don't understand anything in it,' he repeated with obstinacy. 'You know very well that Romain Rolland is another of my pet aversions. Proust is as long-winded as Rolland.'

During the War Charles Du Bos and Jacques-Émile Blanche succeeded where I had failed. Boylesve came one day to see me in a state of indescribable exaltation: 'You were quite right, my dear Marie; how could I not see it for myself? *It is only now I understand how to read Proust.* I am most enthusiastic, but very wretched: he has written the book I longed to write. It is prodigious. As for me, the best I can do is to destroy my works.'

Boylesve was sincere; he had a genuine sense of justice. He told me, that day, that he had written to Proust to express his admiration.

The reading of *Swann* filled me with enthusiasm. I wrote to Marcel to come and see me, so we might talk about it; I wanted to convey my joy. I joined violets to my letter, the first in this month of November. He at once telephoned and came in the evening, but a bunch of roses had preceded him with this letter:

Madame,

My roses are not a reply to your divine violets! By a sort of pre-established harmony (which I should like to see existent not merely in our words) the little card you sent me said exactly (and almost to the letter) what I want to say with my flowers. You tell me that my book brought you great joy and I wanted to write to you that you brought to my book its greatest joy when I read in your eyes you were looking forward to it, would protect it, would read it, and perhaps even like it. I wish you all possible happiness. I know so little of your life that those wishes are very vague, but they are most ardent. As for me, I have been so wretched these last months that the best thing to wish me is to become numb, but that cannot happen.

If you see Bonnard, tell him how much I like his novel. What constitutes its value is, naturally, what is not obvious at a first glance, this causing one to be unfair to him. But his great distinction is in having preferred this unobtrusive beauty. I often mention his book, and especially like to talk to you about it, since you also admire and like it.

Your most respectful and grateful

MARCEL PROUST

Such was the way he had, as his usual reaction, when he saw me disposed to approach a subject his heart was set upon, to divert his thoughts to another book, while he embarked on considerations which fitted his. That evening he was indeed so very modest, or rather tried to appear so (for at heart I am sure he was convinced of the full significance of his book), that I was much upset. Yet often there was in his behaviour, when he talked about himself, that old stubbornness, above all early during his visit. However, when he felt certain that the praises you proffered really rested on a deep understanding of his work, his mistrust gave way to outbursts of affection and an unconstraint most moving because of its sincerity. At such moments no one could be more captivating, no one could display such pure joy and a more lofty character. He then forgot his illness, his diet, his melancholy, and even his malicious wit transformed itself into childlike mirth and cheerful jokes.

The War, the first bereavements, the general anxiety came to part friends. Every individual had much to endure in his or her own field, and Marcel regretted not to be able to take an active part in this emergency. His distress was intense as he watched the cataclysm, and his sympathy found heartrending accents as he mourned departed friends. I can never forget the tender solicitude he displayed toward me when my brother was killed. It is not that he tried to console me — he knew quite well this could not be done in such a misfortune; but he spoke with such gentleness, such discerning lucidity that his words did not make me feel rebellious as so many others did.

One day Marcel told me how discouraged he felt, as now all literary enterprises lacked interest; I protested and told him how much I had at heart his work and its completion. I showed him my copy of *Du Côté de chez Swann*, which I had sent to be bound in white vellum and which had just come back. He was much touched. 'Very well,' he whispered, 'since you want to know what became of Odette, lend me your copy and I shall write in it a summary of the remaining parts.' It is thus he came to write, as a sort of preface, the pages which follow:

To Madame Scheikévitch
You wish to know, Madame, what became of Madame Swann as she grew old. It is rather difficult to give a summary of this. But I can tell you that she became more beautiful.

This was mostly because, somewhere about middle age, Odette discovered for herself, or invented, a characteristic physiognomy, an unalterable 'personality,' a 'style' of beauty; over her loose features — left so long at the mercy of the perilous and futile whims of the flesh that the least exertion or transitory flabbiness made her old for an instant, that, willy-nilly, fitting her moods and health, they had given her a disparate, ordinary, shapeless, and charming face — she now superposed that fixed type of some sort of immortal youthfulness.

You will see that she makes new friends; yet (without your discovering the reason until the end) you will still find Madame Cottard exchanging with Madame Swann talk such as this:

'How very smart you look,' said Odette to Madame Cottard. 'Is that a dress from *Redfern fecit?*'

'No, you know quite well I am faithful to Raudnitz. Besides, it is only an old dress done up.'

'Indeed, yet it is so stylish!'

'Guess what it cost. No, drop the first figure.'

'Oh! that's not nice of you, leaving already; I see that I have not been successful with my tea. Take a little more of these little rubbishy things, they are really quite nice.'

But I would much prefer to introduce to you characters you do not yet know, above all the one who plays the most important part and brings about the winding-up: Albertine. You will see her when she is still in 'budding girlhood,' in the shadow of which I spend many happy hours at Balbec. Then, when I begin to mistrust her over trifles, and again over trifles give her back my trust: 'for it is the very nature of love to render us, at one and the same time, more distrustful and more credulous.'

My acquaintance with her should have stopped there: 'It would have been wise to look upon it with wonder, and deliciously to treasure this small share of happiness without which I might have died before I knew what happiness can be for hearts less hard to please or more fortunate. I ought to have run away, shutting myself in solitude, preserving thus the melodious memory of those lips on which I had awakened words of love and from which I should only have asked, henceforth, that they cease addressing me lest a new utterance, which could not but be different, jar discordantly upon the meditative silence where, thanks to some play of pedals, I might otherwise have sustained the tonality of happiness.'

Besides, little by little, I become tired of her, and the idea of marrying her no longer appeals to me. But, one evening, coming home from one of those dinners at the 'Verdurins' country house,' where you will at last discover the real nature of Monsieur de Charlus, she tells me, as she wishes me good night, that the friend of her childhood, of whom she has often spoken to me and with whom she is still on affectionate terms, is Mademoiselle Vinteuil. You will see the terrible night I spend after this, the outcome being that I entreat my mother with tears to let me be engaged to Albertine. Then you will witness our life together when engaged, the serfdom to which my jealousy reduces her and which, contriving at last to make me recover my composure, vanquishes, so at least I believe, my longing to marry her. Therefore, one day — so fine that my mind dwells on all the women passing by, on all the journeys I might undertake — I resolve to ask Albertine to leave us. But Françoise, on entering my room, hands me a letter my fiancée has given her for me, for she left that very morning, having decided to break off the engagement. That was exactly what I so firmly believed I longed for! Yet I suffered so much that I had to assure myself that before the evening some way would be found to bring her back. 'Only a few moments ago, I thought, this was the very thing I wanted. Seeing how I was mistaken, I realized that suffering has a deeper understanding of psychology than the best of psychologists, and that the knowledge of the elements composing the soul is not granted us by the subtle perceptions of the mind, but — hard, dazzling, queer as salt suddenly crystallized — by our sharp reaction to pain.'

On the following days I could scarcely stand on my feet in my room. 'I tried not to touch the chairs, not to notice the piano nor any of the objects she had used, and which all, in the peculiar language which was theirs in my memory, seemed once more to tell me of her departure. I fell into an armchair, but could not remain there, for I had sat in it when she was still there. And thus, every second, appeared one or other of those numerous and humble egos forming myself to whom I had to notify her departure, whom I had to bring to listen to these strange words: "Albertine is gone." Thus with every act, however unimportant and which previously had been submerged in the atmosphere of her presence, I had, through renewed efforts and renewed suffering, to begin my apprenticeship of separation. Then the concurrence of other ways of life.... As soon as I grew aware of these, I became struck with panic. The composure I had just recovered was but the first manifestation of the strong though intermittent will which was going to fight against suffering, against love, and at last master them.'

This part deals with forgetfulness, but the page being already half covered, I must skip all this, for I want to tell you the end. Albertine does not come back; I am driven to wish her dead so that she might not belong to others: 'How could Swann at one time have believed that if Odette died through an accident, he would be restored, if not to happiness, at least to peace through the blotting out of suffering? To blot out suffering! Have I truly believed this possible, believed that death is content with striking what has being?'

I learned the news of Albertine's death. For this death to put an end to my torments it would have been necessary that the shock killed Albertine outside of me, as indeed it had done, but also within me. Never had she been more alive. When a being takes possession of another, he has to shape himself to fit within the compass of Time; he can only reveal himself through the succession of minutes, and only gives of himself but one aspect at a time, or presents but one picture. This, no doubt, is a great hindrance for us that a person can be summed up only through a collection of moments, yet it is also a great strength. Such a person appertains to memory, and the memory of one certain moment has no knowledge of what happened after; the one moment it has registered is still lasting and with it the being who embodied it. Such parcelling out not only caused the dead Albertine to live on, it also multiplied her.

When I had succeeded in bearing the grief of having lost one of those numerous Albertines, I had to begin all over again about another, about hundreds of others. Henceforth, the perpetual revival of bygone moments, which had been for me until then a sweet comfort in life, became my torment. I waited until the summer drew to an end, then the autumn. But the first frosts brought back other memories so cruel that, like a diseased being (who in the book places himself from the point of view of his own body, his lungs, his cough, but morally is myself), I felt that what I ought to dread most in my grief and for my peace of mind was the arrival of winter. To lose Albertine's memory, linked as she was with every season, I ought to have been crushed by each in turn, chancing a re-education to them just as the hemiplegic patient learns anew to read. My real death alone could have consoled me for her own. But the real death of oneself is not an extraordinary thing, it consummates itself daily in spite of ourselves.

Since I always brought her back to life simply by thinking of her, all her betrayals never became those of a dead person; the instant at which she had committed them became the actual moment, not only for herself, but for that one of my 'egos' I conjured up and which contemplated her. So that no anachronism could ever pull apart our indissoluble couple, in which each new culprit was at once paired with her jealous mate, myself in the flesh. After all, it is no more absurd to regret that a dead person will never know we saw through her deceit than to long for our name to be famous two hundred years hence. What we feel is only real for ourselves; we project it towards the past, towards the future, and the fictitious barriers of death cannot stop us. And when my most important recollections no longer brought back Albertine, small insignificant things acquired that power. For love-memories are no exceptions to the general laws of Memory, itself ruled by Habit which weakens everything. Thus, what we end by recalling best about a loved person is precisely what we had forgotten because it was unimportant.

I began slowly to feel the power of forgetfulness, this masterful implement which shapes us back to reality by destroying within ourselves a surviving past in constant contradiction with actuality. Not that I ceased loving Albertine; but I already no longer loved her as towards the end, but as during the most ancient days of our early love. To forget her entirely I should have needed, like a traveller who retraces his steps to his starting-point, to journey through again, but in a reverse way, all the feelings I had known until I rediscovered my initial indifference. But each halting-place in the journey can never find us motionless. As one stops at a certain stage, one has the illusion that the train is starting off again, but in the direction from which one has just come, exactly as of old. Such is the cruelty of remembrance.

Albertine would have had nothing to reproach me with. We can only remain faithful to what we have known. My new self, while it was growing against the background of the old in process of dying, had often heard the latter speak of Albertine. From the talk of this moribund being it had come to believe it knew her and loved her. But it was only second-hand affection. Just as certain happy events happen to us when we are past expecting them, misfortunes may also come too late in our lives to grip us with the magnitude which, at an earlier period, they would have had.

By the time I came to realize this, I had already got over my loss. There is nothing surprising in this. Regret is indeed a physical ill, but among all physical ills we must mark out those which attack the body only through the medium of Memory. In such cases the prognosis is generally favourable. After a certain lapse of time a patient who has cancer will be dead. But very rare are the instances of a disconsolate widower who in the end does not find consolation. Alas! Madam, my paper is running out just when all this was promising to become, perhaps, fairly interesting!

Yours ever
M. P.

This narrative, written in my copy of *Swann*, sums up the work published later in the books not yet issued at that time. The main extracts are taken from *A L'Ombre des Jeunes Filles en Fleurs* and *Albertine Disparue*, the proofs of which he was correcting seven years later. In answer to my question, 'What became of Madame Swann?' he borrowed from his manuscript, not only conceived at that date of 1915, but in part written out. One can follow the leading ideas of his work and its whole conception in the extracts quoted in this summary, which is also an answer from beyond the grave given by the author, in view of his death before the complete edition of his work, to critics who argued among themselves, notably Louis de Robert and Benjamin Crémieux, whether Proust had really a guiding plan for his complete work.

I should like now to relate the origin of the friendship which later brought together Proust and Walter Berry.

I was one evening dining with friends at Berry's when, on looking through his books, I found a small volume bearing the arms of the 'Guermantes.' This cultured man, who was President of the United States Chamber of Commerce, did not know Marcel Proust. I wanted him to offer this small opuscule to the author of *Swann*, and I suggested they should meet. But there was always a great deal of cunning required to bring about a meeting with Proust. I wrote to Marcel to praise my host's intellect, and promised him a surprise if he came to my home one afternoon at three. This was an hour almost out of the question for a rendezvous with him, for he very seldom agreed to move from home in the afternoon. I do not know whether I proved very eloquent, or whether curiosity got the better of him, but he promised to come before long.

Walter Berry, a sceptic by nature, was pleasantly surprised. From their first meeting there existed between them a bond so mutual and so striking that the three of us did not part company until two in the morning, after having concluded the day by dinner at a restaurant. Marcel, nevertheless, had not agreed to accept the little book, and on his side Berry had refused to take it back. For eight days the book travelled backward and forward between my house, the Boulevard Haussmann, and the Rue Guillaume where Berry lived. At last Marcel kept it and sent to Walter Berry two hundred cigarettes and to me two hundred white roses.

Every new acquaintance was for Marcel an inexhaustible source of documentation, for he liked to ask numerous and direct questions; provided the person he met was alert and active, he always found a way to sound him. He was also not only anxious personally to guide his interlocutor, but also to place in his way information which might be useful to him.

I do not think that at this period he read copiously; nevertheless, he had a special gift for finding the important passages in any book and memorizing them. How often have I heard him referring to an author (I speak of modern ones), though he confided to me he had only just glanced through that man's book, yet he had marvellously grasped his attitude and his views! He even managed to quote his text. When he studied an individual who might help him to complete a character he was creating, he never hesitated to go direct to him or make him come. His chauffeur Odilon, husband to his maid Céleste, was often asked to go and bring the person he wanted to question. He would explain to Odilon with a smile:

'You are not an interesting subject of study for me, for you always tell me the truth, but there is a person I have seen several times and who interests me greatly. Until now he has only told me lies and he thinks I believe them. I am going to have him come here once more, and I will knock down his scaffolding of lies like a house of cards.'

He had a passion for reaching the truth about people, and many a time went to the actual spot where, taking care not to be seen, he could gather first-hand evidence, while later, once more back in his retirement, he continued to ponder over these cases. When one reckons the countless hours during which he secluded himself to formulate his observations and rely solely on his own judgment, one guesses that he sifted out carefully the information he had been able to find. This searching method was applied not only to people, but to the most trifling objects. I must here give an example and show how he incorporated such information in his text.

One evening Marcel came for me to dine at a restaurant. I was still very anxious about my young brother, news of whom had not reached me for three weeks. While I was getting ready to go out, the post brought the long-awaited letter and a little parcel from the front. The parcel contained one of those tinder-boxes, then almost unknown, which soldiers were making from fragments of shells and coins; this one was made out of two English pennies. Marcel was enraptured with it.

'Are you fond of me enough to give it to me?'

Delighted that I could prove I was, I replied: 'But of course, take it.'

During all the evening Marcel would take the tinder-box from his pocket, examining it with much feeling.

'Do you know,' he told me suddenly, 'you will find it back in my book.'

And in fact, in the first volume of *Le Temps Retrouvé* I read, a long time after: 'There were rings and bracelets made from fragments of shells or driving-bands also tinder-boxes fashioned from two English pennies to which a soldier in his dugout had succeeded in giving such a patina that Queen Victoria's profile looked as if chiselled by Pisanello.'

The original tinder-box had been preciously kept by Marcel, and he desired Céleste to give it back to me after his death. I confess I was greatly touched when, faithful to his wishes, she brought it to me. We talked together about Marcel's daily way of life. He had never had any fixed hour to ring for her when he got up; any time between eleven in the morning and seven in the evening, though usually about five. She used then to bring to his room a lighted candle for his fumigations with Legras powder, as recommended to asthmatic subjects. The chambermaid brought the powder in saucers and he breathed it for a long time. Then he had his *café au lait* with three crescent rolls, and often this was the only food he took all day. The coffee had to be as strong as essence and it took an hour and a half to prepare three small cups; he liked it boiling hot. Sometimes, when he had to go out, he had a dish sent him from a restaurant — stewed beef or a Russian salad, on rare occasions a small chicken — but, towards the end, he hardly touched anything. In the evening, Céleste placed at his side a tray on which was a cup, a bottle of Évian water, sugar, a kettle, and a box of lime blossoms. He worked in bed, in his nightshirt, with a cardigan of natural Pyrenean wool over it.

When he left his bed, everything was altered. He had his hairdresser come to his dressing-room, and used, every time he washed himself, some fifteen towels. His linen was always kept warm in the oven. He was extremely particular as to the softness of materials. One day Céleste bought for him at the Bon-Marché handkerchiefs which she thought very soft, but Marcel thought them too thick; so she washed them several times and they became much better; however, as she entered her master's room one day, she found him engaged upon cutting these handkerchiefs to strips with a pair of scissors.

'Don't you see, Céleste,' he explained, 'this is the only way I can prevent your giving them to me again. If I am not careful, my nose takes good care of itself and cannot put up with them. My mucous membranes are so sensitive that this rough linen causes me to sneeze, and with my asthma this is not prudent.'

Marcel's grief on account of the War was almost an obsession, a perpetual anguish; he could only still his regret at not playing an active part in it by the thought that the torments of his illness represented, in a certain way, his share of trouble. His friends did all they could to beguile his sorrow. During the summer of 1917 I went to Versailles, where news of my brother, then in a dangerous sector, would reach me more easily; Marcel came to see me several times at the Trianon Palace Hotel, where I had put up. A journey, if only as far as Versailles, was always for him a great event; his pining for nature was attenuated by the fear he had of it. Sometimes, with the longing for a change, his nostalgia carried the day.

I still picture his arrival at the Trianon Palace one September evening in the car of General Zankévitch, then Commander-in-Chief of the Russian troops on French territory, with whom I had made him acquainted. The

General had conceived a strong admiration for Marcel; he wanted to repeat for me several things Proust had discussed during the journey and which had struck him, but Marcel escaped him, and taking me by the hand asked me:

'Should you not like, Madame, as it is still daylight, that we go together into the park? I must absolutely, since I have today fenced off my asthma, take that chance of rediscovering sensations I have not been able to indulge in for so long.'

He was as cheerful as a child. And he, always so reserved, squeezed his arm under mine.

'You don't mind, do you? It is such a fine evening. I am so delighted I could come, I must look at everything and miss nothing; even the scent of this thorn-apple will not be able — I will it so — to hurt me.... Everything worked beautifully. Céleste was kind enough to wake me early so that my fumigations were over in time. The carriage was punctual, I have been very comfortable in that big car, and how very interesting I have found the General.... As we drove up the Saint-Cloud hill it seemed to me that all sorrow had dropped from me. But don't go and tell I was here tonight. I have had to refuse several invitations to the country this week, for I was feeling too ill....'

We had a long walk under the trees, until nightfall. Marcel, now and again, bent towards a flower-bed, looked at a flower, asked me the name to make sure he was not mistaken, picked up leaves and moss which he examined with minute attention. The noise of a scythe reached us from a distant lawn.

'Marcel,' I exclaimed, 'you must not go that way; grass freshly cut is not good for hay-fever.'

'No, no,' he replied, shaking his head, 'we can go everywhere, fear nothing; tonight nothing can do me any harm.'

Nevertheless, we went back for dinner. Besides the General and Marcel, I had that evening as guests my sister-in-law, Madame Hellmann, Carolus-Duran's daughter, who, like myself, lived at the Trianon, and her children, who brought young friends of both sexes with them. Marcel was delighted to feel such charming young people around him. After dinner we went up to my private sitting-room, and Alexandre Dumas's grandson, Serge Lippmann, sat at the piano and played and sang some of his own compositions. Then a general conversation started, grew animated, and Marcel, surrounded by these adolescent heads, displayed his matchless charm as he multiplied questions, encouragements, and gracious words.

It was growing late, the General kept looking at his watch, but Marcel pretended not to notice. At last he came to me.

'Do you know if in the morning this place is very noisy on this floor? It seems to me well situated...'

'Our rooms look on the park and we are on the fifth floor.'

Marcel hesitated.

'Do you think the manager could fix me up somewhere for a few days?'

'I fear you would not feel at home, and the hotel is crammed full; there are people coming and going all the time.'

He pondered over this.

'It is so lovely to see young people who have not suffered...'

Dear Marcel...

One winter evening, during the War, Marcel arrived while hooters were giving warning of an air-raid.

'This evening, I want to carry you off. If you like we will go to Ciro's; I have been told their chef is excellent, and since you are kind enough to spend the evening with me, we shall talk.... Be careful not to catch cold.... Whatever you do, don't look at my collar; if you see a bit of cotton-wool poking out, it is Céleste's fault, for she absolutely insisted I put some on, quite against my will.... No, there is no need for you to call a taxi, mine is downstairs, and your feet will not be cold, for I had a foot-warmer put into it. How nice of you to put on this handsome white fox!... Truly, are you not ashamed to be seen with someone so badly dressed?'

We drove through war-time Paris, deserted and darkened, but invested with torturing poetry, and all at once found ourselves at Ciro's, where we neither of us had been before. 'Monsieur,' said Marcel to the head waiter, 'be kind enough to take Madame to the nicest table. Have a bottle of champagne of the best year at once put on the ice... yes, yes, you must have some, if only to please me.... Have you got *fillets de sole du vin blanc*? And a *boeuf mode*, a small salad, and... taking care it is really very creamy, a *soufflé au chocolat*.' (Marcel's guests always ate the same menu, the one he would himself have preferred if he had been in a state of health to eat it.) 'Oh! as for me, I touch hardly anything; ask for a glass of water for me, I have some *cachets* I must not forget to take.... And bring also some coffee, strong, good coffee, and if you don't mind, several cups of it.'

So we were settled down.

'I should have arranged, if I had known you would agree to come here, to have roses placed on the table, dark red and white; you must forgive me.... Just now, in your drawing-room full of flowers, I noticed those I had sent you; I ought to have chosen them nicer still, you have so many....'

His fragile hands were clumsily handling the *cachets*, which he emptied into his glass.

'I beg of you not to pay attention to my undervest if you see it poking out from my cuffs. It is as usual Céleste's fault. I know that you notice everything; a most pleasant thing, but also rather dangerous.'

Suddenly he got up, walked to the head waiter who was standing a few steps away, pulled his pocketbook out, and in a much altered voice said:

'Be kind enough to hand my card to one of these gentlemen at the table behind Madame.... They behave in the most indecent way, and I will not tolerate it; how dare they?'

It was my turn now to get up.

'What is the matter, Marcel?'

'These foreigners seem to be ignorant of who you are, they are making fun of you being with me...'

My eyes looked in the same direction as his, and I

recognized friends from the Italian Embassy. I went towards them.

'Dear Marquis de Médicis, allow me to introduce you to Marcel Proust.'

Marcel's face lit up.

'I was fearing, Monsieur, and quite wrongly, that you were making a mistake about Madame, or perhaps taking her for someone else.... I am so glad to know you. I am very fond of Italy and should very much like to see Florence where I have never been.'

We settled again at our table.

'Madame, what I have done was very stupid; I should have consulted you, and in any case it is war-time now. Thanks to you I had for a moment forgotten all the horror of it, all the suffering; but of course one can't have duels in our days. Will you ever forgive me for what has just happened? I feel most wretched about it.'

When I met Marcel at a party one evening, some months before his death, I found him so sad, so lost, that I realized that neither his growing reputation nor the Prix Goncourt could make him forget the incessant struggle which life meant for him. He seemed disillusioned and smiled in such a distant way when people congratulated him that I felt a strong longing to have him all to myself for one evening, so as to help him to find again the interest he used to display about most things.

'Marcel, I should very much like your advice about something.'

I knew this was the best way to make him agree to call,

for I do not believe he has ever refused his help to anyone. He looked at me at once.

'You know, I am rather tired, still, can you receive me tomorrow evening?'

His nature was so complex that it would not have done for him to know that one had invented a pretext to make him come; therefore, when the morrow came, I pretended that, contrary to all my expectations, I had been able to settle my difficulties by myself, but was now looking forward to his valued presence to make us live over again one of those delightful evenings of the past.

'You do not realize, my friend,' I told him, 'that you are now very famous, but I have here something which, even if it does not prove your fame, will no doubt make you laugh.'

I unfolded a cutting from a newspaper and showed him the advertisement from a girdle-maker, who, in order to attract new customers, had worded his lines as follows: 'If you wish to retain that charming and supple carriage of "budding girlhood," buy the girdle X...'

Marcel burst out laughing.

'Indeed,' he said, 'I was not expecting this. Where did you cull this pearl?'

'Just in *Le Figaro*.'

That evening, the last we spent together, proved very sweet and full of memories.

Marcel Proust died at the very moment when success was beginning to come to him. Although he had often said that fame meant nothing to him, I know that he had been happy at its first appearance. Had he not also written for me, 'After all, it is no more absurd to regret that a dead person will never know we saw through her deceit than to long for our name to be famous two hundred years hence?'

I felt so greatly upset by Proust's death that I had to allow several months to pass before I could bear to hear the story of his last moments; but then I went to see Céleste who had tended her master to the last minute with the utmost devotion. I had retained a picture of a slender Céleste, worn out with sleepless nights, her face pale, her way of talking deliberate and thoughtful. Dressed in black taffeta, she had glided about the place and only the rustling of silk told of her presence. Standing at Marcel's door, her quiet and protective appearance revealed her mission as a guardian angel.

When I now saw her at her home, it was a more robust Céleste I found, mother of a family and busy with the care of her own household. Upon seeing me she started to weep, silently; her grief was so acute that she had great trouble to begin talking: 'Yes, I also, Madame, knew that he was very ill, but I could not believe he was about to die. I shall never find consolation again.' Céleste's husband appeared. He also had eyes brimming with tears. Proust had the gift of inspiring people with love and devotion. Both Céleste and her husband spoke of him with veneration. Gradually, Céleste grew more animated. From everywhere in this modest dwelling, Marcel looked upon us at different ages. Here was a photograph of him as a frail little boy, wearing short knickers which emphasized the delicacy of his limbs; his exquisite hands played with a walking-stick in gestures I could so well remember.

Other photographs were carefully preserved in wornout letter-cases which had belonged to him.

Céleste had treasured the most trifling things; she had kept the pieces of paper, all of different sizes and often torn scraps, on which he daily wrote instructions for her. Sometimes it was only one single word, at other times minute directions, for he had periods when he hardly spoke and did not like to be disturbed. Then there was a name he had traced on the very day of his death.

We spoke of him in soft tones. Céleste used turns of speech which had been habitual with him; I recognized his way of expressing himself, his extreme politeness; Céleste's face, which Marcel used to describe as of 'lilac shade,' was distracted. 'Madame, to anyone who has known Marcel Proust, most other people are vulgar.'

I was plunged back into the past. I remember Marcel's delight in Céleste when she imitated, for his benefit some one of his friends, their whole manner! I recalled the dedication he had put in his own copy of *Pastiches et Mélanges*: 'To Céleste, the Queen of parodists, the imitator of Madame Scheikévitch, Monsieur J——, Madame Z——.'

On coming home from a party, Proust often called Céleste, related to her where he had been, what interest he had found in all this; then, bearing his work in mind, he would add: 'My poor Céleste, I believe I shall never reach the end of it. You know that I want to write a book about you; it would be just adorable, Céleste, and I must start on it. I believe nothing has ever been more useful to me than yourself. Listen...' and he would talk to her for a long while; and the hours of the night went by while she stood and listened.

In 1913, Céleste had married Albaret, Proust's taxi-driver. This man, knowing how much she was bored in her small lodging, had proposed that Proust should always employ him when he went out. Little by little Marcel took a liking to this arrangement and could no longer dispense with it.

I questioned Céleste regarding Proust's last moments. Towards the end of September he had felt more tired than usual. Going out one morning, early in October, he had felt chilly. He came home with a bad throat. The next day he had a cold and an attack of asthma followed. He worried much at finding himself so shaky, because of the proofs of his book *Albertine Disparue*. Instead of looking after himself, he thought it best to work harder, fearing that his state of health might prevent him from completing the reading of his proofs. A few days went by during which he suffered, but took no care of his health, absorbed as he was with his work, and refusing to interrupt it. He was developing a temperature; Céleste insisted that he call Dr. Bize, his usual adviser. Three days later, when the doctor came at Céleste's request, he declared (it was on October fifteenth) that Proust had as yet nothing very serious the matter with him, but that, having a bad cold, he should stop working and take care of his health. Provided Marcel did this, the doctor promised he would be cured in eight to ten days. He was also to take nourishment, which was most important. Marcel protested that food would increase his fever, which in its turn would prevent his going on with his corrections. Was not his work all that mattered to him?

Against the doctor's advice and in spite of fever, he dressed and went out one day, towards the end of the afternoon. His strength betrayed him and he had to come back almost at once. He went to his room and lay on his couch; he was chilled to the bone, was shivering and felt so bad that he had to go to bed. He asked Céleste to prepare his fumigation and tried to go back to his work, forbidding her, however, to light the fire: 'Céleste... Death is after me,' he told her. 'I shall not have time to send back these proofs and Gallimard is waiting for them....' That day he felt so weak that he had to give up work; in this shaky state he kept on sneezing. He sneezed in such an abnormal way that Céleste felt most anxious.

He was at that time living at 44 Rue Hamelin, on the fifth floor, in a flat furnished in the most scanty fashion. In order to telephone one had to go down and out into the street to a shop. It needed great cunning to leave the flat for so long. Céleste, however, tried that day to reach Professor Proust, but could not get the call through. The next day she begged Marcel to allow her to call Doctor Bize. The latter came, and renewed his entreaties that the patient take care of himself. Marcel still refused, saying that it would be a loss of time; but he promised the doctor to hurry with his work so that, once his corrections were finished, he would take care of his health. He had completely ceased taking food, and swallowed iced beer which Albaret had orders to bring from the Ritz Hotel, and in bottles placed in a pail filled with ice. He also gave orders that he wanted no fire in his room, saying that heat upset him. The doctor insisted he should be cupped, take hot drinks, and above all some light food to keep up his strength. He told him that he thought his work was wearing him out more than would a navvy's work. Marcel, although he felt weaker and weaker, protested. If he had to choose between his work and nursing, he did not hesitate: he had only lived for his work.

Nevertheless, he had choking fits, called Céleste every instant: 'Céleste, I am dying,' he explained; 'if only I have time to finish.... Céleste, it is horrible to think that doctors, to prolong a dying man's life, sometimes for a few hours, sometimes just for a few instants, persist in torturing him, with injections, cupping.... They know very well these things won't cure him... it is horrible. I beg of you, if that is to happen to me, don't let them do it.' He was very nervous, but gentle. His doctor, upset that he would not be nursed, went to warn Professor Proust of the danger he foresaw. That very evening Professor Proust begged Marcel to be reasonable and proposed to have him taken to a nursing home, where he would make sure he was given all the comfort and medical care required.

This affectionate concern irritated the patient, who asked his brother to leave him in peace, repeating that he would never agree to leave his room. The Professor suggested that he might at least have a nurse. This made Marcel even more angry: 'Céleste nurses me better than anyone, and she is the only one I want around me.'

When the doctor had gone, Marcel rang for Céleste: 'Céleste, you must promise me never to let anyone come near me, neither doctor, nor nurse, nor family. You must, Céleste, get rid of all those who wish to prevent me from working. I beg you not to leave me even a second, and if I become more ill still to remain. Do as I tell you, and don't worry.' He was looking at her with eyes full of anger plunging into hers to see if she would, really, keep the promise he had just extorted from her. He even took the further precaution of asking two of his friends, by letter, to prevent his being carried off from his home, an idea which had occurred to him during insomnia, for sleep had completely deserted him. He had more and more choking fits. Professor Proust came every day to see his brother, but Marcel's obstinacy in refusing to be nursed remained the same. He allowed no discussion on this point, and no one could influence him.

During all that period his illness was becoming rapidly worse. Eight days before his death Marcel sent a big basket full of flowers to Doctor Bize. He said to Céleste: 'Well, Céleste, that's another thing settled if ever I come to die.' He considered he had caused his doctor much trouble to no purpose, and since he was very fond of him, and yet did not want to follow his advice, he tried to make amends in this way so peculiarly like him, always full of politeness and sensitiveness.

Marcel kept to his bed, almost sitting up, and wearing the numerous woolly vests which Céleste always changed for him; he was surrounded by newspapers, books, papers of all kinds, and his proofs. Since he had left the Boulevard Haussmann he took no notice of the outside world, and every new flat he fixed up was always a sort of extemporized and provisional installation. During his last illness he once received Monsieur Tronche, and twice Jacques Rivière to give him full instructions about the publication of *Albertine Disparue*.

Callers tired and exhausted him. Nevertheless, one evening, he rejoiced at a call from Paul Morand. He kept him a long time by his side, and once the visitor was gone, he called Céleste: 'Céleste,' he told her, 'I feel that Paul Morand has a great heart, which I had never believed. He must have found me much altered; he spoke so kindly to me... I understood that he was grieved at seeing me thus.' Then, lost in thought: 'I did not know he was fond of me, it has given me great joy; and I also am very fond of him.'

On November seventeenth Marcel believed himself much better. He kept his brother near him a long while, and told Céleste that if he could only go through five more days like this, he would conquer his illness and once more prove to the doctors that they were wrong in wishing to keep him from his work. He added: 'But it remains to be known whether I can go another five days like this.' He was full of smiles and went on: 'And since the doctors and yourself wish me to eat, prepare me a fried sole; I am sure it won't do me any good, but I wish to please you.'

Professor Proust thought it was unwise to eat the sole. Marcel agreed that this decision was prudent. He talked further with his brother, told him he would spend the night doing good work and would keep Céleste by his side to help him. His courage was sublime; he went back to correcting his proofs, adding a few notes to them. About three in the morning, feeling worn out and choking, he called Céleste and dictated to her a few supplementary notes about Bergotte's death. He felt great happiness at being still able to dictate: 'Céleste, I think that it is quite good what I have just dictated to you. Don't forget to see that it is put in its correct place. I count upon you. Do not fail to add it to my manuscript where it is to follow in the text. I must stop, I feel quite done.'

The next day the doctors reckoned that this must have been at the very moment the abscess broke which had appeared on one of the lungs. About six he asked for a cup of milk, adding with a wan smile: 'Always to please you... but you can go away, I prefer to be left alone.' Céleste, who could see he was more and more in pain, wanted to come back softly close to him, but he grew cross at this: 'Why not leave me alone?' She went away; but at once, and at every instant after that, the bell rang to call her back. Towards ten the next morning, Marcel asked for some of that iced beer Albaret often brought for him from the Ritz. Albaret went off at once, and Marcel whispered to Céleste that it would be with the beer as with everything else, it would arrive too late.

He had more and more difficulty in breathing. Céleste could not take her eyes off his bloodless face on which a beard was growing, making it look even more pale: he was extremely thin, his eyes were so piercing that they seemed to penetrate right through to an invisible world. Standing by the side of his bed, Céleste, hardly able to keep on her feet (she had not gone to bed for seven weeks), went through the torture of being unable to do anything to ease him. She kept watch on each of his gestures, trying to guess and to anticipate any of his wishes. Suddenly one of Marcel's arms stretched out outside his bed, and it seemed to him he could see in the room a hideous fat woman. 'Céleste, Céleste, she is so fat and so black; she is entirely black. She frightens me...' Céleste, thinking he was feeling faint and delirious, believed she would reassure him by promising to chase her away. At once he forbade her to do so: 'You must not touch her, Céleste; she is implacable, but more and more horrible...'

Professor Proust, warned at his hospital, arrived in haste; Doctor Bize also came. Céleste, in despair at having to go against Marcel's orders, witnessed the arrival of an array of medicaments, oxygen gas-bags, syringes for injections. In her ears echoed the words: 'To prolong life in a dying man doctors torture him with injections, cupping...' The patient's eyes expressed his exasperation when Doctor Bize arrived at his bedside. Marcel, always so exquisitely polite, did not say good morning, and to make it quite clear he was displeased, he turned to Albaret who was following the doctor with the beer: 'Thank you, my dear Odilon, for having gone to get me this beer.' The doctor bent towards the patient to give him an injection, Céleste was helping him to pull away the sheet, when she heard, 'Oh! Céleste, why?' and she felt Marcel's hand bearing on her arm and pinching her, to protest one last time.

Now everybody was eagerly busy around him. All that was possible to be done to save him was attempted. It was, alas, too late! The cupping had no effect; gently Professor Proust raised Marcel up on his pillows with all possible care: 'I move you rather a lot, little one, I hurt you,' and in a whisper Marcel uttered his last words, 'Oh! yes, my dear Robert!'

He passed away about four o'clock, gently, without stirring, his unforgettable eyes wide open.

Marcel Proust had written for me, speaking of Albertine's death: 'Never had she been more alive.' In the same way, after his own death, he lived again a manifold life. Not only did his work acquire a world reputation, but his life itself, which during his last ten years had nourished the monument he left behind, became one of its most entrancing chapters. From everywhere appeared admirers and disciples. Such a strong personality emerged from the complete amalgam of his novel that each admirer chose to extract what elements seemed to him best suited to the conceptions and various sensibilities which had such marked literary tendencies. This parcelling out of the author's genius according to various appreciations led people to attribute to him, in turn or simultaneously, the most opposite gifts, though he could easily claim them all. Some people admired the poet in him; others looked upon his psychological insight as the reason of a success which had exceeded the most favourable previsions.

The attention of the most absent-minded found itself little by little captivated by the subtle understanding delineating, in strokes deeply humane, the most minute analyses. Likewise, the creation of types, at first drawn with a light hand, then gradually completed with touches searching nearer and nearer to their physical and moral skeleton, left in the reader's mind characters of such reality that, once their destiny was revealed, they stepped out of the pages and continued to live, as do the heroes in Pirandello's famous play, *In Search of an Author.* Yes, every conscientious reader of Marcel Proust became thereby a little his creator.

The article which Élie-Joseph Bois published in *Le Temps* of November 12, 1913, remains entirely true, where he pronounces *Du Côté de chez Swann* 'a strange, deep book in which analysis is carried to such lengths that one sometimes longs to shout "Enough," as to a surgeon who would insist on informing you of all the details of an operation.' But we do not say 'Enough' when Bois lets Proust talk for himself; this is how he expresses himself on his own work:

> Novels in several volumes are no longer in fashion. I am like someone who has a tapestry too big for his actual dwelling and is obliged to cut it to pieces. Young writers, towards whom I am otherwise sympathetic, advocate on the contrary a brief plot with a few characters. This is not my conception of a novel. How can I explain to you what I mean? You know that there is a plane geometry and a three-dimensional geometry. Well, for me psychology is not only plane psychology, but a three-dimensional psychology; I have tried to isolate this invisible substance which is Time, and for this indeed the experiment had to have duration. I hope that, at the end of the books, any small social fact taking place between characters who, in the first volume, belong to different spheres of life will indicate time has gone by and will acquire the beauty of the mellowed lead roofs of Versailles which Time has ensheathed with an emerald casing. Then, again, just as a town, during a train journey as the line curves about,

appears now on our right, then on our left, the aspects which a character will offer when viewed by others are so various that they will make him appear as several successive and different persons, and will give, but only by that means, the sensation ʼof time flowing by. Certain characters will reveal themselves as different from what one had believed, as of course happens so often in life.

And it will not only be people who will reappear in the course of the work under different aspects, as in certain of Balzac's cycles, but within any particular person certain deep impressions, almost unconscious. From that angle my book might be looked upon as an attempt at a series of 'Novels of the Unconscious'; I should not be ashamed of calling them 'Bergsonian novels' if I believed them to be so, for at every period literature has endeavoured — naturally after the event — to link itself with the philosophy then in vogue. But to describe my work in that way would be inaccurate, for its predominating consideration not only does not figure in Monsieur Bergson's philosophy, but is even inconsistent with it. From my point of view voluntary memory, which is above all a memory through intelligence and the eyes, gives us of the past only faces without truth; while, on the contrary, if a scent, a savour, recaptured in quite different circumstances, brings us back the past almost in spite of ourselves, we find that it is a very different past from what we believed we recalled through the pictures of our voluntary memory, which are, like the work of bad artists, painted in colours lacking truth. Already, in this first volume, you will find that the person who tells the story, who says 'I' (and who is not myself), will suddenly recapture, through a cup of tea in which he has found a bit of sponge-cake, forgotten years, gardens and beings, which no doubt he did recall, but without their colour and their charm. I have been able to make him say that, as in that Japanese game where tiny little bits of paper, when placed in water, open out, twist about, and become flowers and figures, all the flowers of his garden, the water-lilies of the Vivonne, the good people of the village, their small houses near the church, in fact Courtray and its neighbourhood, the whole of which took shape and solidity, had emerged, towns and gardens alike, from his cup of tea.

Don't you see, it ought to be almost entirely involuntary recollections in which the artist should look for the raw material of his work. For one thing, precisely because they are involuntary, because they shape themselves of their own accord attracted by the resemblance with an identical moment, they alone bear the stamp of authenticity. Then again, they are linked up with events and things in the exact proportion of memory and oblivion. And furthermore, since they made us taste a sensation again in quite different circumstances, they liberate it from any contingency, they give us its extra-temporal essence, that essence which is precisely the tenor of fine style, the general and necessary truth which beauty of style has only to translate.

If I presume to reason thus about my book, it is because the book is in no way a work of reason; it is because its most trifling details have been supplied to me through feeling; because I first of all noticed them deep within myself without understanding them, having as much trouble to change them into something intelligible as if they were foreign to the realms of the intellect, just as is — how shall I put it? — a theme of music. Perhaps you think these are all subtleties. Not at all, I assure you, but on the contrary sound realities. What we do not need to elucidate for ourselves, what was perfectly clear before us (as for instance logical ideas), does not truly belong to us, we do not know if it is real. It is from what is 'possible' we choose despotically.

Besides, you know, the style at once gives the show away. Style is in no way the embroidery some people think it to be; it is not even a matter of technique; it is — just like colour to the painter — a quality of vision, a revelation of the special universe which each individual sees as his own and is not seen so by others. The pleasure which an artist brings us resides in making us aware of another universe.

After the tribute paid to Proust in a special number of *La Nouvelle Revue Française*, other friends and other writers proclaimed their admiration independently. Among the earliest and most touching recollections must be noted those of Proust's boyhood friend, Robert Dreyfus, which appeared accompanied by letters from Marcel. The long friendship which had united the two writers dated from the time when, with a few other companions, Paul Leclercq, Louis de la Salle, or the charming Jean de Tinan, they used to meet in the Champs-Élysées at the merry-go-round. However, the earliest of Proust's letters which Dreyfus preserved dates from the top classical form at the Lycée Condorcet. Their schoolmates were: Jacques Bizet, Daniel Halévy, Henri Rabaud, J. Baignières, Louis de la Salle, Robert de Flers, Marcel Boulanger, Gabriel Trarieux, and a little later Fernand Gregh.

With shrewdness Robert Dreyfus comments on his recollections:

> When I remember so many petty assaults against Marcel Proust's sensitiveness between my sixteenth and my twenty-fifth years, just because he was too different from my other friends and from myself, I am surprised that our 'intermittent disagreements' did not one day degenerate into a great quarrel without forgiveness. It was, indeed, a miracle this did not happen, and I attribute the miracle to his genius for friendship. In the lives of most men comes a time when, youth giving place to manhood, this gloomy winding-up of a period of disinterested work and easy joys, the subsequent diversity

of careers and the hazards of love, all tend to separate the best of friends, once united through childhood and school days. If I may use ordinary stock phrases, but all quite good, each man, as he tries 'to shape his life,' adopts new friends, 'loses sight' of the old ones whom he sees only now and again without pleasure or displeasure, though he goes into raptures at the mirrored reflexion of 'the good old days,' swears he 'must keep in touch' with his former pals, though on the very next day he is once more engrossed in his adult and all-absorbing occupations. The lives of human people are all too fugitive to grant one leisure for an accumulation of friendships dating from various periods. But what a reward bring friendships which do nevertheless succeed in lasting a lifetime!

Marcel Proust's life was overcrowded and short, but the renewal of friendships was for him a necessity in a life for ever dominated by a longing for a thorough knowledge of the secret of each different heart. The strength of his early feelings, from the very outset of his life, had prolonged itself so spontaneously as to spring up to activity again without the least effort in the opening part of *Swann*, those two hundred pages which certainly contain the most extraordinary resurrection of a child's impressions ever published in any language, and which are likely to remain his one undeniable masterpiece.

And later he adds:

If he continues to display towards me such affectionate solicitude, it is because he guessed I also had not forgotten the intimacy of our childhood; it is because he knew that, in spite of our temporary disagreements during youth, I should always realize the full worth of his friendship. I very seldom saw Marcel Proust between the time of our school-leaving party in the year 1893 and that of his death (November, 1922), but during these thirty years a bond persisted between us: his letters.

These are almost entirely devoted to Marcel Proust's literary preoccupations and it is because of this they are so interesting.

Léon Pierre-Quint has also published a very remarkable work on Marcel Proust where he displays much insight and depth of judgment, a great power of analysis and a deep understanding of Proust's work. He wrote also an introduction and commentaries to the volume of Proust's letters addressed to René Blum and to Bernard Grasset, Proust's first publisher. In this volume it is interesting to follow the negotiations of the author to secure the publication of his book and a publicity campaign.

This is how Léon Pierre-Quint sums up the documents he collected:

> We became aware, throughout these letters, of the amount of work Proust undertook in this domain of publishing strategy, and how he sacrificed his immediate self-interest, his peace, his vanity, and even his pride — so alert in this man always ready for a duel — solely for the sake of his novel. The main features of these letters reveal his early waverings, his few mistakes quickly amended, but also his unequalled perseverance, his constant tact, his astounding politeness, his almost juridical conception of what 'favours' to expect and what others to grant, his friendly loyalty, on one occasion even superseding his love for his art, his extraordinary requirement of precision, his perpetual fear of misunderstandings; in short, the whole make-up of Proust, the 'man of Letters.'

On his side Louis de Robert published part of his correspondence with Proust in a booklet, of limited edition, in which he showed Proust's difficulties in finding a publisher and how he had in the end to issue *Du Côté de chez Swann* at his own expense. These letters are of interest because in them the author avows his hopes and his despairs, exposes his conception of art, holds forth and discusses, and replies to Louis de Robert's objections. In another book, *From Loti to Proust,* Louis de Robert reshaped his essay on Proust and completed it by the addition of a few letters. Here is one in which Proust thanked him for his remarks about his book:

Dear Friend,
    I have just now waked, rather ill. Your two letters were handed to me. How can I ever thank you! I do not know what has touched me most, your lofty and comforting words, or the patient annotation which, made by you, acquires magnitude even in its simplicity. If only I could see you I should take the liberty of giving you a hug. I now reply to what you tell me in order to show you, even if I must bore you, that I have taken to heart your criticism. As regards page 5, I cannot obey you; when you shall have come to the end of the chapter 'Combray,' you will understand that the page is of the utmost importance, and will see how the description of these dim rooms, begun on page 5 and at once interrupted, is pursued to its conclusion at the end of the chapter. In what concerns *trouver* and *retrouver* you are absolutely right. I have altered it, or rather I shall alter it, for it had escaped my notice. The same as regards *lui supposer.* The same again as regards Françoise; that was a misprint. As for the alteration you propose concerning the two old maids, your correction makes the sentence more clear, more elegant, but I am not sure I shall adopt it, for it has a logical inconvenience, which I shall not mention to you to save you the need to answer.
    My dear friend (and, talking of friendship, why should we not address each other by our Christian names?), if by any

chance you write again, tell me just in one line if my idea of eliminating certain lengthy passages (which would make the volume shorter) is bad (I believe it so); and if my other idea of suppressing blanks in the dialogue is also bad. The volume will not be eight hundred pages, but somewhere about six hundred and eighty. If you think it absolutely necessary, I shall have to resign myself to seeing it cut in two, though not quite in the middle, making the first volume somewhere about five hundred pages. To end this volume after Combray is quite impossible (unless the second volume can be sold at the same time). As to the question of the title, do you consider that *Le Rouge et le Noir, La Connaissance de l'Est, Les Nourritures Terrestres, L'Annonce faite à Marie* are poetic titles? I had no thought, of course, of imitating that type of title. (Forgive me for not rewriting my letter over again, now that I notice there is a blue mark on the paper, but I have no strength left to write another line.) Thanking you with all my heart, most affectionately yours

MARCEL

The Princess Bibesco, in *La Nouvelle Revue Française*, wrote an article, 'At a Ball with Marcel Proust,' in which she related how she met Proust during a ball, the attempts he made to come near her and how she escaped him. As a cousin of the Princes Emmanuel and Antoine Bibesco she gave extracts from some of Proust's letters addressed to them, and made of the author a pathetic portrait.

Proust's letters to the Comtesse de Noailles appeared in a volume of Marcel Proust's general correspondence, where they are presented and commented upon by Anna de Noailles herself. These letters bear witness to Proust's admiration for the poet and are followed by an article of his which had been published in *Le Figaro* at the time of the publication of *Éblouissements*. Previous to this volume Proust's letters to Robert de Montesquiou had formed the first volume of this *Correspondance Générale*.

Likewise, Lucien Daudet made a searching study of Proust based upon commentaries of a rare sensitiveness which had accompanied his book, *Autour de soixante lettres de Marcel Proust*.

But it is quite impossible to mention all that was published subsequent to the death of the author of *Du Côté de chez Swann*. I think I am not mistaken in thinking that certain letters, such as those addressed to Robert de Montesquiou or to Walter Berry, can in no way heighten Proust's reputation. With great humility, often a mere pretence, he could lavish excessively flattering compliments upon his correspondents, and, delighting in this game, re-create their personality to the extent of altering them beyond recognition. Nevertheless, from among the essays and books about him, I wish to select those of people who have had the good fortune of knowing Proust, and also those from eminent minds who have endeavoured, through an analysis of the monument he left behind, to reconstitute the writer by means of information and documents gathered from reliable quarters.

There is no doubt that other productions unluckily exist which are the work of fantastic amateurs longing to divert towards themselves, for their own glory, some reflexion of his fame. If I were only to consult Marcel's intimate preferences, I should even further limit my choice and preserve, from the flowers on the wreath now adorning his pale brow, only those he would himself have chosen:

I mean the studies which discuss his novel, and in relation to them those which explain his intellectual formation and his nature.

Proust was in love with his work more than anything else on earth and he slipped from life into death, after an unbelievable neglect of his health, in an endeavour to complete the corrections of the proofs for *Albertine Disparue*. If he could reappear among us I am certain he would like and approve of the book written by his friend Robert de Billy: *Marcel Proust* (letters and conversations). Not only is this work a prolongation of the unclouded friendship which united them from the date of their first meeting in 1890 until 1922, but it is above all an enlightened commentary worthy of both of them and of the friendship which sustained and fortified Proust during the elaboration of his work and which also proved such a help to De Billy. 'Sometimes,' says Robert de Billy, 'two people of very opposed natures confusedly feel themselves complementary to each other; or rather, being in essence similar, even though different in all expressions of feelings, they never suffer from that lack of understanding out of which painful entanglements are born and perpetuated. It is largely to Marcel I owe the joy of being able to differ from a friend otherwise than on principle.'

With a modesty similar to that of the painters of the thirteenth and fourteenth centuries, Robert de Billy placed his own portrait in the most obscure corner of his picture, and as a sort of signature which smiles at his model in the fresco of *Le Temps retrouvé*. In fact, Marcel Proust stands out in this study much as would saints of whom another and rather mischievous Piero della Francesca told the story by means of a series of small pictures. From the very opening pages one already recognizes Marcel with his essential characteristics, his artless face, while his eyes are already turned towards what will become his ideal, his passion. We cannot help following the growth of this passion throughout Marcel's letters, while Robert de Billy's commentaries conjure it up and are deeply sound. These commentaries open new and wide vistas upon our knowledge of the Proustian world; not only are the books which influenced Proust indicated, but Robert de Billy knows how to re-create the familiar and social atmosphere which has gone to mould the writer's mind. Nothing is more just than the important part there attributed to a love of conversation and letter-writing in the elaboration of Proust's work and in his conception of it. Robert de Billy is certain that Marcel, indeed, learned much in that way, for his inquisitiveness claimed exact answers. For the laying-out of his work, Marcel trusted only to himself and asked no advice. People who have known him and have sometimes laughed at the dissipation of his thoughts in the external world should, in all fairness, picture to themselves the hours he spent in solitude and concentration, sifting carefully the impressions garnered by a pitilessly critical mind.

In the Preface to his translation of *Sesame and Lilies*, which appeared in 1896, at the time when Marcel was withdrawing from society life to set himself at his life-task, he wrote:

> Since we, the quick are really only like the dead who have not yet started on their special functions, all habits of polite-

ness, of salutations in the hall of life, which we call deference, gratitude, devotion, and in which we mix so many lies, are sterile and tedious. What is more, with the first words we learn to utter, with the first letters we write, we weave around us the earliest threads of a web of habits, of a manner of being which we are later unable to shake off with new friends; and furthermore, the extravagant utterances we have previously used become transformed into so many bills of exchange we have to pay, or at least into remorse at having protested such bills. But books can, all at once, restore friendship to its original purity. Books do not insist upon civility.

Robert de Billy would have liked to see these lines reproduced as heading to the *Lettres à Montesquiou*. They give, so he thinks, the clue to what has been termed Marcel's snobbishness he also adds that Marcel had been investigating 'how blood and tradition have moulded a social order now losing its gilt, cracking and breaking up. To study aristocracy was part of his investigation concerning the true worth of that world, and of his attempts at finding a mode of classification fitting modern society.'

Nothing conjured up a better portrait of Marcel than the last pages of Robert de Billy's book:

When I think of Marcel I see him smile. But alas, I do not know any photograph of him which has captured the sort of radiance which then transfigured his pale face. At the period when he had a beard, his smile seemed even broader. It appeared to step out of a picture by Carrière and was in no way bookish; rather it glowed with a gaiety and a mischievousness so peculiar to him that no one who had seen it could forget the vision. It was a window looking on marvellous gardens which you recognized as you followed his gaze; or again, if you had

Time Past

happpened to tell him about a journey, his smile closed itself for a while, then reappeared radiant once more, to show you, transformed and embellished, the landscapes conjured up in his mind. The shades of feeling revealed in that smile were infinite, and according to what things or people provoked it, the interpretation upon it might signify either utter contempt or the most cheerful trust. There was nothing childish in it, nothing incomplete. It strikingly and vividly embodied the laws of life, the splendour of triumphant humanity. Sometimes, very rarely, I saw him smile when speaking of his work. It was then a confidential smile which imparted, 'I can't tell you yet anything about it, but you'll see, you'll see'; and I knew that this motion of his eyes and lips was really meant for the tribe of his spiritual children, unknown to us all, but of whom he was then holding a review. I feel certain that if, during this inspection, one of them did not display an appearance which made him clearly distinctive, Marcel would jump to one of his manuscript books, once I was gone, and modify with some illegible paste-on this person's make-up.

« VI »

WIDOR

For about thirty years Charles Marie Widor has been kind enough to treat me as a friend and to call me 'his niece.' What charming hours I owe to this excellent man whose unfailing memory has retained so many varied aspects of life! His great passion, as is well known, is history, and he continues, by means of daily reading, to widen the field of his knowledge. Though he comes in contact with most famous people in the world, he has preserved his independence of mind. His sprightly temperament, his swift response, bear witness to his inquisitive and active spirit.

Every Sunday, at the ten o'clock Mass, Widor plays the organ at Saint-Sulpice. I like to go up the narrow stairs and sit near the organist. With quiet ease he uses to the best effect the complex devices of the monumental organ. His admirable execution is in the great tradition of Bach. Sonorities follow upon each other amazingly blended by the *artiste's* mastery. His deftness is unrivalled in his use of the five key-boards and the precise motions of his nimble feet on the pedal-board. He claims that it is thanks to this enforced physical exercise that he has remained lithe in body.

Generally, on these Sundays, admirers or ardent disciples

gather around him, and inevitably some foreigner passing through Paris drops in to listen to the master's playing, so lofty and wondrous, and heard from this gallery ever since 1870. As he plays, Widor gives explanations concerning the music chosen; his commentaries are lively; wit sparkles in his short, hurried sentences often seasoned with jests. So numerous are the things he has seen and remembered. He is devoted not only to music, but to all the arts. Society life also amuses him, and since he has been appointed Perpetual Secretary of the Institut National de France, he is often called upon to act as a skilful diplomat and mediator. On all occasions his sound judgment, his tact, his courtesy, have made him a first-rate art adviser; his services to French arts are countless and his endeavours to make French artists known and appreciated.

He is a very simple-hearted sort of man, yet likes to see to the bottom of things, and any cause which seems to him worthy always finds in him a supporter. His powers of work are prodigious; rising early, he works all day at the Institut in his rooms which look on the Seine, the Louvre, and further out on the long vista of the quays. As a friend of my father-in-law, Widor had played the organ at my wedding, and has ever since given me opportunities of meeting him. It was he himself told me what follows:

Born in Lyons, where his father was organist and his grandfather an organ-builder who set up numerous organs in Alsace, Widor was only a child when he was taught to play this instrument, and at the same time won a scholarship for the Lycée Ampère at Lyons. He can still remember the ancient Jesuit chapel at his school, and the library adorned with a terrestrial globe which had been burst by a shell during the siege of Lyons in 1793. After he had secured his school-leaving certificate, he was sent to study composition in Brussels, on the advice of Cavaillé-Coll, the famous organ-builder, admired by Widor's father as much on account of his intelligence as for his instruments.

Charles Marie Widor worked in Brussels under Fétis, Director of the Academy of Music, and Lemmens, a pupil of Adolphe Hesse, the latter being known all over Europe as the custodian of Bach's tradition. For one year Widor worked under the direction of these two men in a quite peculiar system of training. In the Palais Ducal, where the concerts of the Academy of Music were usually held, the seventeen-year-old pupil was allowed to practise on the organ from twelve to six daily; then he went to have dinner, and from eight to ten he had to compose a fugue for four singing parts, which, whether good or bad, was to be finished by the appointed time. This was his daily task. On the following day he showed it to Father Fétis, who read the score and said, 'It is atrocious'; or, 'It is very good.' Lemmens, the great *artiste*, had married a well-known singer, Madame Sherrington, and sometimes lived in London, at other times in Brussels. When he was at the Academy of Music, he came daily to listen to Widor and to remark on his work. His criticism, when the young man tried his hardest to play correctly and had prepared his work, hoping to deserve praise, was often a great deception.

'It is bad,' commented Lemmens, 'you don't impose your will.'

'The torment of my life,' explains Widor, 'has been to puzzle out what he meant by will, and I have been tortured by the riddle all these years.'

Lemmens gave particular attention to the difference between rhythms. Uniformity of measure, such as illustrated by the tick-tock of a clock, exasperated him, for on the organ, since the sound is mechanically prepared beforehand in a pipe, the touch of the finger on the key has no power. The only way of imposing one's will is by insisting just slightly on the duration of a down-beat and thus put *will* into it. The action is similar to that of the rider making his horse obey by means of the bit.

In Brussels, Widor never had a free day, and the first time he managed to go to Antwerp to see the Rubens pictures was the day before he was due back in France. What captivated him in the world of letters was the spirit of the eighteenth century, above all Chamfort, Rivarol, and Beaumarchais. Once back in Lyons, he worked hard, using to good profit all he had learned during his year of study in Belgium. He already began to acquire a reputation as an organist.

About that time an international exhibition was held at Oporto. In the great central hall of one of the most important buildings was a gallery boasting an English organ. The young man was selected to give on it a daily recital of one hour, this during a period of three months. An excellent 'cellist, Alfredo Casella, great-uncle of the present day composer of this name, a gifted French flutist, and the well-known pianist, Arthur Napoléon, made up the group of first-rate *artistes* who inspired Widor to compose his *Sérénade* for piano, violin, flute, 'cello, and organ, his first published work. (Widor was then drawn in two directions between Bach's and Beethoven's influence.)

Still living in Lyons during the Second Empire, he went on with his work, going on frequent journeys everywhere in connexion with it, and stopping frequently in Paris, where he had numerous friends. He often acted as substitute for Saint-Saëns, who was organist at the Madeleine. Monsieur de Nieuwerkerke, Superintendent of the Beaux-Arts, held a weekly reception every Monday evening at his office, where he entertained the artistic and intellectual *élite* (though only men were invited). Cavaillé-Coll introduced the young composer, who had just written six duos for piano and harmonium which Monsieur de Nieuwerkerke asked the pianist Lavignac to play.

In 1869, at Christmas time, Saint-Saëns was invited by Liszt to go to Weimar for the last rehearsals and the staging of *Samson et Dalila*; he asked Widor to replace him at the Madeleine. As he was one day coming down from the organ, the choirmaster came to him.

'Do you know that our former organist at the Madeleine, Monsieur Lefébure-Wély, since then organist at Saint-Sulpice, died last night?'

Cavaillé-Coll endeavoured to get Widor chosen to replace Lefébure-Wély. This created quite a scandal among organists in Paris when it became known that this monumental organ, the largest in France, might be entrusted to a young provincial. But both Gounod and Saint-Saëns backed the young candidate: he was duly appointed on January 13, 1870, on a year's trial. He fixed his home at 8 Rue Garancière, in the old house of the Marquis de Garancière whose son-in-law, the Marquis de Sourdéac, had, with Perrin and Lulli, introduced opera in Paris. In Lulli's time operas had actually been given in that house, and according to Sainte-Beuve it is there, under Louis XV, that Adrienne Lecouvreur first appeared on the stage. The house had also belonged to the President Le Geai. The painter Henner told Widor that in 1848 the Town Hall had been housed in it, and that as a soldier of the National Guard he had been on guard at the door.

During the war of 1870 Widor was in the artillery, and General Riffault, who had been the friend of one of his uncles at the Military Academy of Artillery and Engineering (École Polytechnique), had him enlisted in the battalion of the former pupils of that school. So, during the siege of Paris, Widor took his share in defending the capital, which did not prevent him, every Sunday, playing the organ at Saint-Sulpice, still in uniform and with spurs at his heels. He had by then composed his first quintet dedicated to Gounod, and the joy of having at his disposal the five key-boards and the hundred draw-steps of the marvellous organ, one of Cavaillé-Coll's masterpieces, led him to compose his earliest four symphonies in quite a new frame of mind, although he remained faithful to the essential organ-music tradition.

'This instrument,' says Widor, 'which alone plays with Time and disposes of it, gives one an idea of boundless space, as boundless as human folly, and through this boundless space conveys a religious atmosphere.'

During the period 1872–73, Thiers, then President of the

Republic, and Madame Thiers resided at Versailles. They were often asked to contribute to charitable entertainments, and wished to choose such opportunities for using the Castle Chapel in order to attract Ambassadors and Members of Parliament to these religious concerts. Madame Thiers requested Cavaillé-Coll to restore the historical organ which dated from 1711 and had been built by Robert de Cotte and Clicquot. The admirable ornamentation of Robert de Cotte's organ-case had cost fifty thousand livres and the organ itself almost as much.

Visitors to Versailles are today surprised to see in front of the white and gilt decorations of the original organ-case an ugly console in dark oak. When Madame Thiers asked Cavaillé-Coll to repair the organ, he had only six weeks granted him. He had to make use of this makeshift and provisional console on which Saint-Saëns and Widor gave a recital of religious music on February 21, 1873, to an audience composed of a great number of members from the Assemblée Nationale accompanied by their families.

That organ at Versailles has been associated with the whole history of French Monarchy from the end of the reign of Louis XIV down to the Revolution. During the latter it was silenced, left without repair, and the chapel, without fire, fell into complete neglect. In 1796 a decree from the Convention interfered: all organs in France were to be destroyed with the exception of those which offered any special architectural interest. The Versailles Town Council asked for a statement concerning the value of the instruments inside the palace and the town churches, and they employed to that effect a modest clerk from the

Conservatoire des Musées Nationaux. Monsieur Bêche sent in a most favourable report concerning the external and internal worth of these instruments, and was thus responsible for saving them. Does not this illustrate the fable of the lion and the mouse?

'I must also relate to you,' Widor told me, 'the story of Cavaillé-Coll. He was the descendant of generations of organ-builders from Gaillac (Languedoc), dating back almost two hundred years. His grandfather, Jean-Pierre Cavaillé, had married a Mademoiselle Coll from Barcelona. Most of the organs in Languedoc and Catalonia bear the name of Cavaillé. In 1832, Louis-Philippe's Government decided to set up a monumental organ in the Saint-Denis Basilica. It happened that, by luck, the young Aristide Cavaillé, then twenty-one years of age, was on a trip to Paris. This young man, reared in his father's workshop at Toulouse and initiated from childhood in all the secrets of the trade, was then a pupil at the Toulouse Academy of Mathematics, Physics, and Chemistry, where his mathematics master had entrusted him with a letter to be delivered to a former friend of his from the Military Academy of Artillery and Engineering, Monsieur Savart, the famous acoustician, then a member of the Institut National de France.

'"You are coming for the competition at Saint-Denis, I presume?" asked Monsieur Savart.. "The plans must be handed in on Friday evening, and today is Monday."

'"I know nothing about this competition," the young man replied, "and I have never been to Saint-Denis."

'"Then go at once and draw up your plans."

'"I must first ask my father's permission."

'"You will ask him on Saturday morning."

'Cavaillé's plans, scientifically sound, were found by far superior to the others and unanimously classed first, to the great amazement of the board of examiners confronted with so young and unknown a candidate. The Minister, Monsieur Thiers, telegraphed to the Prefect of Toulouse, who in his turn sent back the most favourable information concerning the respectability of the organ-builders, Cavaillé-Coll. The board of examiners appeared before the Minister, telling of their unanimous vote, yet at the same time of their anxiety at having chosen an inexperienced young man as a prize-winner.

'"I have received," explained Monsieur Thiers, "an excellent report about this firm. Therefore, gentlemen, let us choose the father as well as the son and I sign the contract."

'It is thus that the Saint-Denis organ was built by the young Aristide Cavaillé-Coll.'

For years Widor used to lunch every day at Foyot's, a restaurant established on the premises known as Joseph II's house where Marie-Antoinette's brother lived when he stayed *incognito* in Paris. There he used to meet the younger Alexandre Dumas when his plays were given at the Odéon, François Coppée, A. Dorchain, Jules Simon, the future President Loubet, Anatole France while librarian at the Senate, Leconte de Lisle, Paul Baudry, Carolus-Duran, Humbert, Ranc, Henry Bataille, and many others. The Abbé Moissenet, choirmaster at Dijon, sometimes came to lunch with him, not far from where sat Ranc, the Radical-Socialist Senator known for his anti-clerical views. They had never been introduced. One day Moissenet and Widor were chatting in quiet tones, when suddenly Ranc, who had followed it all, thrust away his newspaper and exclaimed:

'Look here, Monsieur l'Abbé, there is some sense in what you say!'

The Abbé bowed modestly.

'But how do you instruct the children in your choir school?'

'I tell them only what I believe to be true. I make them read only beautiful literature and sing only the best music.'

'That suits me,' said Ranc. 'If ever I become Minister I'll fix you up as a Bishop.' (This was before the disestablishment of the Church.)

Thus it happened that the sentry who, in front of the Luxembourg, keeps guard over the Republic, witnessed that day a most unusual spectacle: Ranc walking down the Rue Tournon arm-in-arm with the Abbé Moissenet, and Widor coming at the rear.

As we walked along the quays, Widor went on talking to me.

'After the Commune the most hospitable salon on the Left Bank was that of the Marquise de Blocqueville, daughter of the Maréchal Davoust. Look, she lived there, at number 9 on the Quai Malaquais, at the angle of the Rue Bonaparte. This place used to be the Hôtel de Transylvanie, built by a nobleman from over the Alps, whose son was a boarder at the Hôtel des Quatre-Nations (actually now the Institut National de France.) This nobleman ruined himself and disappeared. Several lawsuits followed thereupon, during which the house became a bawdy-house frequented by gamblers and prostitutes. It is there the Abbé Prévost found his subject for *Manon Lescaut*, but he made his Manon die in Louisiana while he himself remained contentedly to play cards at the Quai Malaquais.

'The Marquise de Blocqueville never went out. Her husband, Louis-Philippe's aide-de-camp, had by then been dead a good many years, but she still received guests every evening, and on Mondays gave a formal dinner followed by a reception. For thirty years most of the famous people in Europe were seen at her house: Claude Bernard, Liszt, the Comte de Gobineau, the Comte d'Haussonville, Caro, the professor of philosophy who was the model for the illbred pedant in Pailleron's *Le Monde où l'on s'ennuie*, and I could give you many other names... but since I have uttered that of Liszt, I had better tell you about him. The Trocadéro Palace was to be opened for the Exhibition of 1878. One morning Cavaillé-Coll came for me.

'"My organ is completed, cher Maître. I believe it suits the big hall to perfection. Liszt is waiting there for us. Come and try it."

'Thus it was done, and afterwards, about midday, Cavaillé-Coll took us off to lunch, Liszt and me:

'"What can I do to thank you, Widor?" asked Liszt.

'"I live in Liszt's century," I replied, "yet I have never heard him."

'"Well," said Liszt, who was living in the Rue du Mail

in Madame Érard's flat while she was at her mansion of La Muette, "come to lunch tomorrow, I am free all the afternoon, I will play you whatever you like."'

During that whole week Liszt played for Widor, not only from classic music, but from his own compositions. Widor was never to forget that wonderful playing.

One evening in July, at La Muette, Liszt was at the piano, improvising. The door opened and Madame Krauss came in on Gounod's arm, for she was rehearsing his *Polyeucte* at the Opéra. She had asked to be introduced to Liszt. The latter rose to greet her.

'I know that you sing the *Roi des aulnes* as no one else does. May I be allowed to play the accompaniment?'

And he started Schubert's piece on a fairly slow rhythm, accentuating the composer's thought and allowing the singer unexpected opportunities of expression. Madame Krauss, much affected by the occasion, sang the poem. Deeply moved, the listeners in the vast drawing-room did not stir, no one daring to applaud.

'What a memory of perfect beauty!' exclaimed Widor. Then he went on:

'Similarly François Planté's faultless sonority, though in no way similar to Liszt's fire, also avoided undue speed. It was the very essence of perfection, of clarity of sound, absolute clarity, the faithful reproduction of the text. Planté, coming to see me at the Institut, explained to me: "It is not without deep emotion I come up these steps. Many, many years ago, when I was nine years old, I used to spend all my Thursdays at Isabey's, who, not as a member of the Institut, but as designer of Charles X's study, lived in the Palais Mazarin. His daughter was my age, and we both had the same piano teacher, Mademoiselle Saint-Aubin, a pupil of Liszt." Planté won his piano prize at the Academy of Music when eleven years old.'

When I tried to speak to Widor about his own music, he preferred to relate further recollections.

The huge riding-school in the Avenue Marceau used to belong to bankers, the brothers Berthier. It was often rented for orchestrated plays, with chorus or soloist. Massenet gave the first of these concerts with the finale of the *Roi de Lahore*. Clemenceau, who was fond of riding and was a friend of the brothers Berthier, was generally present at rehearsals at the riding-school. The Berthiers had asked Widor to arrange in about thirty days a sort of musical fresco representing the life of Joan of Arc — first act, Vaucouleurs; second, Orléans; third, the stake. The play was in fact finished and was acted every evening for two summers.

Widor recalls the comical side of the rehearsals. Two orchestras a hundred metres apart from each other! As he needed to go from one to the other, he was first offered a Roman chariot; then the state coach mounted on eight springs which had once belonged to the Duke of Brunswick and was then used by clowns and acrobats when parading in front of an audience; and at last a horse who had been trained to bow in front of ladies. Widor, tired and inconvenienced by the heat and the smell rising from the track, complained to Clemenceau. 'Take to smoking cigarettes,' advised the latter; 'that is the only way to clear your head.' And Widor added: 'It is from that day I smoke.'

« VII »

BONI DE CASTELLANE

THE death of the Marquis de Castellane marks the end of a period. He was its most brilliant representative, the most famous of Parisians, a man of breeding whose personality was often distorted by legend, the man who to all appearances was the most sought after, yet who felt himself the most solitary, for he longed to uphold the prerogatives of his race, though he had to submit to the exigencies of his time. He was so generous and disinterested in bestowing ideas, fashions, tastes, and money lavishly, that his daring encountered severe criticism and a great deal of calumny; but it also brought him devoted friends who knew his true disposition. Although circumstances were often adverse, he was by nature serious, with lofty aspirations and a constant devotion to the welfare of his country. After the calamity befalling his private life, he displayed the strength of will to rise above its consequences, to create for himself a sphere of action and to maintain his independence of judgment. His biting wit, his swift perception, lent to his conversation pungency and novelty. From his whole person emanated a potent charm which was a mixture of simplicity, brilliance, and a certain ingenuity rather in contrast to his other qualities. Through education and origin he was imbued with the traditions of his caste, and the imprint of Rochecotte — the Castellanes' estate, where his grandmother, the Marquise de Castellane, *née* Périgord, and grandniece to the Prince de Talleyrand, maintained her ancestor's political views — persisted with him through his whole life as did his faithful adherence to the Papacy and to religion. His life, in turn so dazzling and so wretched, its last years so tried by illness, was always swayed by calamity; so much so that when he died one of his near relatives could exclaim, 'It is not his death is ghastly, but his life.' Yet it was precisely during the years of suffering that his true character was best revealed.

Fastidious, born, so it seemed, to live at some former period, he endeavoured to impose his way of thinking by creating around him an atmosphere of elegance. No one received guests with more perfect art. For several years he managed to bring together, as well in his rooms on the Place du Palais Bourbon as in his private house, Rue de Lille, or his flat, Avenue Victor-Emmanuel, the most outstanding figures from very divergent circles. It was with a graciousness quite his own and in a setting harmoniously contrived that he received his guests under the soft light of many candles, for he preferred their intimate brilliance to the crude glare of electricity. His table was noted for the preparation of the most simple dishes, though he was quite an epicure. It was true French cooking he offered, carefully prepared, kept at a simmer. He held long conferences with his cook. To make sure of results, he often had prepared for himself a few days beforehand the dishes he intended for his guests and gave directions so as to have them perfect. Each lady found at her place at table a flower for her dress, in harmony with the colour effect of the room. He had the knack of bringing together people whose exchange of views often gave to the conversation far-reaching results. And he laid himself out to please: with a smile on his lips, his blue eyes illuminating his face, he gave himself no rest, saw to every detail, anxious that nothing should escape him.

He dressed with great taste, and now and again amused himself by wearing shirts the colour of his eyes or the colour of his cheeks; enjoying such trifling achievements like a child. He had a rare gift for harmonizing colours and has often explained to me that arranging grades of tones, matching or contrasting them, was a source of great delight to him; he was never unaffected by anything pleasing to the eye. His sensitive vision found with accurate precision the complementary colour, the golden spot or the darker one required to lend tone to a general effect.

And what mirth he displayed as he thought out schemes, as well in the realms of art and life as in those of politics! His courage, his intrinsic simplicity, his zest for life were such that one always thought he would at last defeat Fate. He believed himself destined to play an active part which would do credit to his country. Towards servants and subordinates he displayed a generosity and a politeness which moved them to deep gratitude, and towards his friends a never-failing faithfulness. Friendship was for him one of the most lofty of feelings; he showed endless care and exquisite consideration in cultivating it.

One winter, as I was for a long time kept indoors through facial neuralgia, Boni sent me every day a specially selected rose to keep me company. A rose, a daily rose! What ingenuity he displayed to give pleasure, and in the least of his gifts what excellent taste! Consequently, he was often shocked by post-War manners and the remarks he made on this subject were so many shafts of satire. There was nothing peevish about him; quick as he was at repartee, his remarks could be deep, biting, yet never betrayed ill-will or spite against his fellow beings or his own fate. I never heard him utter a bitter word, and his resignation during his illness was nothing short of heroic.

He was deeply religious; so that when struck ten years before his death by merciless encephalitis lethargica, he remained serene of soul, although he knew the hopelessness of his case. After being laid up for several weeks, he went back to his usual activities. Although condemned to a slow death, the Marquis de Castellane maintained a moral courage which neither frightful suffering nor worries could shake. He preserved his clear mind and daily witnessed his physical decay, from the dreadful paralysis involving his limbs, the torture now and again of impeded speech, and the distortion of a body which once had been lithe and active. At no time did he complain. His interest in politics remained keen; whenever his features were not drawn with pain, he was bright and smiling among his guests. His admirable mother, the Marquise de Castellane, came daily to spend part of the afternoon with him. Her son never allowed her to leave without rising from his chair and taking her as far as the hall, though it cost him a great deal of pain. Then, worn out by the effort, he dropped back into his armchair: he would never have countenanced a failure in dutiful respect to the being he loved and admired most in this world.

« VIII »

GABRIELE D' ANNUNZIO

THE poet of *Laudi*, the novelist who wrote *L'Enfant de Volupté* and *Le Feu*, the author of *La Ville Morte*, arrived in Paris surrounded by fables, the most charming of which reported him as having been born far out at sea in one of those *paranzallas*, rigged with ochre sails, which had rocked the infant's wails. This romantic birth was supposed to mark him out for singing the sea, beauty, love, and death. The truth is that Gabriele d' Annunzio saw the light of day in his parents' house at Pescara, an attractive fishing village on the shores of the Adriatic. When the child was first shown to his mother, she exclaimed, so we are told:

'My son, you are born in March and on a Friday; who knows what great things you will accomplish!'

His success as a writer and a captivating man, his long and stormy liaison with La Duse, what was known of the sufferings of this famous actress and her reasons for deciding to come and live in Paris — all this offered the more food for speculation since it aroused curiosity.

I was not expecting to meet d' Annunzio the day he appeared without warning at Count Primoli's flat. His face struck me on account of its paleness and nakedness:

the top of the head was polished, the nose prominently outlined, the lips adorned by a moustache almost shaved off, and the chin ending in a pointed beard. In this severe countenance, which looked as if rubbed with pumice-stone, the two dark spots of the eyes alone showed mobility. It seemed as if, to intensify the characteristics of his features, d'Annunzio had endeavoured to lend them the fixity of a head on a medal. His carriage was very upright, so as not to lose an inch of his stature; and his small body appeared moulded by his close-fitting suit.

When he spoke, his sonorous, harmonious voice unrolled learned sentences. He expressed himself with assurance and a great deal of preciosity; his knowledge of old French enabled him to use archaic expressions; he made use of parables, quotations, and an accumulated wealth of similes and epithets. His praises sounded magnificent and terrible, his invectives were ferocious and colourful; technical terms rendered his conversation somewhat affected, and this impression was reinforced by his habit of hammering on certain words to which he wished to draw attention. His mind, well schooled, betrayed his resolution and habit of stubborn work; yet I also felt in him a disposition, clumsily repressed, to a bubbling, boylike fun. Later, I saw him amuse himself with the unconcern of a child at a friend's house in the country. He had arrived there with his pockets full of small trifles used for practical jokes, such as are sold in the streets of Paris, and he had in great secrecy placed them about in the rooms. As no one could suspect the poet of such tricks, he laughed till he cried every time one of his comical pranks came off. Once he arrived at a smart dinner wearing a blue wig.

The eager welcome he received in Paris from artistic and society circles made d'Annunzio aware that his work was well known and admired. This was in 1910 or '11; welcoming parties followed upon each other; everywhere they were organized in honour of the famous foreigner. He was surrounded by a small court. Writers, young women, journalistic and theatrical circles vied with each other to make his stay in Paris agreeable. He proved a guest full of high spirits, eloquent and always ready to be carried away by his poetic enthusiasm.

While in Paris, he lived in different places. In each of them he succeeded in creating an atmosphere which was in part that of an antique shop and in part an alchemist's laboratory. As soon as one entered the hall, one was greeted by a smell of incense. The rooms were cluttered with all sorts of things: velvet draperies dragged over the furniture; old books, weapons, daggers, poniards were displayed on tables side by side with delicate glass vases in which rare flowers were arranged. There were, above all, numerous objects whose use it was impossible to know, but concerning which the poet entered upon long speeches. The legendary origins he attributed to each of these things formed the prelude to a perfect fairy-tale it pleased him to relate. I am convinced that d'Annunzio's enjoyment was that of extemporization; and who knows if, really, he did not come himself to believe in what he said?

Nevertheless, this gift for exaggeration often made him find formulas and names one could never forget. Had he not thus nicknamed Debussy 'Claude de France'? In the spring of 1911 the production of *Le Martyre de Saint Sébastien* promised to create a sensation. The music was by Debussy and Madame Ida Rubinstein embodied the saint. A few days before the first night the Archbishop of Paris issued orders forbidding the faithful to attend the play. D'Annunzio had supervised all the rehearsals, full of passion, active, seeking perfection, and inspiring in his interpreters such enthusiasm as to cause them to live in a state of excitement for weeks on end. The sight of the saint tied to the laurel tree and pierced by arrows was of great plastic beauty. The audience was thrilled with the famous replies: 'I am the archer sure of my mark'; 'The arrow does not fall back!' The spectators, a sumptuously elegant crowd, followed the unfolding of the tragic history of the martyr. How could one fail to marvel at the knowledge of this archaic tongue which the poet used with learned virtuosity? He had dedicated the work to Maurice Barrès, apologizing for having worked on this fine material from beyond the Alps with his sharpest tools. This is how he addressed Barrès:

> I send you my verses written in France because I so greatly like the prose you wrote in Italy, my dear Barrès. This poem was born in the land of Montaigne and heady resin; I dedicate it to you because it is in Pisa, Siena, Parma, at the sepulchre of Ravenna and in the gardens of Lombardy you have found inspiration for your most harmonious verses. My Sébastien — whom I have drawn while I kept before me Antonio del Pollaiuolo's plaquette where a slender centaur towers in an expanse of breast over two-legged archers — my Sébastien mentions somewhere that the shaft of his crossbow was pro-

vided with animal tendon so tightly fitting it as to be indistinguishable from it. This makes me think of the physical nervous energy which supports the spirituality of your art. And again I think, remembering certain of your sayings, of those divine bees caught in clear amber which one of my humanists seems to have acclaimed in honour of your Muse in a votive epigram. No one, indeed, except you, will be able to understand the queer pleasure I have found through my daring and the sense of so great a danger. One evening, close to Sparta, and in view of Taygetus and the Eurotas, one word stood out illuminating the heroism of your spirit: 'The most beautiful in the Occident.' But there is another word of the most lofty Latin species, which does not seem to me less beautiful, since I always picture it coloured with the best of my blood and the blood of my peers: that is intrepidity.

This intrepidity, fearlessness in words and deeds, was instrumental in enabling d'Annunzio to live at the height of his dreams. But before reaching that zenith, he found much enjoyment in artistic achievements and sometimes also sporting ones. Was he not the first to install in France greyhound farming and kennels in view of racing?

Moreover, nothing ever made him swerve from the feelings of injustice and indignation he entertained towards a certain school of politics. On all occasions he displayed those feelings in letters I received, where he gave vent to his indignation against a 'vile and loathsome Austria,' calculating upon the revenge he looked forward to at the hands of Destiny.

One day, loaded with red carnations, I took the poet to the house of the Comtesse de Noailles. From their first meeting they tried to outdo each other in smartness.

It is impossible to describe the young woman's eloquence, the swift working of her mind, her humour. D'Annunzio told me as we left her that her conversation could only be compared to the most intoxicating nightingale's song he had ever heard. Frequently, after this, the three of us met again.

In September, 1913, I found Anna de Noailles in Milan where we had agreed to meet. It was during a marvellous autumn and we explored the town and its surroundings. While the noise of the Balkan War was beginning to die down, we enjoyed the deceitful peace of those mellow mild evenings on the shores of Lake Bellagio and under an Italian sky twinkling with stars.

In reply to a little note I sent to d'Annunzio, he let us know he was at Arcachon, as hard at work 'as a mulish slave,' to complete his play, *Le Chèvrefeuille*, after he had read Anna de Noailles's book, 'sweetly scented with herbs and flowers,' and every day more beautiful to him. (He was referring to her last published work: *Les Vivants et les Morts*.)

Then came 1914. Tragic events followed upon each other. In August, Gabriele d'Annunzio was in Paris. When the invasion threatened the valley of the Oise, his heart felt oppressed, wounded as much as ours.

He summed up his impressions in his admirable *Envoi à la France*. But when after the battle of the Marne the news reached us that Rheims Cathedral was in flames, his longing to act became irresistible. He had himself taken at once to the front; obliged to stop at Jouchéry-sur-Vesle, he had full view from there of the horror of the scene. His grief equalled his indignation. His whole being protested against this barbarous crime with such might as to lend him new strength to feed his hatred of the invader. This hatred transmuted itself into words and deeds. In Genoa, in May, 1915, his inspired speeches bore immortal witness to this.

In 1920, a very heavy envelope reached me from Fiume; it contained, besides a letter, his photograph and a badge of honour he had just created: The Star of Fiume.

« IX »

JOSEPH REINACH

WHEN I call to mind Joseph Reinach, it is his laughter that I hear, and his wide eyes, sparkling with intelligence, enthusiasm, and kindness, that I see. His prodigious vitality prevented his appearing ungainly, though rather stout, for he was always actively busy. He moved nimbly, spoke with briskness and wit. His erudition was extensive, yet he despised pedantry. With equal competence he could discuss the most varied subjects; intellectual contacts fired his generous nature; he could defend his views with passion and courage. He was constantly requisitioned in literary debates, and his memory brought forth arguments with ease from classic authors, and he could present these in an original and pointed way. His reputation for knowing everything was so firmly established that, when *Le Figaro* launched the fashion of a new society game consisting in naming the sources of quotations, Joseph Reinach was often at dinner parties put on the mat. Nearly always a quotation was not given in full before he had already fastened on the author. Nevertheless, one evening, at Madame de Caillavet's he was rather baffled; one of the guests had asked who wrote the line:

C'est moi qui te dois tout, puisque c'est moi qui t'aime.

The discussion lasted a long time, some maintaining it to be from Racine. Anatole France denied this, though he could not give a satisfactory answer. This time Reinach remained silent and thoughtful. The party broke up. The next day the guests of the preceding evening received a telephone call from him: the author was Voltaire and the line came from *Adélaïde du Guesclin*. Another day everybody agreed that

Le vrai peut quelquefois n'être pas vraisemblable

was a line from Boileau. Joseph Reinach protested and stated it was from Destouches. Once more he was right.

As secretary to Léon Gambetta, he became the principal private secretary of his chief when the latter was made Prime Minister. His worship of the great democratic leader remained always as ardent as during his youth. On the anniversary of Gambetta's death, he regularly went, with Adrien Hébrard, Étienne, Léon Bérard, and others, on a sort of pilgrimage to Jardies. He was for many years deputy for Digne in the Basses-Alpes and took frequent part in parliamentary debates. As reporter on the laws for the reorganization of the army, he became, with Jaurès, Vice-President of the Army Committee. His activity and his powers of work were prodigious. At his flat, Avenue Van Dyck, he worked tirelessly in a huge study with windows overlooking the Parc Monceau. The walls of this lofty room were entirely covered with books, always in such perfect order that, without any hesitation, Reinach could put his hand on the volume he required. How many times did I not go there to ask him for the loan of a book which he proffered at once, with rare kindness!

When one entered his study, Reinach forsook his work, the page already covered with his fine and squeezed writing, but one felt certain he would quickly go back to it as soon as he was alone. There was little room for other objects besides books in this study, though on some pieces of furniture were displayed photographs: the Princesse Mathilde, Lady Grey, the Empress Eugénie, Madame Strauss, Madame Waldeck-Rousseau, the Princesse Murat, and also the original bronze of Rodin's famous *Poet and Chimaera* which had once belonged to Guy de Maupassant. Reinach also possessed the unmatched nude of a woman by Dalou, and Prince Troubetzkoy's statue of Tolstoy; there, too, in a frame, was a letter from Voltaire to Madame de Pompadour asking a free pardon for an innocent man.

In an adjoining room, on a panelled wall, was to be noticed Delacroix's portrait of George Sand. Somewhere about 1890 this painting was in a collection about to be sold. Madame Vaudoyer drew Reinach's attention to it, hoping he could bring the Conseil des Musées to buy it. A thousand francs were asked for it, but the funds of all museums were low. Joseph Reinach bought the portrait for himself, promising to bequeath it to the Louvre, which he did, with the addition of the three statues I have mentioned.

Reinach was very hospitable and entertained a great deal. One could always be certain to meet at his home any foreigner of mark arriving in Paris. At times of a change of cabinet it was again at his place the chances of the candidates for the Government were discussed, and often the candidates themselves were among the guests. I was too young to know Reinach at the time of the Dreyfus scandal, but the volumes he devoted to it are the work of a real historian and bear witness to his courage and the keenness apparent from his whole personality. He worked cheerfully and was always ready to intervene in causes he considered sound.

At the very outset of the War, he was cruelly hit by losing on the battlefield both his son-in-law, Pierre Goujon, deputy for the department of Ain, and his son Adolphe, a distinguished archeologist destined to a brilliant future. Reinach had taken upon himself the heavy task of writing for *Le Figaro* a daily article which he signed 'Polybe.' These remarkable commentaries won numerous readers to this paper; in a compact and precise form they expressed highly personal suggestions. Their style and thought do credit to their author and raised the courage of the public.

Here is the dedication to the armies of Joffre, Foch, and Pétain, to the Allied armies as well, which Joseph Reinach wrote for the illustrated history of France to which he gave the name of *Francia*.

> This book, written for you, is not really a History of France. It is, taken from such a history, all that it appeared essential a decent man should know, the better to understand France, therefore the better to love her in her glory and her trials, in her sustained effort to shape herself, to conquer independence and freedom. What I have endeavoured to draw in broad

TIME PAST

outlines is but the picture of the France of former days, the glorious and often tragic mother of our present-day France.

What France is today, brave, patient, and enduring on the battlefield, lovable and charming even in her greatest hardships, yet in victory calm and as steadfast as justice — all this is known to you, British men, as to you Americans who come to defend on our invaded soil the rights and independence of nations. Likewise, you also, Belgian men who fought by our side, you Serbians and Portuguese and others, Poles, Czechs, soldiers of the Empire of the Rising Sun, know of this, you all who have suffered, hoped, and conquered with us, since from the immortal Marne to the Vistula, from the Yser to the Vardar, from the Piave to the Danube, from the Aegean Sea to the Sea of Japan, there was only one battle for us all.

But what was France in former days, do you know that, and we ourselves, do we know it?

What France has been has been explained through numberless pages, in huge works in many volumes, some of which are counted among the masterpieces of our literature; likewise in educational works of which several are also fine and very good books. My aim is far more modest; I am neither learned nor a teacher; I write for those who have no leisure to read learned works, for those to whom even school manuals appear either too detailed or too elementary.

It is the *poilus* who have asked me for this book; the *Tommies* and the *Sammies* have expressed a wish to see a book from which would emerge in a clear light the past of a country whose body became the main battlefield in the Great War. Perhaps I have been wrong in letting myself be won over; but, even should this prove so, I have no regret, so much have I enjoyed living over again this magnificent history. I thought I knew the History of France, yet one thing only did I really know thoroughly: which is that, in order to love France throughout her agitated destiny, one has only to let the facts speak for themselves.

« X »

THE SALON OF MADAME DE PIERREBOURG

THE Avenue du Bois, with its fine lawns adorned with flowering trees, white and pink chestnut trees, offered at all hours of the day, when spring came, an engaging spectacle. In the morning, among the countless people out for a stroll, one might see a group made up of Forain, Boldini, Helleu, and Sem promenading and chatting cheerfully. These four artists, as different in appearance as in their method of work, were greeted and stopped at every step. Helleu, with a yellowish face framed by a black beard, stared with his pale eyes at the pretty women going by, future models for his dry-points. Forain, from lips slightly awry, whistled mocking remarks. Boldini turned about on his short, crooked legs each time an elegant figure went by, while Sem, diminutive, spick and span, threw out harsh comments in his Périgord accent.

The incessant promenading went on: ladies of fashion, groups of young men laughing merrily and exchanging jokes, nursery maids surrounded by children, old beaus, Amazons, and stout ladies walking furiously along the avenue in order to lose weight.

It was at the entrance of this avenue that the Baronne Aimery de Pierrebourg lived in a spacious and charming flat.

From her balcony she had a view of Mont Valérien and the Arc de Triomphe. The scheme of decoration of her home, in the eighteenth-century style, suited her perfectly distinguished appearance. She used to receive every Sunday, and her salon was considered one of the most interesting in literary circles. Before she became the soul of this intellectual group, the Baronne de Pierrebourg had lived in the countryside near Blois with her husband, descendant of a military provincial family, and had led the empty life of aristocratic country gentry hostile to intellectual pursuits. This way of living, entirely devoted to hunting and sports, stifled the young woman's inclinations towards art and literature. She could not grow accustomed to this narrow and severely simple life from which her only escape was reading. At thirty she really looked upon herself as old.

The few short stays she made in Paris as a pupil at Julian's studio no longer satisfied her; she decided to leave the country and settle in the capital. Thanks to her culture and her passion for literature, she soon attracted people. Her salon quickly became a brilliant intellectual centre, frequented by several academicians. As one arrived at her flat, animated and interesting conversations greeted one from groups around the tea-table. Alfred Capus's piping voice stood out as he brought forth the paradoxes of his bantering and optimistic philosophy with gusto and wit. 'When a prejudice ceases to hold,' he declared, 'you may be sure some virtue goes overboard with it.' The author of *La Veine* viewed his period without indulgence, though he was nevertheless convinced that 'all would come right in the end.' Ah! if there were no women, he sighed, the human race would not be funny at all. Someone told him one day at his club of the death of an acquaintance of his: 'What did he die of?' asked somebody. 'No one knows,' said Capus, 'just as no one knows of what he lived.' If one referred to *La Veine* (Luck), this acute observer parried: 'Luck — well, of course. But what really is luck except an unconscious theft? That is perfectly true, and the proof of it is that the man who is too happy resembles the professional thief: he always gets nabbed in the end.'

Étienne Grosclaude played up to Capus with inimitably whimsical imagination, seasoned with hearty puns. He frequently added an original detail to a story, and his serious face never betrayed the screaming fun in some of his remarks. He liked to relate that, in a recent duel, a man was hit by a bullet right in the chest, but the missile flattened itself against a five-franc piece the victim had forgotten in his waistcoat pocket, and so he was not hurt. 'I was,' explained Grosclaude, 'one of the seconds and could not help remarking: "That, sir, was money well placed."'

He went on: 'The other day, a banker assured me that he could never share in a bad deed.

'"Quite so," I replied, "banks have enough to do safeguarding bad shares, though, of course, I do not mean this for you, my friend."'

'Examinations granting degrees in honesty are far too easy nowadays,' put in Capus! 'a greater number of candidates pass every year.'

Maurice Donnay might then arrive and join the conversation. His plays were very successful because of his sense of reality. He talked on the most risky subjects and rendered them dazzling through his biting irony, his cold-blooded jokes, the liveliness of his dialogues interspersed with witty, cynical, or exquisite sayings.

In another group Gabriel Hanotaux discussed events with the barrister, Henri-Robert. Or else the Comtesse Mathieu de Noailles, then in all the splendour of her fame, was as always surrounded by an even greater throng of admirers. It was at the Baronne de Pierrebourg's she had recited her early poems revealing in their fresh novelty that a great poet had been born. In those days there was scarcely a young man who was not in love with her.

Jacques-Émile Blanche, Abel Hermant, Maurice Paléologue, Abel Bonnard, René Boylesve were to be found among brilliant groups of charming young women. Madame Bartet, who on the stage acted the parts of Hervieu's heroines, sometimes came for a short time, while Forain, in the group of our hostess, chatted with the Princesse Murat and the Baronne de Primont. The Duchesse de Rohan sounded Paul Hervieu as to the chances of one of her protégés in the forthcoming elections for the academy.

Hervieu was a regular guest in Madame de Pierrebourg's salon. She had first met him at Jacques Normand's. After his *Diogène le chien*, a cruel and bitter book, he had published in *La Revue des Deux Mondes*, *l'Inconnu*, and its disturbing mystery had greatly moved the young woman. On Hervieu's features was impressed a gentle expression of melancholy. The psychologist of *Peints par eux-mêmes*, whose icy irony recalled that of *Les Liaisons Dangereuses*, was one of the most influential members in this learned and distinguished company. His lofty spirit, his keen sense of justice, caused him to be looked upon almost as the 'Minister of Literature.' Thanks to his authority, his literary gospel carried weight. When he was elected President of the Société des Gens de Lettres, he played there a predominant part. He accepted and assumed responsibilities capably, and was frequently requested to settle awkward misunderstandings. Under a certain coolness of manner, Paul Hervieu hid a sensitiveness, a courage, a delicacy and subtlety of feeling, a control over himself, which rendered his friendship precious and sure. He was always very precise and his uncompromising disposition made him express himself with elevation and distinction.

Among the Baronne de Pierrebourg's friends no one was more sought after than Monsieur Hébrard, editor of *Le Temps*. His wit, the acuteness of his repartee, his wisdom, in part from experience and in part from forbearance, made him the most brilliant and good-humoured of conversationalists. He could sum up any situation in a few illuminating words in a picturesque and caustic fashion. His similes appeared both surprising and natural, so that this mixture of the unexpected and the plausible almost at the same time astonished and satisfied one. Often a certain tartness of speech lent the more flavour, since Monsieur Hébrard had preserved a touch of Toulousian accent. His small blue eyes shone with cheerful wit from under bushy eyebrows which remained black until his death; his nose, with its quivering nostrils, was hooked, a grey moustache in part hid the shapely mouth, while dimples appeared on his round cheeks with every movement of his mobile face. The forehead, very receding, was deeply indented by a furrow which he attributed to caps too tightly fitting during his babyhood. He was of medium stature, his gestures were swift, and each of his attitudes was precise and in keeping with an inquisitive mind always on the alert. When he heard from some group near-by a remark which struck him, he would turn round with youthful eagerness.

Adrien Hébrard was passionately interested in love-affairs, inviting confidence and showing himself more than indulgent towards sins committed in the name of love, while with smiling aloofness he sighed with regret over the hero of an adventure: 'Ah! the sly dog; he has all the luck!'

He never approached anyone with preconceived ideas; on the contrary, by setting his interlocutor at his ease, he at once gave him the impression that nothing interested him more than his story, and therefore met the spontaneous confidence which delighted him, and to which he responded with a desire to reach complete understanding. 'There is in me the making of a father confessor,' he explained, 'but no leaning whatever to read a lecture even to those I find guilty.'

Exquisitely polite, his graciousness was always perfect when expressing blame or admiration. His moderation and his tact were as well known as the foresight with which he judged a case and evaluated its consequences. Adrien Hébrard never repeated himself. His sparkling improvisations burst forth unexpectedly; his conversation was bold, as on wings. Nevertheless, whenever he embarked on controversies, his speech, enriched by facts, gave the impression of having summed up beforehand its full import, notwithstanding the unexpected side issues, and one felt perfectly confident he would carry the day in spite of his fantastic whims. More so, like the juggler he could perfect his 'trick' with every new experience.

What he termed his incurable laziness denoted on the contrary the alertness of his mind; nothing escaped the acuity of his analysis and perspicacity. His presence was like a fête always renewed. He could make use of telling expressions which, by their juxtaposition, rendered his speech savoury, precise, and of such surety of touch that its compact substance struck the imagination. He knew how to use adverbs without insipidity. 'She is fallaciously artless.' Hébrard's witticisms were part and parcel of his conversation, they were not prepared beforehand and they always came pat.

At Madame de Pierrebourg's also successively appeared: Gaston Calmette, editor of *Le Figaro*, the poet Fernand Gregh, Robert Dreyfus, Fernand Vandérem, Henry Bernstein with Madame Simone, and Gabriele d'Annunzio who, during his stay in Paris, came often to the Avenue du Bois. The young Jean Cocteau, dazzling in spirit and imagination, would make his way through the throng to exchange views with the Comtesse de Noailles.

Madame de Pierrebourg was a great admirer of the

Marquis de Ségur, author of the life of Mademoiselle de Lespinasse. He suggested to her that she also should write sketches on historical or literary figures. The Baronne de Pierrebourg followed his advice, and in turn published, under the name of Claude Ferval, *Ninon et son Cortège*, *Mademoiselle Aïssé et son Tendre Chevalier*, and quite recently another remarkable volume on Madame du Deffand. These works, where the past is recalled with such charm, show a wide erudition, and the author reveals in them a subtle mind and an ingenious psychology.

René Boylesve was one day my neighbour at a 'literary' dinner. I had very much admired his early novels: *L'Enfant à la Balustrade* and *Mademoiselle Cloque*. These studies of provincial life revealed such delicate observation, such gifts for re-creating the life of humble people, that I had wished, during previous meetings, for an opportunity for a long chat with him. That evening I told him how much his books attracted me, and little by little our conversation became more intimate. The marked attention he showed prompted me to trust him, for with exquisite sensitiveness he could penetrate into the most hidden recesses of the heart. A passionate feeling of interest led him to probe into the emotional life, and his remarks, so delicately shrewd, were proof of the depths of his understanding. Playfully, and almost with tenderness, he laid before me the summary of a rather disillusioned philosophy, while in his serious and emaciated face his eyes smiled at me. Now and again sparks of mirth fused amidst the modulations of his solemn voice.

Then he seemed to withdraw within himself, and the shyness I divined attracted me and gave me a foretaste of pleasant friendship, once he could relinquish the fierce reserve with which he protected himself. He represented himself as disillusioned, and boasted of his years, but these affirmations did not fit with the freshness of his impressions; on the contrary, they betrayed how attractive women were to him. He studied them as might a lover, met their confidences halfway, forgave them their weaknesses and guessed their secrets with penetrating foresight. What means have I to describe the subtle charm of a chat with René Boylesve? To keep a check over his heart he disciplined himself through his critical mind, mastered his passionate nature, and carefully hid the turmoil within.

When I made his acquaintance, René Boylesve was already a master much sought after by young writers. He received them with sympathy and encouraged them in their work. In his small private house, Rue des Vignes, his At-Home days held an attraction quite their own. Madame Boylesve, with her subtle charm, created an atmosphere of pleasant intimacy. The author of *La Leçon d'Amour dans un Parc* gave his advice willingly, though with discretion, and scrupulously listened to all objections. To literary coteries Boylesve remained indifferent. What interested him above all things was the evolution of society, and he noted the most minute details of it with smiling irony. He was far too impressionable, however, to look with favour on constant transformations. As he looked closely at humanity, an attentive observer, events often had a way of sharply hitting him.

The War threw his mind into confusion and left him without anchorage in face of the unknown. The thought that he could not do his share was a crushing blow, but he was no longer young and his health was precarious. The whole unfolding of events at that time ran counter to his disposition, wounded his convictions, blasted his views of a civilization always progressing. At Deauville, in the hospital founded by Madame Boylesve, the spectacle of physical suffering was agony to him and fired his patriotism. Filled with anguish, he reckoned up the ruin and devastation of his country, and in the evening, leaving the hospital, he would walk on the beach lost in feverish thoughts. He told me of these solitary walks when he had the impression that the world was falling to pieces, and could find no consolation for what he called 'the bankruptcy of reason.'

In society circles, after the War, he looked sorrowfully at people whom he judged incapable of understanding him. He, who had been fond of dainty living and leisure for constant dreaming, was scared by the haste people brought to their pleasures, and the fierce activity of which he could not make sense. The new manners, and even the sight of a Paris which was rapidly changing in aspect, wounded his preferences and all his recollections. He held in horror the barbarians who felled trees in his peaceful district of Passy. Every blow of the axe slashing close to his house, at what remained of the ancient park of Monsieur de la Popelinière, hit him cruelly. When I was one day lunching with him, he took the precaution to make me sit with my back to the window so that I might not see this spectacle which broke his heart.

Friend beyond compare, how best can I tell of your constant solicitude, your wise and merry disposition, the dreamy wanderings of your clear intelligence? For many long years we exchanged observations and felt sure of the frankness of our feelings towards each other, but now, when I must speak of you, I become the prey to all the scruples of your shy nature. I have qualms at recalling our confidences, and fear of betraying the trust you placed in me.

« XI »

FORAIN — JACQUES-ÉMILE BLANCHE

WHEN I met Forain, about 1906, he was already famous. He moved in society a great deal, much in demand on account of his wit, yet also feared because of scathing remarks which always hit the nail. His voice was biting and bantering. His handsome brown eyes shone with acute intensity in his clean-shaven pale face. When Forain entered a drawing-room, the atmosphere became charged with electricity; his presence prolonged any discussion, for he never let pass any opinion he did not share without opposing it. Yet he never argued; his remarks were darts he shot off. His laughter lent strength to his words. Sometimes one imagined that, lost in dreams, he had not heard; but suddenly, like a dyke bursting its banks, his fearless moral judgment burst forth. Every week *Le Figaro* published one of his admirable cartoons with a caption commenting on some notable event with scathing and biting irony. A contributor to this newspaper once asked him how he wrote these captions, and Forain replied: 'Sometimes I make a drawing to fit words which have come into my head, but often I make my drawing and just open my ears...'

Thus, this historian of morals and manners knew how

FORAIN

to grasp their meaning and to illustrate them. Pitiless observer that he was, his words shot forth, sometimes deep, often quizzical, always bold and free, and imposed themselves through their elliptic style. Nevertheless, to meet Forain only in drawing-rooms was not to know him. The shrewdest people could hardly guess at the sensitive heart he so skilfully hid from those who were indifferent to him. If ever he allowed you inside his home — a rare favour — one realized how kind and courteous was this man, capable of the cruellest satire. His conversation abounded in illuminating views on art; his enthusiasm and his faith towards works and men worthy to be admired were genuine. I sometimes asked his advice about my drawings.

'You must never cease studying the great masters,' he told me: 'when one is young, one understands nothing of nature. It is equally important to acquire the habit of drawing from memory. This is essential to convey movement and life. And when you draw,' he explained, 'never forget the spiral. I mean by this that the lines of shapes are never straight.'

While he talked, I watched him painting, in the studio of his private house in the Rue Spontini, either a scene in a law court, a drama of poverty, or an attitude in a ballet dancer. He conjured up from the void, in neat touches and striking relief, the very synthesis of life. Sometimes, after the lapse of a week, the picture had entirely altered in composition and light effect. Or else again, on the new picture he came back to his original idea, only slightly altering a few details.

TIME PAST

This great moralist chiselled in chiaroscuro types of physical decay and threw over them a cynical elegance in most impressive relief. As a political satirist, he laid stress on events to stigmatize them; thanks to his inexhaustible humour, he could speed up a sequence of drawings as for a brilliant campaign, choosing the most significant gestures, suppressing as superfluous everything except the one important detail, and with his gift for caricature picturing with a minimum of strokes the figure who typified the person he wanted to brand.

In his least sketches one feels the sharp claw of a master. Sometimes, when he came to see me, he picked up any piece of paper within reach, and according to the events of the day his pencil raced along, swift and pitiless. He seldom retouched a drawing; he preferred starting it anew. When he tried to recapture the expression or face of a man he wanted to portray, he drew, one after another, a dozen outlines which more and more resembled his model. On the day Maurice Barrès was received at the Academy, Forain drew for me a series of Barrès as *académicien*, front views, three quarters faces, and profiles. As he worked, he elaborated the most delectable portrait of the writer. I have often regretted that no recording device was there to tap the artist's conversation. When he was in good form, he let himself go, and his enthusiastic temperament was revealed in all its generosity, with his horror for shams and his pity for human suffering.

This was the time when he felt the influence of J. K. Huysmans. He often went to see the writer when the latter was seriously ill, and always came back much disturbed. One afternoon, he brought me *Les Foules de Lourdes* and began to read long extracts from it, making comments as he went. From that day, his mind was haunted by the unforgettable mystic drawings which he came to produce later. His engravings bear witness to such greatness of mind and loftiness of spirit as to class Forain among the great masters. With one great stroke he summed up emotions; crookedness in his fellow creatures interested him more than themselves; his aim was to represent his period with entire veracity.

As he took on years, Forain became absorbed in a preoccupation with the after-life to which we owe the admirable Biblical scenes so fresh to everyone's memory. Never did Forain draw or paint to express nothing. He always acutely felt the misery of women in dire straits, of forsaken children, and of all the obscure dramas of the human soul. For him children were sacred. No one was ever a more affectionate and indulgent father. He was always radiantly happy when he brought his little boy to lunch with me. He related all the smart sayings and pranks of his son; unconsciously touched up by himself, some of them were very charming. This one, for instance: As someone was telling the little boy to be very careful not to hurt a lady who was going to have a baby, the mite exclaimed, 'Yes, I see that she is already full of milk to feed him.'

During the War, the great artist could not bear remaining a spectator; despite his age he volunteered in the camouflage service, where he made himself most useful.

War proved for him a new source of inspiration. How many of his unforgettable pictures depicting heroism or desolation amidst ruins do we not owe to it! How many pages illustrating the tragedy are but his indignation never at a loss for expression! By dint of stubborn work he could express himself with a mastery and swiftness which are the hallmark of genius. His pencil obeyed his thought, cutting, direct, never repenting.

Parisian by choice, he had all the great French qualities. Tradition found again in him the elements which go to the making of the great masters of painting, and the works of this engraver, this scrutinizer of souls and faces, will remain as the most searching document of our period.

Painter, man of letters, critic, moralist — Jacques-Émile Blanche is all these with equal success.

One feels something like respect in viewing the burden of work involved in labours so various and of such breadth and lofty probity.

Blanche kept from a first stay in England an ineffaceable recollection which was bound to leave an impression upon the manifold facets of a mind given to analyzing all things and understanding everything. From an early age, keen observer that he already was, he denounced what appeared to him false, ugly, or in the nature of caricature. Here he can be linked with the moralists, and this disposition, as evidenced by his work, is perhaps his most striking characteristic. His leaning towards analysis turns him into a watchful witness always ready to pass exact judgment, and often most severe. This fact puts him in rather a delicate position in his relations with smart society.

When such a disposition marks a life, it can find expression either on canvas or in writing and it bestows a quite special value to any work, but involves the risk of being appreciated during the lifetime of its author, not so much for its artistic character as from the point of view of its anecdotic and documentary interest.

As a painter one might perhaps look upon the enormous output of Jacques-Émile Blanche as the fruit of a stubborn, slow, painstaking, untiring search for the technique of painting and the perfection of the art. Yet Jacques-Émile Blanche is as little of a theorist as are most painters of today. I mean by this the systematic theorist putting forth mental and metaphysical conceptions, in opposition to what is worthy of the artist's brush, for in what remains a matter of his craft Blanche would easily become more than a theorist; he would prove a pedagogue, 'an educational force,' as the English put it.

This painter, who has formed so many generations of pupils, represents himself above all as a teacher. At eighteen he made at the Louvre a copy of Mantegna's 'Parnasse' with such mastery that Gustave Moreau and Bonnat wanted to buy it. Both Manet and Fantin-Latour were friends of his family, and both had the best influence upon his training. Degas, whose implacable harshness so much wounded him, played a leading part in his destiny. Jacques-Émile Blanche worshipped him. But above all he was destined to preserve always present the memory of the English women who had surrounded his childhood. His early stay in England (1870–71) remained for him a dazzling experience, an illumination.

Some years ago (1929) Paris had the rare fortune, during a retrospective exhibition, of viewing these English landscapes, all at once colourful and dim, which leave one convinced that Blanche is the best painter of London, his second country, and that he alone has truly caught the effect of those brilliant reds standing out against a background of grey mist.

He remains again the best painter of London in his novels, for although so consciously French, no one better than he has known how to translate with happy results the motives of foreign souls. This artist is in this way peculiar, that the man of letters is also a greatly appreciated painter, as well as being rightly praised for his musical gifts, his taste in general, and his skill in conquering forms of art in various fields. Was he not chosen as adviser for the staging and costumes for *Tannhäuser* at the revival at Bayreuth after the master's death?

He was still adolescent when he was companion to the most famous men and had secured such friendships as that of Claude Debussy who dedicated to him his *Jardins sous la Pluie*, or of Marcel Proust who wrote a preface for his *De Ingres à Degas*. As a frequent collaborator to *La Revue de Paris*, he became one of those men whose opinions carry weight; his were particularly feared, for he had the courage to expound them with complete freedom. If he defended *dadaisme*, he is the only one whom the *sur-réalistes* have spared.

Whatever may be learned from his painting, it is above

all in his writings that the explanation of Jacques-Émile Blanche is to be found, and I do not think I am much mistaken in stating that *Georges Aymeris's* childhood is, with scarcely any alterations, that of the author. A marvellous series of portraits is collected together in *Mes Modèles*, while at Rouen Museum a collection of paintings is on view where the landscape and flower painter is revealed by the side of the portrait painter.

The longing to understand, the anxiety to probe every problem to its depths, such are needs that no one feels more than Blanche. The inquisitiveness of a mind never easily satisfied causes him to draw near, almost to touching, those he wishes to study. He thus forms his estimate from precise notes carefully checked.

In his book, *Dates*, the subjects he treats, from his essay on Forain to the one on music, taking in his stride an 'artistic survey of the season in Paris,' where he refers to the Russian Ballets and especially the *Sacre du Printemps*, contain a priceless documentation for the study of our period.

Therefore, Jacques-Émile Blanche's work will live after him as a monument erected by one who observed and could not keep silent. His luminous career is in a way paradoxical, since it did not proceed along the road to success, nor adopt the usual means for reaching it. In fact, Blanche's career was strewn with enmity, people taking dislike to him even in his very studio at Auteuil on account of the frankness of his critical mind always on the alert, all of which greatly adds to the value of the man and the artist.

« XII »

LORD BALFOUR

WHEN Lord Balfour passed away his strong constitution had already for long fought against a progressive weakness which caused his friends to fear a fatal issue. His advanced age (he was nearly eighty-three) became a burden on his broad and drooping shoulders only during the last months, for there was much solidity and vigour in this fine intelligence. By those who had the good fortune to know this great man — one of the last of the fine stock of English statesmen — whose personality far transcended the high positions he occupied, he was sadly missed. Lord Balfour was, above all things, a 'man.' His dreamy and poetic appearance, his handsome features, revealed a generous soul enamoured of humanity. The nobility of his face, something clear and celestial in his eyes, the pleasing charm of his smile, struck one as soon as he appeared. His tolerance, his wish to understand everything, his calmness, at once captivated the people he talked to, while his delightful simplicity, his natural gaiety, gave this genial man everlasting youth. His taste for healthy recreations — for tennis above all — stood out all the more in full significance since one knew him engaged on important tasks in a perfect equilibrium of mind and ac-

LORD BALFOUR

tions. I have heard him say that after philosophy what interested him most was music, then nature and physical culture.

I met him for the first time, in the early part of 1919, at the Duchess of Sutherland's (Lady Millicent Hawes). She was then living in a small furnished flat, Rue Fortuny, on a ground floor prolonged by a tiny garden. We were having tea when the door opened and Mr. Arthur Balfour came in. The room, which was low of ceiling, seemed too small for his tall stature; his vigorous body was dressed in rather loose garments which, far from giving him a dowdy appearance, seemed on the contrary to enhance the gracefulness of his bearing. The neck, quite free, supported a head of harmonious proportions; snow-white hair framed a luminous forehead. After a long day of work, he was coming to find rest close to a friend of old standing. The Duchess complimented him on the choice and colour of his tie. She explained that he was very dainty; each of her words indicated her intention to make much of him. I felt, in her discreet praises, her pride at reckoning such a man among her countrymen. Mr. Balfour, appreciative of these attentions, smiled and ate at tea with the appetite of a child.

He was then in Paris as second plenipotentiary attached to Lloyd George for the peace negotiations. The conversation concerned the anxieties of the time. I was struck by the questions asked by Mr. Balfour. What interested him was the analysis of the temperaments of the partners with whom he found himself in daily contact at the council chamber. He wished to know what peculiarities in each revealed his psychological pre-occupations. He himself elaborated some swift portraits, in a few touches and with great loftiness of spirit; then, as if to push to one side an inexhaustible theme, subject to constant modifications, he suddenly declared:

'One evening I should love to hear some music. I have often met Reynaldo Hahn while in London. Do you know him? It would be delightful to hear him sing. I should also like a talk with Aristide Briand; I greatly admire him.'

Then, like someone used to having his wishes granted at once, he added: 'I am free after tomorrow evening. Can you do it?'

I was only too eager to try. My hostess suggested the names of a few other guests I might ask. It was agreed I should arrange a dinner. I can claim no credit for having gathered my guests. They all looked forward to the honour of meeting the great Englishman. My main difficulty was in procuring butter. I had been, for several years, ruled over by my cook Joséphine, famous for her skill and her strictness. She was most conscientious and Paris was still rationed in the matter of certain foodstuffs. Joséphine threatening to go on strike, I had to go to town myself and hunt for butter. Perhaps the occult influence of Mr. Balfour protected me; I had a great deal of trouble, but I succeeded.

Around the table were assembled, to meet my guest of honour, the Comtesse de Noailles, the Princesse Lucien Murat, the Marquise and the Marquis de Ganay, Aristide Briand, Paul Painlevé, Louis Barthou, Maurice Barrès, the Abbé Mugnier, Sir William Tyrrell (since then Lord

Tyrrell), Émile Vandervelde, the Duc de Guiche (now Duc de Gramont), Reynaldo Hahn, and the Marquis Visconti-Venosta, who had arrived from Italy that very morning.

To my great regret, the beautiful and engaging Duchess of Sutherland did not come, having caught a cold. The main duty of a hostess is to take care over the menu and draw out each of her guests. There was scarcely any bother that evening. It often happens that at dinner parties the prevailing tone, either right or wrong, creates itself, and even if all the most favourable elements are gathered together, an atmosphere once created becomes final and elusive.

But Mr. Balfour's magic presence turned the gathering into a success such as is the best reward for the hostess. He chatted in turn with each of my guests, as does a perfect gentleman. I admired his skill, his diplomatic sense. The Comtesse de Noailles, sparkling with life, lyricism, and humour, led the conversation with her usual eloquence. Aristide Briand, witty and humane, answered her back, supported by Louis Barthou, who was as ready-witted as cutting. Maurice Barrès often remained silent. His touching face, with its long eyes, was slightly bent forward. Whenever he stepped into the conversation, his serious voice, with its lustrous stresses, sounded like the rippling of a brook upon a bed of tiny pebbles. He was fully attentive, just like a young student on a holiday. I do not think he was bored that evening. Paul Painlevé, always modest, lent himself with good grace to answering all the questions where his erudition was of help.

Time Past

As we left the table, the Comtesse de Noailles, in one of those poetic or funny epitomes such as her genius knew how to frame, summed up her impression in these words: 'I feel in this great man such tender and affecting purity that I should like to scatter edelweiss upon his head.'

Mr. Balfour had a very friendly private chat with Paul Painlevé. They remained a long while by themselves and, when I drew near, I understood they were discussing the settlement of the Greek question at the time of the murder of the French sailors. Paul Painlevé, then Minister of War, had taken the initiative in drastic measures. Mr. Balfour, who heard the news in America, said that he had trembled before the enormity of the risks.

As on that very morning Mr. Balfour had telephoned me to inquire if he could invite for the gathering after dinner, his nephew and niece, Lord and Lady Hartington, newly married, I had also asked, to complete the party, some ten people, among whom Venizelos, and Maklakoff, Ambassador for the Russian Provisional Government, who had met Mr. Balfour at the homes of Asquith and Astor.

Reynaldo Hahn, that day in an admirably good mood, did not complain at the height of his collar and himself proposed to sing, asking simply to be allowed to shift the piano so as to face his audience. Scarcely had he made this request when Mr. Balfour came to the rescue and helped to alter the position of the instrument. And there again is one of his characteristics: no sooner had this alteration been made, and the guests became all attention for the treat the composer was going to give them, than Mr. Balfour settled himself close to the piano so that it was understood he was going to give himself entirely to the music.

Reynaldo Hahn, always so marvellous, that day excelled himself. He began by singing some of his own melodies, in his warm, sonorous voice and with unrivalled charm. Then he gave us old French songs: *La Tour Saint-Jacques*, *Fan-fan la Tulipe*, which was encored. What variety of choice in his pieces! His memory was faultless, his diction perfect, as was his very personal way of embellishing each new song with unexpected commentaries. He sang *La Carmagnole*, and his rendering was inimitable; then came the national anthems of various countries, and *Le Chant du Départ*. His mastery and the stirring tones of his voice adorned this improvised party with the magic of music.

After five years of mourning and anguish, Paris, in this spring of 1919, offered an extraordinary animation. Such liveliness reflected the hopes born of the council then assembled for the peace negotiations.

In Parisian salons one came across, in select society, politicians from many countries. I often met Mr. Arthur Balfour during that time. He stood among us as the incarnation of tradition, patriotism, national spirit, and that other thing greater than the English themselves: England.

He did me the honour of coming to my home several times. One day, on the occasion of a rather intimate luncheon, I placed under his napkin a copy of *Theism and Humanism*, a book of his dating from 1915 which had been translated by J. L. Bertrand, the present secretary to the *Observatoire de Paris*, under the title, *L'Idée de Dieu et l'Esprit humain*. Mr. Balfour had not yet seen this translation, issued in Paris. I shall never forget his expression of cheerful surprise. Never did I understand more clearly that all his most secret leanings went towards philosophy.

When I arrived in London I dared not ask to see him again. At a party, given by Mrs. Baldwin, I was chatting with Rudyard Kipling, a relative of Mr. Baldwin, as is well known. I knew the famous author of the *Jungle Books* and greatly admired him. I had several times met him in Paris, notably with Anatole France. We were recalling the past, and he was complaining of his health which was at the moment preventing him from writing. Yet he did not look ill, and I admired his face where thick bushy eyebrows shaded eyes which have so skilfully seen and interpreted animal life. What savour there was in the least of his remarks.

Suddenly I noticed Lord Balfour coming in. He had scarcely altered. His angelic face had, if anything, become more refined still. I was glad to see he recognized me, for with that simplicity which is gracefulness of heart, he came to me and reproached me with my discretion. I then dared ask him the favour of sparing me a few moments that I might make a sketch of him. He inquired my address, and when he found that I lived at the White House in Chelsea, where the owner, my friend Miss Anabel Douglas, had welcomed me most charmingly, he offered to come on the next day at eleven o'clock.

I was most grateful, and, I confess, very much moved.

Then the fear came over me that I might make a failure of my drawing. In that state of agitation I spent a wretched night.

White House, which had belonged to Whistler, is situated in delightful Tite Street in Chelsea, the artists' quarter, and at the end of the street is the Thames with its flocks of sea-gulls. My hostess's exquisite taste had watched over my comfort.

Lord Balfour made it a point to arrive just on the stroke of eleven. He congratulated me on the big bright room in which I had decided the light was best suited for my drawing. I tried to gather courage by listening to my model; then I took hold of my pad, and such was my agitation that, mistaking the right side, I made my sketch on the blotting-paper. After a quarter of an hour I stopped, greatly disturbed at finding my mistake. Lord Balfour took up my drawing. I felt absolutely done.

'I like it,' he said; 'don't alter it. It's really me.... And to prove this, it is not you will sign it, but myself.'

I took his fountain-pen, signed, and noted the date.

Another morning I lunched with him at Lady Colefax's, who, with her usual skill, had arranged a brilliant gathering. There were present, among many others, Lytton Strachey, the author of *Queen Victoria*, a man with deep eyes in a pale face framed by a very black beard, who spoke to me about Marcel Proust; Edmund Gosse, already rather ill and whom I had met at Joseph Reinach's, who had a vast knowledge of French literature, greatly admired Paul Bourget, was eager to know Paul Morand's work, and spoke of André Maurois with fervour. Lady Lavery, the portrait painter's wife, was also there, in all the splendour of her marvellous complexion and russet hair; likewise Geoffrey Scott, who died prematurely in the United States, author of *The Portrait of Zélide*, a charming book about a friend of Benjamin Constant; he spoke to me about Italy where he had lived a long while.

The handsome house known as Argyll House was flooded with sunshine. Lady Colefax presided over her gatherings with vivacious intelligence and attracted the *élite* of the best society. Just as we were leaving, Lord Balfour suggested that we two should go together for a walk. His seventy years were but a myth. He walked briskly while relating various interesting things. We reached the Embankment. London atmosphere holds some intangible softness, the beauty of the site suited the grand old man. His eyes took it all in and gazed beyond. A white scarf around his neck was almost the same shade as his silky hair. He talked in a sort of dream. In November, 1917, he had promised to restore a Zionist *home* in Palestine. In a few weeks he was to start for the Holy Land to see the fulfilment of his promise.

I saw Lord Balfour again at Sargent's, in his house in Tite Street where the painter had assembled such a remarkable collection of works of art. I had to grant Lord Balfour's wish to bring my own drawings next door, at White House. Then — and this was the last time I had the great honour of meeting in private this man who achieved so much for England — he came, once more without warning, to have tea at my hostess's.

He loved to speak of his student years, of Scotland, his

family, his sisters. It always seemed to me that his youth would never leave him, that he himself would never go for good. There was still so much for me to find out about him, so much to admire!...

« XIII »

ANNA DE NOAILLES — JEAN COCTEAU

ANNA DE NOAILLES proved for me not only the inspired poet, the marvellous being whose genius had dazzled me, but also the peerless friend — little Anna, the darling, the sublime and familiar creature whose presence adorned my life, and whom I thanked for being alive every time it was my good fortune to be with her.

Since she has left us, since her eyes, 'whose gaze bore the stamp of the sun,' are closed, I am haunted by the beauty of her face as it appeared to me in its final fixity, and I measure the gap which her departure left in our lives.

Anna de Noailles moved people to enthusiasm. To be near her was to feel her lofty spirit, her passion for justice, and her extraordinary courage. One in turn admired her and desired to serve and protect her, for she was not proof against injuries, being often worn out with fatigue or in poor health, though so brave about it. Yet she always sprang to life again, being taken out of herself through the urge of her clear mind and her boundlessly eager interests. She was so complete in herself, and at the same time so various, that one had hopes she would find within herself the means to carry off the weight of mortal days; yet we have now to think of her, she who was life itself, as among the dead.

My recollections of her are profuse! I recall her under a thousand aspects, yet always unique, always herself. Who will ever be as dazzling, witty, humorous, novel? Who will ever speak as she did? I picture her again, pale and young, in the garden of her native Amphion, long before the War. Every day, in the family circle, sparkled the warmth and fire of her conversation, and she gave of herself with as much success as when in public. Nothing equalled her tender respect for her mother, the Princesse de Brancovan; often I have held her adorable small hand in mine while she surrendered herself to the delight of her mother's rendering of Chopin. The great *artiste* did not always allow us to come near her, for she was nervous, and it was from an adjoining room we listened to the sublime song rising from the key-board. Anna's luminous eyes were filled with dreams. Then she retired to her own room to write:

> *Un prélude houleux et grave de Chopin,*
> *Profond comme la mer lumineuse et remuée,*
> *Pousse jusqu'en mon coeur ses sonores nuées...*

It was also at Amphion she wrote, during that same year:

> *Comme le temps est court qu'on passe sur la terre*
>   *Si peu de matins vifs,*
> *Si peu de rêverie heureuse et solitaire*
>   *Dans des jardins naïfs.*

And it is not without emotion I note the last stanza:

> *Mais vous serez dissous, coeur éclatant et sombre,*
>   *Vous serez l'herbe et l'eau*
> *Et vos humains chéris n'entendront plus dans l'ombre*
>   *Votre éternel sanglot.*

Time Past

During that same summer we took long walks on the shores of the Lake of Geneva and in Savoy, the gentle hilly landscape she preferred to any other in the world. It was there inspiration had first come to her, and there again that later, in days of mourning and sadness, her mind sought rest as in a paradise regained. I met her the following year at Milan, and I now so clearly recall the Restaurant Cova, where, gay and full of life, she was recognized by young people who begged for her autograph upon their menu cards, and later the escort of young admirers who followed us as we visited the town. She responded to them with that charming simplicity she brought to all things and which made her beloved of all even the humblest. One evening, we went as far as Bellagio to dine with Monsieur and Madame Louis Barthou, and I shall never forget how she spoke of Nature on our way back at night, towards a sleeping Milan.

She was gracefully natural, full of understanding, and her joy of life was so intense as to give the impression she had never exhausted youth. Throbbing with vitality, her aspirations went towards what was lofty and eternal. Her clear mind fearlessly attacked the deepest problems, eager to reach beyond the limits of human knowledge, athirst for logic and certitude. Enthusiastic and keenly observant, she sought such human beings as seemed to her to have attained those powers of strength and beauty which filled her with wonder and helped her to soar always higher. No one could, as she did, ask questions with precision, method, and alert attention. Perhaps this explains why she liked to meet famous people, whose knowledge and secret motives she longed to probe. Her splendid eyes took in the external appearance of a person at one glance, and thence she proceeded deeper with her survey. Through her gift of visual observation she proved irrefutable, often cruel, though her mind could lend poetry to physical defects and choose them as themes for her musing. Her swift critical faculties and her quick way of guessing or suggesting the answers she expected, combined to give to anyone talking with her the feeling of being understood; she thus won her listener's heart, captivated as he was by her intelligence and charm. Sure of herself and of her irresistible eloquence, often amused at her own felicitous expressions, she never beat about the bush, but succeeded in learning what she had decided to know; then, imagination helping such knowledge, she reconstituted all obscure details with a faultless logic. It was delightful to see her read the newspapers and sort out in a moment what was worth attention; or turn over the pages of a book, as if taking a sniff at it, and thereby extracting its full essence. I remember that, one day, her young son was to write a school essay on Chateaubriand. Anna de Noailles, taking up his book, opened it at a description of blue teal, read through a few pages, and, carried away by enthusiasm, began to explain Chateaubriand's genius with marvellous eloquence.

No one was her match for oral literary criticism. Victor Hugo, Goethe, Ronsard, were themes upon which she was for ever varying her comments. Sometimes she was as bright and merry as a child, enjoying public festivals and the pleasures of the mob, taking delight in an account of a society gathering. Her sense of humour was striking, and numerous were the piquant comparisons, the unexpected parallels, which dropped from her lips.

One incident stands out for me amidst so many. She wanted to meet Kerensky who had just arrived in Paris. I asked Monsieur Maklakoff, Ambassador for the Russian Provisional Government, to bring him to her. She invited also Rostand and Barrès. We found her greatly excited and impatient to ask a thousand questions of this captain who had just left his ship to be wrecked; but, disheartened by the look of the man and the difficulty he encountered in following her, she improvised for our benefit a sort of fresco on the Russian Revolution, and of so impressive a sincerity that we remained struck with awe. She was quite right in saying that her life was made of the very substance of the universe; nothing left her indifferent. A watchful and discerning onlooker, she always found the tracks of great and glorious mortals.

As soon as she appeared in any social circle, she no longer remained her own mistress, possessed as she was by a dazzling and inexhaustible eloquence which carried her beyond herself. First she would get hold of one person, then attract another, and soon she was the life of the whole gathering. Her improvisations were monologues unequalled in spirited ardour. Through them she enjoyed, almost to the verge of exhaustion, the pleasure of conquest and coquetry. What points of satire, illuminating epitomes, brilliant images, could not her prodigious wit pour forth with irresistible ease! Yet, whenever I dined alone with her, sitting by her bed in the dim room adorned with cretonne, a charming intimacy prevailed. She took much interest in the lives of her friends, and she was a splendid adviser, full of pity and always ready to give benefit by her influence. She opened her heart freely; with full trust and affection she confessed her griefs, her weariness, and through such unreserved confidences I felt her fierce courage and lofty dignity to such an extent that I never left her but filled with wonder. I often attempted to convert her to a more normal life. Yet I rarely succeeded in making her go out. About midday, in a car, we sometimes went for a drive in the Bois, which she scarcely noticed, though the sight of a trifle, perhaps a shutter left ajar, might prove sufficient to bring back to her mind memories of a past season. And thus, one day, she wrote all at once her *Chant du Printemps*:

> *Le silence et les bruits soudains*
> *Dans l'air humide*
> *Ont ce soir un accent plus vaste et plus ardent.*

She always declared that she never worked; that what she did was the fruit of inspiration, of natural gifts and happy improvisation. Thus she became a painter. Her entirely spontaneous technique revealed tones of brilliant freshness; her settings were in delicate taste and the outcome of impulse. Her gift for caricature appeared in her portrait work. Seated in bed, surrounded by boxes and crayons, she pulled them out with surprising swiftness. This was one of her last pastimes; for about two years she found great pleasure in it. Then, suddenly, she whose glorious life had so mingled with the history of her period, she who had displayed such courage, such powers in her struggle with the universe, such melodious love of Nature, no longer wished to live. As fervent as had been her enthusiasm to sing of life was now equally strong the vertiginous attraction death held for a mind suddenly bereft of illusions.

One day, when one of her friends jokingly assured her that she would become a delightful old lady: 'But I don't want to!' she told him, greatly shocked.

Eighteen months before her death bitter disillusion drove her to a negation of life. She no longer wanted to bear up under suffering and grief, and she refused to allow her will to uphold a fragile body undermined by mysterious pains and aches. This obsession of the emptiness of life wore her out, and finally greatly harmed her constitution. Her clairvoyant mind foresaw death and welcomed it without fear.

Those unrivalled eyes are closed, one of the warmest hearts that lived has ceased to beat. Marvellous child, so tiny and so great, she has left the earth, but there remains with us her immortal work.

Dazzingly whimsical, Jean Cocteau, only a youth when I first met him, grasped elusive ideas on the wing. His irrepressible spirits, his prodigious gift for talking in turn as poet or as mimic, his quaint expressions, his puns, his opinions, all revealed a complex nature which, thanks to numberless gifts, made light of difficulties. His keen eyes discerned on the instant what he wanted to make note of; his wit transformed his visions into original presentation. His cleverness never stood in the way of true likeness in the amusing scenes he liked to enact. His slim and harmonious body seemed bewitching. All that came within his reach was food for his imagination, and he transformed and lent life even to the most humble things. This untiring gift for creativeness marked the extent of his vitality and of an alert mind never at rest. Even in depths of depression he still found within himself a constant fount of new life, and sprang up again with new schemes. As a shrewd observer he seemed to have feelers with which to guess, from the confused web of new tendencies, those which would become dogmas. Standing in the van of artistic movements, his part was often similar to the water-diviner's, and he generously placed his influence at the service of new ideas. Original draughtsman as well as poet, he drew portraits which were true revelations in the elliptic style.

It is at the time of *Le Sacre du Printemps* that I like to remember Jean Cocteau, ready for a fight, eloquent, and expounding Stravinsky's new formulas. In *Le Coq et l'Arlequin* he wrote: 'When a work of art seems in advance of our time, it is, more truly, our time which is lagging behind.' He asserted that *Le Sacre*, staged in a new, rather too comfortable theatre, had been met by a decadent audience used to the Eastern bad taste of divans and cushions. Even if *Le Sacre* did not quite move on the same plane as other restless endeavours — for music lagged far behind painting — it nevertheless brought an indispensable dynamism, and Cocteau acclaimed this work a masterpiece.

He declared that he owed more to Erik Satie and Picasso

than to any other writer, and stated that the influence of a writer would have made him run the risk of acquiring a mannerism, while the astounding discipline through freedom he acquired by the side of this musician and this painter saved him from such danger.

When he spoke of Guillaume Apollinaire, whom he called an exile from the eighteenth century, he explained that he had never known a man more ill at ease at the extreme point of his own epoch. 'He tolerated it, gulled it, and decked it out with delightful flowers. He foresaw its collapse.' One day, as we were walking near the Colonial Office where he was employed, he told me how depressed he was. This on account of the modernism of which he wanted to be the apostle, but which nevertheless exasperated him. Indeed, having himself opened the sluice, he was then cursing the floods under the excuse that he had only let them loose as a sort of joke. The charm of his personality resided in the contrast between his duty as anarchist and the sparkling fantasies he wrote. Watch the drop of ink quivering at the tip of his pen. It falls, and a star appears on the paper. All the work of this great poet was a series of exquisite ink blots.

After having written *Le Cap de Bonne-Espérance* and *Le Coq et l'Arlequin*, Jean Cocteau, with Darius Milhaud and Jean Wiener, opened a café, Le Boeuf sur le toit, which became the haunt of young artists. According to him, the music-hall, the circus, the negro bands, helped artists to creative work like life itself. The café of the Rue Boissy-d' Anglas became at once a great success.

Jean Cocteau was in the habit of saying: 'People demand

to have poetry explained to them. They are completely ignorant that poetry is a closed sanctum where few people are admitted, where it even happens that no one is admitted.' Cocteau's many-sided talent draws its inspiration from the evolutions of his period. He culls and gathers emotions from the most subtle sources. His *Vox humana* renders in a monologue of growing intensity the anguish of a deceived heart. We can trace in his films and novels of the last few years an acute power of observation untrammelled by mere literature, and a need to express himself in his full strength by means of a style more and more compact and terse.

« XIV »

PAUL VALÉRY — A POST-WAR PUBLISHER: BERNARD GRASSET — PAUL MORAND — JULIEN GREEN

JEAN COCTEAU was already prancing before the War; but his elder, Paul Valéry, was later in entering the life of letters. It was during the War that I learned to know and admire the author of *Charmes*.

In 1917, Jean-Louis Vaudoyer, while on leave, invited some friends to spend an evening with him in his charming flat at the Palais Royal and he read to us *La Jeune Parque*. The author, in his dedication to André Gide, considers this poem as a simple exercise in view of acquiring a greater facility of thought and expression; we did not share this opinion, but enjoyed in these verses the delight of a complex and bewitching symphony. Certain lines condensed precious and fugitive states of soul through a light and haunting music. This song of lucid reason at grips with death, love, and life, revealed such beauty that we spent the whole evening discussing it and reading over again several passages.

> *J'étais l'égale et l'épouse du jour,*
> *Seul support souriant que je formais d'amour,*
> *A la toute puissante altitude adorée.*

Rien ne me murmurait qu'un désir de mourir
Dans cette blonde pulpe au soleil pût mûrir.
Mon amère saveur ne m'était point venue,
Je ne sacrifiais que mon épaule nue
A la lumière; et sur cette gorge de miel
Sont la tendre naissance accomplissait le ciel
Se venait assoupir la figure du monde.

At about the same time, at a party given by Arthur Fontaine, Léon-Paul Fargue read *La Jeune Parque*, and the echoes of this reading were far-reaching.

In his foreword to *Connaissance de la Déesse* Valéry remarks: 'Any judgment passed upon a book must above all take into account the difficulties which the author has set himself to conquer. It might be said that a survey of those self-imposed tasks reveals at one glance the poet's intellectual height, the quality of his pride, the delicacy and despotisms of his disposition.' From the spiritual strength of Valéry's poetry emanates a peculiar atmosphere in which the finest minds move with ease and breathe with delight.

Henceforth Paul Valéry's success grew with the years. Invited everywhere, much sought after in social circles, he showed himself of a cheerful disposition and perfect equanimity of temper. His Italian and Corsican origins predisposed him to play jokes. As a child he had spent his holidays in Genoa, and was still fond of that town. In an interview he had with Frédéric Lefèvre, he spoke of those 'society circles' people reproached him for frequenting and of the advantages he found in such frequentation. 'The foremost of these is not to crave for society's approval, just as I imagine that the advantage of being rich is to forget to long for a fortune. When society's circles hold no mystery and the life led by these people appears as simple as any ordinary life, the bulk of the inconveniences and pitfalls rumoured to be connected with it are warded off.'

And he explained further: 'A conversation exchanged at a dinner or tea may instruct and mature a man more rapidly than the reading of a hundred volumes. Where can one meet the politician, the banker, the diplomat, the churchman, the wit, the club man, the writer, except over a cup of tea and *petits-fours*? And this medium so favourable for a swift perception of the human comedy is almost exclusively the work of women!'

When I arrived at the Rue de Villejust, the author of *La Jeune Rarque* and *Monsieur Teste* emerged from the adjoining room into the clear drawing-room where I was waiting. His simplicity, his natural ways, formed a contrast to his quest for what is rare, exact, difficult. The elegant ease of a fluent mind makes the attraction of his conversation. Was it not Valéry who wrote, 'Only by the word am I conquered'?

'I have few recollections,' he replied to one of my questions, 'but it appears I was rather witty when I was three years old, though I displayed no other gift. At nine or ten I wrote for the marionettes a drama in verse: *Cartouche ou le roi des Voleurs*. It began in this way: "No one today in the woods." One act took place in Hell where Cartouche defeated the Devil, the most important character, one of the finest inventions of the human mind and the most accommodating, for one can make him as horrid a being as one wishes or yet again a sympathetic artistic personality.

A little later, reading brought me to discover architecture, and during several years I was keenly interested in Gothic art, thanks to Viollet-le-Duc and a book of Owen Jones: *The Grammar of Ornament*. I may remark about this that two or three years later, when I was about eighteen, I was much influenced by Edgar Allan Poe, for certainly there exists a relation between these two influences. This relation resides in an application of scientific reasoning to the realms of art. It is not surprising that this peculiar consideration soon brought me to be interested in the most famous representative of the tendency, Leonardo da Vinci, whose manuscripts, although fragmentary, sum up the most extraordinary endeavour to co-ordinate man's various faculties; in fact seek to establish a marvellously creative exchange between practice and theory. The fulfilment of the predictions of these great men is, in fact, our modern civilization when it is original and powerful.'

I asked Paul Valéry why he did not go into the navy as he first intended.

'Because of my absolute lack of understanding of the mathematical sciences.'

Paul Valéry's engaging and refined face was lit by grey-blue eyes sparkling with wit. He played with his monocle, causing it to turn swiftly at the end of its black ribbon.

'My ideas are my servants. They are the tools of my mental life, the product of my intellectual operations. It may be that they are of use to other minds. It is improbable that they should be so as they stand. You wish to know what activity I like? The activity of the mind in view of a production which, unfortunately, is my allotted task; yet I would willingly put a stop to this! I am at an age when I see most men retire on a pension and spend their days watching the earth go round. I have always thought that literary production, when it is obligatory and therefore almost a trade, is the great enemy of meditation; that is to say that state in which thought becomes formed, as a crystal shapes itself in a saturated liquid, or like the excellence of a fruit developed in the sun on the branch. Modern life, with its material demands and the permanent agitation which it represents, is supremely contrary to such precious formations. If the crust of the earth had been subjected to the conditions to which our minds have to submit, not a single diamond would have been discovered therein.'

We then spoke of translations, and Paul Valéry told me that there had been an excellent one published of his *Variétés*, the work of Mr. Malcolm Cowley. He had been filled with wonder at the quality of the translation, for he writes in a peculiarly abstract and sometimes archaic tongue, and he had been equally surprised and delighted by some articles which appeared in American magazines concerning this book. They were all remarkably understanding and revealed an earnestness and a knowledge of the text seldom met with in Europe. 'Nevertheless,' he added with a smile, 'I do not think that more than two or three volumes were sold, which is quite natural.'

'Monsieur,' I explained, 'although you have stated that you spent long years in varied meditation without thinking of a literary career as in accordance with your nature or seeing any book result from your meditations, but only

PAUL VALÉRY

a sorting out of your thoughts, yet is not your fame the revenge of our period?'

But Paul Valéry waved my statement aside: 'Reading and writing are to all intents and purposes things of the past.'

As a publisher Bernard Grasset inaugurated a new method for launching writers: he invented modern literary publicity. It was he who, first displaying huge posters, thus pushed forward Raymond Radiguet's *Le Diable au Corps* and *Le Bal du Comte d'Orgel*, two novels in which psychological study reverted to the classical style of *La Princesse de Clèves*. In *La Chose Littéraire*, Grasset explained himself on this matter: 'I have, on my part, only come across one authentic *débutant*, Raymond Radiguet. He caused a storm. I had certainly expected it, for he was bound to run counter to all conventions. Do not tell me, "It is you ran counter to all conventions in launching him." Without my provocative publicity he might have been neglected; was it not best to attempt conquering for him in his lifetime the place he now occupies in the world of letters? But most experts avoid inquiring into the secret of such success, finding it no doubt more easy to put it down to some inexplicable infatuation on the part of the reading public, though reflexion should lead them to discover the real needs of our period. But they prefer to dally endlessly over the unravelling of this mystery and to make nothing clear out of it.'

'The publisher of the four Ms,' Morand, Maurois, Mauriac, and de Montherlant, not only discovered new ways, but he enforced them. He was instrumental in re-educating the public to a sense of literary curiosity, and this for a vast public. He succeeded in creating a state of mind favourable to the appearance of a book. To readers who buy books by taste came to be added numerous inquisitive people and snobs who wanted to be in the know. The number of editions increased suddenly. Some of these successes could not be entirely explained by the worth of the books, but by the favourable circumstances under which they came out. The advance royalties which Grasset granted his authors were again an indication of modern ways, of the risk encountered in adapting the author's trade to the exigencies of modern life. He declared that his wish to meet such a need took even the upper hand over his preoccupation with success. 'But the War taught us,' he added, 'that demand more than supply rules success; therefore, it is demand we must create, and it is to this I applied myself.'

The modern writer is no longer sedentary, keeping to his study or the salons. The younger men — for instance Paul Morand — travel over the world, add sport to travel, and are active in as many new fields as their elders were curious about the past. Lucien Fabre, a writer much admired by Paul Valéry, has been a factory manager in Roumania; a philosopher like Ramon Fernandez has been a motor-car tester for the Bugatti firm, and is passionately fond of dancing. Marc Chadourne has carried out investigations in China; Giraudoux never misses a sports festival. André Beucler and Albert Flament have lived a little everywhere. Those who travel all over the world to give lectures or exploring unknown lands are legion, and the press urges them on. If newspapers offer to writers a means of adding to their incomes, they also require of them to adapt themselves to circumstances and proceed from one activity to another without any apparent connecting link. Thus, Guy Mazeline, editor of *L'Intransigeant*, author of *Les Loups*, winner of the Goncourt Prize for 1932, had no sooner received this prize than he had to set off for Rome and interview Mussolini. Last year, André Beucler, when in Prague to interview President Masaryk and write an account of the Sokols Festival, had at the same time to squeeze in an articles contracted for with an American magazine on night life in Berlin.

The rhythm of life is in our days jerky, and on the other hand the reader's appetite has gone on increasing. A Chateaubriand, a Théophile Gautier, a Barbey d'Aurevilly would never have thought of being just like anyone else. A few days ago, as I was reading over again Flaubert's correspondence, I came across letters where he speaks of his sojourn in Rome. He had reached Rome with Maxime du Camp, worn out after his journey to the East. But he refused to follow the advice of his friend Bouilhet, who wrote to him he could easily pay another visit to Italy later on. Flaubert, in his answer, gives a list of the reasons he has to make the most of this visit now, stating that, once back at Croisset, his financial means, much diminished by this present journey, would never permit him to take another one. Imagine his bewilderment if he read in the papers today the columns telling of the travels of writers. The only reason he hesitated to stay was the fear that he was not sufficiently prepared for his visit to the Roman capital.

Literary prizes are now so numerous that many writers, after such a success, support themselves financially during a more or less extensive period. The reading public is eager to know their lives, their tastes, their social circles, and even their relations with publishers — in fact, all that pertains to competition in the realms of the mind. Édouard Bourdet's play, *Vient de Paraître*, has thrown light on these new tendencies, and its success has proved how wide is the public interest in the world of letters. But the value of things changes so rapidly in our days that the general inflation which a while back urged writers and literary works forward is already a recollection of the past. Speculation, during a period when all over the world people spent without possessing, spread even to books, *éditions de luxe*, the sale of manuscripts. Evidently a manuscript is a unique thing, and in order to satisfy the snobs' and collectors' infatuation, even proofs, original hand-written manuscripts, and autographed copies were sold. At night, on the boulevards, writers autographed their works, and still do so today. Big stores and other commercial firms commissioned them to write catalogues or booklets where one described lace, another chemical products, a third the radio. It is nothing surprising in our day to see the names of well-known writers at the bottom of publicity articles which praise automobile tyres or steel furniture.

It was in the first year of the War, during one of his

short stays in Paris, that I met the young diplomat, Paul Morand. It was difficult not to notice a young man so strikingly frank and intelligent, shrewd of judgment, and with a turn of mind so synthetic. His neat and swift way of looking at people, events, and their relations to each other at once gave the impression that he moved only by flying. His gift for gathering together, through comparisons, ideas, facts, elements, and for linking them up by a striking detail, rendered his talk both spirited in delivery and adorned by a vast store of knowledge acquired through insatiable inquisitiveness. He seemed to have opened all doors and scanned all possible horizons. He expressed himself simply, choosing by preference concrete terms. While listening to the working of such an original mind, one wondered what had been his education and in what surroundings he had grown.

His father, Eugène Morand, painter and poet, had, after the fashion of certain symbolists, felt the influence of the Pre-Raphaelites. His vast erudition and his interest for experimenting in the realms of art had made him in turn take up decorative art, oil painting, and pastel. When he wrote *Grisélidis* in collaboration with Armand Silvestre and staged it at the Français (for Lucien Guitry's first appearance), he himself painted the scenery and curtain which caused a sensation. He saw a great deal of Stéphane Mallarmé, Villiers de l'Isle-Adam, the brothers Goncourt, José-Maria de Hérédia, Georges de Porto-Riche, Marcel Schwob. He helped the latter with a translation of *Hamlet* in which Sarah Bernhardt acted the leading part with brilliance. His lasting friendship with the tragic actress sometimes brought him back to the theatre, and it was for her he wrote, at the end of his life, *Les Cathédrales*. Nevertheless, it was only occasionally he left his painting brushes. Appointed head of l'École Nationale des Arts Décoratifs, Eugène Morand devoted twenty years of his life to teaching. He lived secluded, amidst a few friends and books, and looked upon studies and examinations in France as of little value, so that very early he gave his son an English education.

The little Paul was a solitary child, and, if we are to believe him, very lazy. At fourteen he loved reading, but mostly realist writers: Zola, Maupassant, Huysmans. Then for a short period he was full of sports and his mind remained undeveloped. However, somewhere about twenty, he attempted a few poetical productions, much influenced by English literature (translations of Francis Thompson, Shelley, and English mediaeval mystery plays). Then he chose a diplomatic career, from no special liking, but so as not to live in France, for he wanted to know various civilizations. His whole outlook was very 'Oxford'; that is to say, very Oscar Wilde and Walter Pater — 'Art for Art's sake,' 'The artist apart from life.' All he had written so far bore the imprint of his reading: Baudelaire, Henri de Régnier, Albert Samain, and the Médan school. After getting acquainted with Jean Giraudoux in Munich, he read essays in *La Nouvelle Revue Française*, then just beginning publication, and, comparing their novelty with his early work, realized that he had to unlearn everything, and he stopped writing for six to seven years. It was during that period that, having chosen a diplomatic career, he no longer gave thought to literature. But entering upon an active life and practical studies, being suddenly thrust into a new world, contributed more than anything else to alter his style and his outlook on life.

'I suddenly became thirty or forty years younger,' he told me one day when I was questioning him. 'I lived in London during 1913 and 1914 as a young attaché, in the company of pleasant women who were my early models for *Tendres Stocks*.'

During the summer of 1916, he came to Paris on Briand's departmental staff. In the preceding year he had met Marcel Proust and was admitted into society on the confines of both the world of letters and that of politics.

Paul Morand was, after the War, among those young writers who felt the originality of a period picturesque and fertile as none before, and where a new poetry was finding expression. He brought to it his telescopic vision of life at full speed, with such haste as to seize on the passing moment, and produced a profusion of photographic impressions revealing the spectacle of a world completely renewed. When he speaks of the outset of his career he admits: 'To date from 1920, after the world revolution, cropped up numerous youthful generals from the army of men of letters. Grasset and Gallimard daily produced new Klébers or Marceaux. The "modest beginning" advocated by Boileau offers advantages; but, after the War, it was the public who, above all, with a passion for something new, instigated the flamboyant attempts of several writers. I quite understand that today, when we are no longer in a hurry, when the ground has been cleared, when God can once more recognize the faithful, an author prefers to take his time before launching out. But there was no choice for us; a special hour, one of the most bewildering in history, was speeding away in front of us: we had to snap it, take photographs of it: two worlds clashing in thunder. A writer lives by contacts; there was a need for prompt action, in fear of the spectacle disappearing, this spectacle without precedent: new frontiers, countries the day before unknown, a Babel of confused races, emancipated women, doomed men, inflation producing upon manners unsuspected and crushing effects, enemies making friends after four years of silence, revolution at our door, the downfall of the West, and many such apocalyptic marvels.'

This outlook on the world has been shared by other minds, but none have given it expression with as much aptness as Paul Morand. His descriptions are as pleasing as cocktails skilfully mixed and spiced. What is more, his relish for the precise and picturesque information keeps curiosity constantly quickened....

Every one of Morand's attitudes is an indication that he can never remain still, but must seize hold of whatever is essential at the place he happens to find himself and proceed always further. One day, when one of Anna de Noailles's admirers was praising her on her prodigious gifts, she stopped him short: 'What you forget, Monsieur, is to praise me for my very good sight; physically I observe much quicker and far better than most people.' This power of observing better, Paul Morand possesses more than anyone else. His intuition made him foresee, as far back as 1925, that the post-War period was virtually closed.

He has set the idea of the narrow dimensions of the earth against the exaltation of the romantic globe-trotter. He has aimed at freeing his narratives from the rubbish of exoticism and local colour, so as to react against the arbitrary fashion through which certain writers have come to conceive people, landscapes, and manners. 'What we came to ask of the earth was not a justification for some mental or sentimental disorder; we had, on the contrary an evident need of order, a longing to take stock anew of this earth on which we were to live, and which we hoped to enjoy more fully than ever had been done so far. To watch a world go to pieces does not perforce compel the observant artist to go to pieces himself. His duty is to take note that this chaos does not prevent the earth spinning round according to the eternal laws which rule submissive Nature, even though Man is unruly.'

His varied travel books — *Toute la Terre, Paris–Timbouctou, L'Hiver Caraïbe, L'Air Indien*, and *New-York*, and so on — move with inimitable impetuosity. Anyone reading his *Londres* makes a deep study, all the more interesting since Paul Morand mingles with his images a documentation almost encyclopaedic. One feels how much he loves the English capital, and that all the occasions he has had of living there he has used with eagerness in his ardent desire to learn. Success has not caused him to limit himself to a fixed type of work; his constant researches prove, on the contrary, that he remains many-sided and attentive in his understanding of the writer's trade. As 'observer,' he should be granted a first prize, while also being looked upon as in the front ranks of the narrators and journalists of our days.

When *Mont-Cinère* appeared, this first novel of Julien Green, then an unknown writer, many erroneous rumours were spread concerning the new novelist's origins and literary formation. Contrary to what certain critics have stated, Julien Green did not choose to write in one language in preference to another, but, born in France and educated in France, he could not write in any tongue but the one spoken around him. It is only when he was nineteen that Green went to the United States to get acquainted with the country of his ancestors. An uncle on his mother's side invited him to come and study at Virginia University. He stayed there three years, not trying to obtain a degree, but studying more especially classic authors, English and German. His father, a native of Virginia, had been long settled in Paris. His mother came from Savannah in Georgia, born from a family of English emigrants.

Julien's childhood was lulled by tales of the Civil War. He went to a French school; disliked science, but was attracted to literature. At fifteen, during the summer holidays, an old priest gave him Latin lessons, and the young man was soon surprised to find himself as advanced in this study as his schoolfellows who had studied the language since the age of eleven. He excelled in French, and in school essays was often ranked top. Reading was his favourite pastime; he devoured books. Gifted for drawing, Green copied museum photographs with peculiar care or drew historical scenes. Two books had especially taken hold of his imagination during his childhood: *Oliver Twist* and Eugène Sue's *Les Mystères de Paris*. Sometimes, after such reading, he longed to write; certain sights also produced this same effect.

After his exams, in 1917, Julien Green enlisted in the American Field Service and was sent to the Verdun zone. But the American Field Service becoming soon after incorporated in the American Army, Julien, who was too young according to the rules to remain in it, was transferred to the Morgan-Harjes Service and sent to the Italian front until June, 1918. Then, coming back to Paris, he volunteered in the French artillery.

When the War came to an end, he lived with his family in a dreamy sort of state and almost in complete solitude. He felt anxious concerning his future, so that his stay in America was a most happy diversion.

On his return Green thought he had discovered his vocation: 'I shall be a painter,' he declared, and went to classes at the Grande Chaumière Studio. It was just then that a small review asked him for articles on English writers. Those he wrote on William Blake and Joyce appeared under the name of David Irland. Then Green thought of writing a story by putting together his recollections of Virginia University. He considers that these pages were the means by which he freed himself of a past he had not yet been able to push aside. He handed this short story to a publisher. The latter put it in a drawer: it was *Le Voyageur sur la Terre*. In 1925 another publisher asked him to write a novel. The task seemed to him beyond his power, but he set about it courageously. Then, one day, the young man awoke to find himself famous; and soon after this the publication of *Le Voyageur sur la Terre* in *La Nouvelle Revue Française* was greatly praised.

In 1927, *La Revue Hebdomadaire* published *Adrienne Mesurat*, which was warmly appreciated by a vast public, fellow writers, and the critics. Almost immediately Green received in London, from Hugh Walpole's hands, the Bookman's Prize, and the same year his book (translated under the title of *The Closed Garden*) was selected for the Book of the Month. I have been told that Paul Morand, who noticed in the United States the effect of this reward upon the success of *The Closed Garden*, jokingly wrote to Julien Green (soon after Lindbergh's triumphant flight): 'I congratulate you on crossing the Atlantic.'

What is the fundamental substance of these books? They offer dream photographs mingled with evocations of reality, both expressed in pure classical language. The characters created by Green and their least gestures remain imprinted in memory. Sometimes one feels Green to be carried away by a power he has had to control, as one feels equally that the plan of his book evolved as the characters themselves and the situations opened out. He one day assured me that he finds it impossible to use in a narrative events which he has witnessed, but that often an object or landscape he has only glanced at becomes the starting-point of a lengthy work. This mingling of the real with the fictitious often results in haunting visions. Their voicing becomes a sort of magic.

In contrast with most writers, Julien Green leads a very

retired life; it is almost impossible to meet him. He prefers to human society that of pictures, Nature, and animals.

Although he is by temperament full of tenderness, one feels at the back of this his tenacious will. He seems more under subjection to his work than the ordinary run of living writers. His application to his task is also pronounced, so that we may expect from his very personal talent many more works through which his exceptional gifts will further assert themselves.

THE END

INDEX

The abbreviations 'f.' and 'ff.' indicate that the reference is to the page designated and, respectively, to that next following or to the two next following.

Abel, 99
Académie Française, the, 88, 114, 129, 143 f., 250, 260
Accent, Périgord, 247; Toulousian, 251
Action Française, 129, 145
Adam, Madame Hippolyte, 109, 110 f.
Adélaïde du Guesclin, 243
Adriatic Sea, the, 235
Adrienne Mesurat, 302
Aegean Sea, the, 246
Aimery de Pierrebourg, Marguerite (Thomas-Galline), Baronne (1858–), writer and mistress of salon, 247–254
Ain, 245
Albaret, Odilon, husband of Céleste, 194, 196, 197, 201, 202
Albert, king of Saxony (1873–1902), 2
Albertine Disparue, 182, 196–201, 203, 213
Alexander III, tsar of Russia (1881–1894), 15
Algeria, 48, 120
Algiers, 119 f.
Alsace, 218
Alvarez, Luis (1836–1901), Spanish painter, 50
American Field Service, 301
Amphion (Haute-Savoie), 277
Angling, 86
Annunzio, Gabriele d' (1863–), Italian writer, 235–241, 253
Antwerp, 220
Apollinaire, Guillaume (1880–1918), poet, 284
Arcachon, 240
Arc de Triomphe, the, 248

Argentina, 89
Argyll House, 274
'Ariel' (Jean Cocteau), 116
Arman de Caillavet, Albert, 76 ff.
Arman de Caillavet, Léontine, friend of Anatole France, 68, 70–97, 101, 103, 104, 108, 137 f., 242
'Art for Art's sake,' 296
Asquith, Herbert Henry, Lord Oxford and Asquith (1852–1928), British minister, 270
Astor, William Waldorf (1848–1919), 270
Aubépin, Henry (1869–), barrister, 114
Aubernon, Madame, 79, 92, 128
Austria, 239
Auteuil, 24, 265

Babinski, Joseph (1857–), physician, 114
Bach, Johann Sebastian (1685–1750), organist and composer, 217, 219, 221
Baignières, J., 207
Baldwin, Lucy (Ridsdale), 272
Baldwin, Stanley (1867–), British minister, 272
Balfour, Arthur James Balfour, first Earl of (1848–1930), British minister, 266–275
Balkan War, 240
Barbey d'Aurevilly, Jules-Amédée (1808–1889), novelist, 293
Barcelona, 224
Baroche, Ernest, 125
Baroche, Pierre-Jules (1802–1870), politician, 125

INDEX

Barrès, Maurice (1862–1923), man of letters, 141, 238 f., 260, 268, 269, 280
Bartet, Madame (Jeanne-Julia Regnault, 1854–   ), actress, 250
Barthou, Louis (1862–1934), politician, 268, 269, 278
Barthou, Madame Louis, 278
Bataille, Henry (1872–1922), dramatist, 225
Battle of Flowers, the, 36
Baudelaire, Pierre-Charles (1821–1867), romantic poet, 296
Baudry, Paul (1828–86), painter, 225
Bayeux, 37
Bayreuth, 264
Beaumarchais, Pierre-Augustin Caron de (1732–99), dramatist, 220
Bêche, clerk, value of his report, 224
Beethoven, Ludwig van (1770–1827), composer, 4, 221
Béhaine, René, novelist, 82
Belgium, 220
Bellagio, 278
Belleau, 123 f.
Belle-Isle, 56
Benedict, Saint, 49 f.
Bérard, Étienne, 243
Bérard, Léon, 243
Béraud, Jean (1849–   ), painter, 51, 114
Bergson, Henri-Louis (1859–   ), philosopher, 45, 205
Berlin, 22, 293
Bernard, Claude (1813–1878), physiologist, 227
Bernhardt, Maurice, 56 f.
Bernhardt, Madame Maurice (Princess Terka Yablonowska), 43 ff., 51
Bernhardt, Sarah (1844–1923), actress, 43, 44, 51–59, 147, 295 f.
Bernstein, Henry (1876–   ), dramatist, 253
Berry, Walter, president of the American Chamber of Commerce at Paris, 183, 212
Bersot, Pierre-Ernest (1816–1880), director of the École Normale Supérieure, 120
Berthier brothers, bankers, 229
Bertrand, J. L., translator, 271 f.
Besançon, 120
Better demi-monde, a, 137
Beucler, André, writer, 292, 293
Bibesco, Prince Antoine (1878–   ), Roumanian diplomat, 211
Bibesco, Prince Emmanuel (d. 1917), 211
Bibesco, Marthe Lucie (Lahovary), Princess, 211
Biblical scenes, 261
Bibliothèque Nationale, the, 29
Billy, Robert de (1869–   ), diplomat, 213–216
Bize, Doctor, physician, 196–202
Bizet, Jacques, 207
Black woman, vision of the, 202
Blake, William (1757–1827), English poet and painter, 301
Blanche, Jacques-Émile (1861–   ), painter, 170, 174, 262–265
Blocqueville, Louise-Adélaïde d'Eckmühl (1815–1892), Marquise de, 226 f.
Blocqueville, Marquis de, aide-de-camp, 227
Blois, 248
Blowitz, Henry Opper de (1825–1903), journalist, 39 f.
Blum, René, 209
Boileau-Despréaux, Nicholas (1636–1711), critic and poet, 243, 297
Bois, the, 123, 281
Bois, Élie-Joseph, editor of *Le Petit Parisien*, 170 ff., 204
Boldini, Giovanni (1842–1931), Italian-French painter, 114, 247
Bonaparte, Lucien (1775–1840), 67
Bonaparte, Princesse Mathilde (1820–1904), 67, 69, 244
Bonnard, Abel (1883–   ), writer, 175, 250
Bonnat, Léon-Joseph-Florentin (1833–1922), painter, 263

INDEX

Bookman's Prize, the, 302
Books and friendship, 214 f.
Bossuet, Jacques-Bénigne (1627–1704), prelate, 142
Bouilhet, Louis (1822–69), poet, 293
Boulanger, Marcel, 207
Bourdet, Édouard (1887–   ), dramatist, 294
Bourget, Paul (1852–   ), novelist, 273
Boutroux, Émile (1845–1921), philosopher, 45
Boyer, Paul, director of the School of Oriental Languages, 41
Boylesve, Madame, 255, 256
Boylesve, René (1867–1926), novelist, 82, 173 f., 250, 254–257
Brancovan, Princesse de, 277
Brandes, Georg Morris Cohen (1842–1927), Danish writer, 82 ff.
Brandès, Marthe (1862–1930), actress, 147
Brantwood, 156
Bravais, Auguste (1811–1863), physician, 123 f.
Brazza, Pierre-Paul Savorgnan de (1852–1905), explorer, 130
'Brazzaville,' 130
Briand, Aristide (1862–1932), politician, 79, 85 f., 268, 269, 297
Brindeau, Mademoiselle, actress, 90 f.
Brisson, Madame Adolphe (Yvonne Sarcey, 1869–   ), essayist, 153
Broutchoux, striker, 86
Brunswick, Duke of, 229
Brussels, 219 f.
Bugatti firm, the, 292
Bulteau, Madame, 113, 145, 148
Butter, hunt for, 268

Cabourg, 35, 36 ff., 160–167, 172
Cadet de Beaupré, Phidias, educator, 48
Cain, 99
Cain, Henri (1859–   ), painter and dramatist, 54, 55

Calmann-Lévy, publisher, 74
Calmette, Gaston (1858–1914), editor of *Le Figaro*, 160, 161, 253
Camouflage service, 261
Camp, *see* Du Camp
Capian, 80, 93
Capus, Alfred (1858–1922), dramatist, 248 f.
Caran d'Ache, *see* Poiré
Carmagnole, La, 271
Carnival, the, 32
Caro, Elme-Marie (1826–1887), professor of philosophy, 227
Carolus-Duran (Charles Durand, 1837–1917), painter, 45, 46–51, 225
Carolus-Duran, André, son of Madame Scheikévitch, 98 f.
Carolus-Duran, Marie-Anne, wife of Georges Feydeau, 51
Carolus-Duran, Pierre, composer, 45
Carrière, Eugène (1849–1906), painter and lithographer, 215
Cartouche, 288
Casella, Alfredo (1883–   ), Italian musician, 220
Casella, Alfredo, Italian violoncellist, 220
Castellane, Boni, Marquis de (1867–1932), social celebrity, 40, 230–234
Castellane, Marquise de, née Périgord, 231, 233 f.
Catalonia, 224
Cathedrals, 37, 156 f., 240 f.
Cavaillé-Coll, Aristide (1811–1899), organ-builder, 219, 221, 222, 223, 224 f., 227
Cavaillé-Coll, Dominique (1771–1862), organ-builder, father of the preceding, 224, 225
Cavaillé, Jean-Pierre (1740?–1815?), organ-builder, father of the preceding, 224
Céleste, servant of Marcel Proust, 171, 184, 190, 191, 194–203
Chadourne, Marc (1895–   ), writer, 292

INDEX

Chaliapine, Feodor Ivanovitch (1873–), Russian singer, 165
Chamfort, Nicolas-Sébastien Roch (1741–1794), called de, 220
Champion, Honoré, bookseller and publisher, 107
Champs-Élysées, the, 23, 24, 34, 35, 207
Chant du Printemps, 281
Charles VII, king of France (1422–1461), 142
Charles IX, king of France (1560–1574), 82
Charles X, king of France (1824–1830), 228 f.
Charmes, 286
Chateaubriand, François-René-Auguste, Vicomte de (1768–1848), writer, 144, 279, 293
Châtelain, 'godson' of Sarah Bernhardt, 55 f.
Chat Noir, the, 39
Chénier, André-Marie de (1762–1794), poet, 40
Chevassu, Francis (1862–1918), literary editor, 161
China, 292
Choiseul, Madame de, friend of Rodin, 104 ff.
Chopin, Frédéric-François (1809–1849), Polish composer and pianist, 277
Cinema, the, 40, 61
Ciro's restaurant, 190 ff.
Civil War, the, 300
Città Vecchia, 49
Clairin, Georges (1843–1920), painter, 52
'Claude de France,' nickname of Debussy, 238
Clemenceau, Georges (1841–1929), minister, 229
Clicquot, François-Henri (1728–1791), organ-builder, 223
Cocteau, Jean (1891–), writer, 114 f., 116 f., 135, 136, 152, 165, 167, 170, 253, 282–285, 286
Colefax, Lady Sibyl, 273, 274

Coll, Mademoiselle, wife of Jean-Pierre Cavaillé, 224
Colonial Office, the, 284
Comaedia Illustré, theatrical monthly, 170
Comédie Française, the, 29, 149. *See* Théâtre Francaise
Commune, the, 148 f., 226
Connaissance de la Déesse, 287
Conservatoire des Musées Nationaux, 224
Constant de Rebecque, Henri-Benjamin (1767–1830), writer, 274
Convention, the, 223
Conversation, value of, 288
Coppée, François (1842–1908), poet, 126, 148 f., 225
Corneille, Pierre (1606–1684), dramatist, 31, 121
Cotte, Robert de (1656–1735), architect, 223
Couane, striker, 86
Couchaud, R. L., 82, 106
Coulommiers (Seine-et-Marne), 93
Courtray, 206
Cowley, Malcolm (1898–), translator and journalist, 290
Crainquebille, 107
Crémieux, Benjamin, 182
Croisset, 293
Croizette, Pauline, wife of Carolus-Duran, 50 f.
Crozat, frame-maker, 132
Cruppi, Jean (1855–1933), advocate, 42
Curie, Marie (Sklowdowska) (1867–1934), scientist, 131
Curie, Pierre (1859–1906), scientist, 131
Cyrano de Bergerac, 118

Dadaisme, 264
Dalou, Jules (1838–1902), sculptor, 244
Dancourt, Florent Carton, Sieur d'Ancourt, called Dancourt (1661–1725), dramatist, 121

INDEX

Danube, the, 246
Dates, 265
Daudet, Alphonse (1840–1897), novelist, 123
Daudet, Léon (1868–   ), journalist, 127
Daudet, Madame Léon (Marthe Allard), 145
Daudet, Lucien, 170, 212
Daudet, Philippe, 145
David, Jacques-Louis (1748–1825), historical painter, 49
David d'Angers, Pierre-Jean (1788–1856), sculptor, 40
Davoust, Louis-Nicolas (1770–1823), marshal, 226
Deauville, 256
Debussy, Claude (1862–1918), composer, 238, 264
Deffand, Marie de Vichy-Chamrond, Marquise du (1697–1780), 254
Degas, Edgar (1834–1917), painter and engraver, 263
De Ingres à Degas, 264
Delacroix, Ferdinand-Victor-Eugène (1799–1863), painter, 244
Dennery, Adolphe (1811–1899), dramatist, 122 f.
De Profundis, 44
Déroulède, Paul (1846–1914), writer and politician, 126
Deschalais, Pauline, 119 f.
Deschanel, Paul (1855–1922), politician and writer, 130
Destouches, Philippe Néricault (1680–1754), dramatist, 243
Detourbet, Jeanne, 122
Diaghilev, Serge de (1872–1929), director of the Ballet Russe, 159
Didier, Charles (1805–1864), man of letters, 122 f.
Dieulafoy, Jeanne (Magre) (1851–1916), wife of the succeeding, 60
Dieulafoy, Marcel (1844–1920), archeologist, 60
Digne (Basses-Alpes), 243

Dijon, 225
Dinniss, janitor, 5, 13, 20
Diogène le chien, 250
Disillusionment, 254 f., 282
Divination, artistic, 283
Doderet, André, writer, 82
Donnay, Maurice (1859–   ), dramatist, 250
Dorchain, Auguste (1857–   ), poet, 225
Dostoievsky, Feodor Mikhailovitch (1822–1881), Russian novelist, 159
Doucet, dressmaker, 123
Douglas, Anabel, 272
Drags Day, 36
Dream photographs, 302
Dreyfus, Robert (1873–   ), writer, 82, 207 ff., 253
Dreyfus scandal, 137, 245
Du Bos, Charles (1882–   ), essayist, 174
Du Camp, Maxime (1822–1894) writer, 293
Du Côté de chez Swann, 162, 168, 170–182, 183, 204, 208, 209 f., 212
Dumas, Alexandre, the younger (1824–1895), dramatic author and novelist, 91, 225
Dumas, Madame Alexandre, 114
Duncan, Isadora (1877–1927), dancer, 114
Dupanloup, Félix-Antoine-Philibert (1802–1878), bishop of Orléans, 118
Dürer, Albrecht (1471–1528), German painter and engraver, 29
Duruy, Victor (1811–1894), historian, 129
Duse, Eleonora (1859–1924), Italian actress, 235
Duval, Amaury, painter, 131 f.

École Nationale des Arts Décoratifs, 296
École Normale, the, 118, 120
École Polytechnique, the, 222
Éditions de luxe, 294
Eiffel Tower, the, 3

INDEX

El Greco, 160
Elizabeth (1864–1919), princess of Hesse, wife of Grand Duke Serge of Russia, 26
Ellebeuse, Clara d', 46
Elliptic style, the, 283
Emma, housemaid, later housekeeper, 103, 107 ff.
Ems, 35
Engel, Madame, 119, 151
England, 262, 264, 271
En Mémoire des Églises Assassinés, 157
Érard, Madame, 228
Eugénie, Empress, 244
Eurotas, the, 239
Exercise books, Lemaître's, 149
Exhibition of 1878, 227; of 1900, 43; French, at Moscow, 2 f.
Extemporization, 237

Fabre, Lucien, writer, 292
Faivre, Abel (1867–   ), painter, 85
Falempin, striker, 86
Fan-fan la Tulipe, 271
Fantin-Latour, Ignace (1836–1904), painter, 263
Fargue, Léon-Paul (1878–   ), essayist, 42, 287
Fauré, Gabriel (1845–1924), composer, 42, 65
Faust, 121
Fernandez, Ramon, writer, 292
Ferrero, Guglielmo (1871–   ), Italian historian, 79
Ferval, Claude, pseudonym of Baronne Aimery de Pierrebourg, 254
Fétis, François-Joseph (1784–1871), Belgian composer, 219
Feydeau, Georges (1862–1921), playwriter, 51
Fire-Bird, legend of the, 43
Fires, 12, 16 f.; pretended, 55
First Love, 159
Fiume, 241
Flament, Albert (1877–   ), writer, 292

Flaubert, Gustave (1821–1880), novelist, 69, 123, 293 f.
Flers, Robert de (1872–1927), dramatist, 207
Flipote, 147
Florence, 192
Foch, Ferdinand (1851–1929), marshal of France, 245
Fontaine, Arthur (1860–1931), politician, 287
Forain, Jean-Louis (1852–1931), caricaturist, 68, 114, 247, 250, 258–262, 265
Four Sergeants, the, 116
Foyot's, 51, 225 f.
Fräulein, the, 12
Français, François-Louis (1814–1897), landscape painter, 50
France, Anatole (1844–1924), writer, 128, 134, 147, 225, 243, 272; connection with Madame Arman de Caillavet, 71–112; personal appearance, 72; voice, 72; full of contradictions, 75 f.; dinner in his honour, 82 ff.; trip to the Argentine, 89 ff.; death of Madame Arman, 95 ff.; on Cain and Abel, 99; trip to Saint-Quentin, 100 f.; 'goddesses from Hades,' 103–111; reconciliation with Lemaître, 136–145; last years and death, 111 f.
Francia, 245 f.
Franciscan friars, 49 f.
François, valet, 90, 104
Freedom, 21
French Academy, *see* Académie Française
French Revolution, the, 223
Fuller, Loie (1869–1928), actress, 3, 79

Gaillac (Languedoc), 224
Gallimard, publisher, 197, 297
Gambetta, Léon (1838–1882), democratic leader, 243
Ganay, Marquis de, 268
Ganay, Marquise de, 268
Garancière, Marquis de, 222

INDEX

Gautier, Théophile (1811–1872), critic and novelist, 293
Gazette des Beaux-Arts, 29
'Gégé,' 68
Gélu, Jacques (1369–1432), archbishop of Embrun, 142
Genoa, 241, 287
Georgia, 300
Gide, André (1869–   ), writer, 286
Gillouin, René (1881–   ), essayist, 150
Girardin, Émile de (1806–1881), journalist, 123
Giraudoux, Jean (1882–   ), writer, 292, 296
Girdle-maker's advertisement, 193
Gluck, Christopher Willibald (1714–1787), German operatic composer, 4
Gobineau, Comte Joseph-Arthur de (1816–82), diplomat and Orientalist, 227
'Goddesses from Hades,' 106, 110, 111
Goethe, Johann Wolfgang von (1749–1832), German poet, 279
Goloubeff, Madame Victor de, 82
Goncourt, Edmond (1822–96), novelist, 69, 127, 295
Goncourt, Jules (1830–1870), novelist, 69, 127, 295
Goncourt Prize, 192, 293
Gontcharoff, Ivan Alexandrovitch (1812–1891), Russian novelist, 159
Gosse, Edmund (1849–1928), English poet and critic, 273
Gothic art, 289
Gougy, bookseller, 140
Goujon, Pierre, deputy, 245
Gounod, Charles-François (1818–93), composer, 221, 222, 228
Gourmont, Rémy de (1858–1915), writer, 102 f.
Gousset, Thomas (1792–1866), archbishop of Rheims, 122
Gramont, Armand, Duc de (1879–   ), 269
Grande Chaumière Studio, 301

Grand Prix, the, 36
Grasset, Bernard (1881–   ), publisher, 209, 291 f., 297
Greece, 98
Green, Julien, or Julian (1900–   ), writer, 300–303
Gregh, Fernand (1873–   ), poet, 82, 207, 253
Grenoble, 120
Grey, Lady, 244
Greyhound farming, 239
Grisélidis, 295
Grosclaude, Étienne (1858–1932), journalist, 128, 249
'Guermantes,' the, 183
Guerne, Comtesse de, singer, 65 f.
Guiche, Duc de, *see* Gramont
Guitry, Lucien (1860–1925), actor, 107, 145, 147, 295

Hadinka disaster, the, 2
Hahn, Reynaldo (1874–   ), composer, 52, 65, 158, 172, 173, 268, 269, 270 f.
Halévy, Daniel (1872–   ), writer, 207
Hamlet, 295
Handel, George Frederick (1685–1759), German composer, 4
Hanotaux, Gabriel (1853–   ), historian and diplomat, 250
Hartington, Edward William Spencer Cavendish, Marquess of (1895–   ), 270
Hartington, Marchioness of (Lady Mary Cecil), 270
Haussonville, Gabriel-Paul-Othenin de Cléron, Comte d' (1843–1924), 227
Havre, 119
Hawes, Lady Millicent, *see* Sutherland
Hébrard, Adrien (1833–1914), journalist, 79, 103, 114, 115, 137, 138, 150, 158, 170–174, 243, 251 ff.
Hélène, dressmaker, 8 f.
Helleu, Paul (1859–1927), painter and engraver, 247

INDEX

Hellmann, Madame, 189
Henner, Jean-Jacques (1829–1905), genre-painter, 222
Henri-Robert (1863–   ), barrister, 250
Hérédia, José-Maria de (1842–1905), poet, 295
Hermant, Abel (1862–   ), man of letters, 250
Hervieu, Paul (1857–1915), man of letters, 250 f.
Hesse, Adolphe (1809–63), German organist and composer, 219
Hôtel des Quatre-Nations, 226 f.
Hôtel de Transylvanie, 226 f.
Houlgate, 160
Houssaye, Arsène (1815–96), man of letters, 121, 126
Houssaye, Henry (1848–1911), historian and critic, 129 f.
Hugo, Adèle (Foucher), 141
Hugo, Victor (1802–85), romantic poet, 41, 141, 279
Humbert, 225
Huysmans, Joris Karl (1848–1907), novelist, 260 f., 296

Ideas as servants, 289 f.
Improvisation, 281
Ingres, Jean-Auguste-Dominique (1780–1867), historical painter, 69, 100
Institut National de France, 218, 224, 227, 228
Intrepidity, 239
Irland, David, pseudonym of Julien Green, 301
Isabey, Eugène-Louis-Gabriel (1804–1886), painter, 228 f.
Ismaïl Pasha, viceroy of Egypt (1863–1879), 124
Italy, 192, 238, 274, 293

Japan, 246
Jardies, 243
Jardins sous la Pluie, 264

Jarre, Madame, 102
Jaurès, Jean (1859–1914), politician, 73, 243
Jesuits, 118
Joan of Arc, 141 ff., 229
Joan of Arc, by Anatole France, 142
Joffre, Joseph (1852–1931), marshal of France, 245
'Jojotte,' 52
Jones, Owen (1809–1874), English architect and writer on ornament, 289
Joseph II, Holy Roman Emperor (1765–1790), 225
Joséphine, confectioner, 130
Joséphine, servant of Anatole France, 87, 95, 97, 102
Joséphine, servant of Madame Scheikévitch, 151, 268
Jouchéry-sur-Vesle, 240
Joyce, James (1882–   ), British writer, 301
Judic, Anna Damiens, Dame (1850–1911), actress, 147

Karlsbad, 35
Kerensky, Alexander (1881–   ), Russian politician, 280
Kinen, Madame, singer, 66
Kipling, Rudyard (1865–   ), English writer, 40, 272
Krauss, Marie-Gabrielle (1842–1906), Austrian dramatic singer, 228
Kremlin, the, 2

La Béchellerie, 111
La Conspiration de Général Mallet, 149
'La Dame au Gant,' painting by Carolus-Duran, 50
L'Épopée, 39
La Ferrière, dressmaker, 123
La Jeune Parque, 286 f., 288
Lake Bellagio, 240
Lake of Geneva, the, 278
La Leçon d'Amour dans un Parc, 255
Lamartine, Alphonse-Marie-Louis (1790–1869), poet, 40 f.

INDEX

La Muette, 228
Languedoc, 224
La Nouvelle Revue Française, 207, 211, 296, 302
La Pérousse, 97 f.
La Princesse de Clèves, 291
La Revue de Paris, 70, 264
La Revue des Deux Mondes, 120, 250
La Revue Hebdomadaire, 120, 302
La Roseraie de l'Haÿ, 153
Larue's, 168
La Tour, Maurice Quentin de (1704–1788), portrait-painter, 100, 102
La Tour Saint-Jacques, 271
Laugoisan (Gironde), 80
La Veine, 248, 249
Lavery, Lady Hazel (Martyn), 273 f.
Lavery, Sir John (1856–   ), painter, 274
La Vie Parisienne, 39
Lavignac, Albert (1846–1916), pianist, 221
'L'Assassiné,' painting by Carolus-Duran, 50
Le Boeuf sur le toit, Cocteau's café, 284
Le Bourget, battle of, 125
Le Chant du Départ, 271
Leclercq, Paul, 207
Leconte de Lisle, Charles-Marie (1818–1894), poet, 225
Le Coq et l'Arlequin, 283, 284
Lecouvreur, Adrienne (1692–1730), actress, 222
Le Député Leveau, 147
L'Enfant à la Balustrade, 254
Lefébure-Wely, Louis-James-Alfred (1817–1870), organist and composer, 221
Lefèvre, Frédéric (1889–   ), novelist, 287
Le Figaro, 78, 126, 161, 164, 170, 172, 193, 211, 242, 245, 253, 258
Left Bank, the, 226
Le Gaulois, newspaper, 54
L'Inconnu, 250

L'Intransigeant, 293
Le Lys Rouge, 137
Lemaire, Madeleine (1845–1928), flower painter, 63–66, 92, 93, 154
Lemaire, Suzette, 65
Lemaître, Jules (1853–1914), man of letters, 109; personal appearance, 114 f.; voice, 115; interest in love affairs, 115; one of the 'Four Sergeants,' 116 ff.; reminiscences, 118–121; influenced by the Comtesse de Loynes, 121–133; conversation, 133 ff.; letters, 135 f., 138 f., 152 f.; friendship with Anatole France interrupted and resumed, 136–145; later years, 145–153; poems, 146; manuscripts, 148 f.; unfortunate liaison, 151 f.; walking-stick, 151 f.; death, 153
Lemaître, Madeleine, 120
Le Mariage Blanc, 147
Le Mariage de Télémaque, 147
Le Martyre de Saint Sébastien, 238
Lemerre, Alphonse (1838–1912), publisher, 40
Lemmens, Nicolas-Jacques (1823–1881), Belgian organist and composer, 219 f.
Le Monde où l'on s'ennuie, 227
Le Pater, 148 f.
Le Petit Parisien, 170
Le Petit Pierre, 87
Le Rire, 39
Le Roux, Henri, called Hugues (1860–1925), writer, 119
Le Sacre du Printemps, 265, 283
Les Cathédrales, 296
Les Débats, 121
Les Dieux ont Soif, 104, 110 f., 112
Les Foules de Lourdes, 261
Les Lettres, 82
Les Loups, 293
Lespinasse, Julie de (1732–76), letter-writer and leader of society, 254
Les Plaisirs et Les Jours, 156
Les Rois, novel, 136 f.; play, 147
Les Vivants et les Morts, 240

INDEX

Le Temps, newspaper, 102, 103, 129, 137, 150, 158, 170, 172, 251
Le Temps retrouvé, 185 f., 213
Ligue de la Patrie Française, 129
Lille, 47, 49, 50
Lindbergh, Charles Augustus (1902–   ), American aviator, 302
Lippman, Serge, pianist and composer, 189
Liszt, Franz (1811–1886), Hungarian composer, 221, 227 ff.
Literary prizes, 294
Livre d'Amour, 141
Lloyd George, David (1863–   ), British minister, 267
Lombardy, 238
London, 219, 264, 268, 272 ff., 297, 302
London Times, 40
Londres, 299
Lorrain, Jean (1855–1906), man of letters, 52
Loti, Pierre, see Viaud
Loubet, Émile (1838–1929), president of France, 225
Louis XIV, king of France (1643–1715), 223
Louis XV, king of France (1715–1774), 222
Louis-Philippe, king of France (1830–1848), 224, 227
Louisiana, 227
Louvre, the, 23, 49, 50, 132, 218, 244, 263
Loynes, Comte de, 125 ff.
Loynes, Comtesse de (Jeanne Detourbet), 121–147
Lulli, Giovanni Battista (1633–1687), composer, 222
'Luncheons Thermidor,' 158
Luxembourg, the, 226
Lycée Ampère at Lyons, 218 f.
Lycée Condorcet, the, 207
Lycée Janson, the, 28
Lyons, 218 f., 220, 221

'Machinka,' diminutive, 135 f., 150, 151, 152

Madeleine, the, 58, 221
Mademoiselle Aïssé et son Tendre Chevalier, 254
Mademoiselle Cloque, 254
Madrid, 50
Magnard, François (1837–1894), editor of Le Figaro, 126
Magre, Maurice (1877–   ), poet, 42
Maklakoff, Russian diplomat, 270, 280
Mallarmé, Stéphane (1842–1898), poet, 134 f., 295
Manet, Édouard (1833–1883), genre-painter, 263
Manon Lescaut, 227
Mantegna, Andrea (1431–1506), Italian painter, 263
Manuscripts, speculation in, 294
Marconi, Guglielmo (1874–   ), Italian inventor, 52
Marfa, gardener's wife, 16 f.
Margaret, 121
Marguery's, 93
Marie-Antoinette, queen of France, 225
Marne, battle of the (1914), 240, 246
Marseilles, 48
Masaryk, Thomas (1850–   ), president of the Czechoslovak Republic, 293
Massenet, Jules-Émile-Frédéric (1842–1912), composer, 51, 229
Mata-Hari, dancer, 131
Mathilde, Princesse, see Bonaparte
Matza, Madame, 51
Matza, Monsieur, 51
Maupassant, Guy de (1850–1893), novelist, 244, 296
Maupeou, Comtesse de, singer, 66
Mauriac, François (1885–   ), novelist, 291
Maurois, André (1885–   ), writer, 273, 291
Max, Édouard-Alexandre de (1869–1924), actor, 147
Mayer, Constance, friend of Prud'hon, 101, 140
Mazeline, Guy, novelist, 293

INDEX

Meaux, 126
Médan school (*Les Soirées de Médan*, 1880), 296
Medgé, Mademoiselle, 119
Medgé, Monsieur, 119
Médicis, Marquis de, Italian diplomat, 192
Menard de France, Madame, 119
Meyer, Arthur (1844–1924), newspaper manager, 52, 127
Milan, 240, 278
Milhaud, Darius (1892–   ), composer, 284
Moderation, taste for, 60
Modernism, 284
Moissenet, Abbé, choirmaster at Dijon, 225 f.
Molière (Jean-Baptiste Poquelin, 1622–1673), dramatist, 134, 140
Money well placed, 249
Monsieur Teste, 288
Montaigne, Michel Eyquem de (1533–1592), essayist, 238
Mont-Cinère, 300
Montesquiou-Fezensac, Robert, Comte de (1855–1921), poet, 212, 215
Montherlant, Henry Millon de (1896–   ), writer, 291
Mont Valérien, 248
Morand, Eugène (1854–1930), painter and poet, 52, 295 f.
Morand, Paul (1888–   ), man of letters, 52, 200, 273, 291, 292, 295–300, 302
Moreau, Gustave (1826–1898), painter, 263
Moreux, Théophile (1867–   ), astronomer, 79
Morgan-Harjes Service, 301
'Morning Bulletins,' 148 f.
Moscow, 1–22, 26, 32, 39
Moskva-Rika, the, 33
Mozart, Wolfgang Amadeus (1756–1791), Austrian composer, 4 f., 65
Mucha, Alphonse (1860–   ), Czech painter and designer, 59

Mugnier, Arthur, cleric, 79, 268
Muller, Charles (1877–1914), editor of *Les Lettres*, 82
Munich, 73, 296
Murat, Princesse Lucien, 244, 250, 268
Muraton, Alphonse, painter, 131
Musset, Alfred de (1810–1857), poet, 40 f.
Mussolini, Benito (1883–   ), Italian minister, 293
Myrrha, story of, 122
Mystery plays, 296

Nabob, the, 123
Nanny, nurse, 5–13, 17 f.
'Nanny,' familiar name for Adrien Hébrard, 115, 138
Naples, 50, 102
Napoleon I, 33, 39, 141, 143
Napoleon, Prince (1822–1891), 123, 124 f., 126
Napoléon, Arthur, pianist, 220
National Guard, the, 222
Nattier, Jean-Marc (1685–1766), portrait-painter, 102
Nero, 49
Neuilly, 120
New York, 55
Nice, 36
Nicholas II, tsar of Russia (1894–1917), 2, 25
Nicholas, coachman, 9
Nieuwekerke, Alfred-Émilien, Comte de (1811–1892), sculptor, 221
Nikita, porter, 7 f., 9
Ninon et son Cortège, 254
Noailles, Anna (de Brancovan), Comtesse de (1876–1933), wife of Comte Mathieu, poetess, 42 f., 116 ff., 135, 150, 211, 239 f., 250, 253, 268, 269, 270, 276–282, 298
Normand, Jacques (1848–1931), writer, 250
Normandy, 35, 37
Notre-Dame de Bayeux, 37
Notre-Dame des Champs, 118

INDEX

Odéon, the, 225
Oise, the, 240
Oliver Twist, 301
Opéra Comique, the, 45, 147
Opéra Italien, the, 99 f.
Oporto, 220
Order, need of, 299
Orléans, 118, 142, 229
Oxford outlook, 296

Padua, 50
Pailleron, Édouard (1834–1899), dramatist, 227
Painlevé, Paul (1863–1933), mathematician and politician, 88, 268, 269, 270
Palais Mazarin, the, 229
Palais Royal, the, 286
Paléologue, Maurice (1859–   ), diplomat, 250
Palestine, 274
Paranzallas, 235
Parc Monceau, 243
Parma, 238
Parny, Évariste-Désiré de Forges, Vicomte de (1753–1814), poet, 140
Passy, 24, 256
Pastiches et Mélanges, 157, 161, 164, 195
Pater, Walter (1839–1894), English writer, 296
Penguin Island, 84
Père-Lachaise, cemetery, 41
Perrin, Pierre (1620–1675), man of letters, 222
Pescara, 235
Pétain, Henri (1856–   ), marshal of France, 245
Petrovskoye Rasumovskoye, 15 f.
Piave, the, 246
Picasso, Pablo (1881–   ), Spanish painter, 283
Piero della Francesca (1416?–1492), Italian painter, 214
Pierrebourg, *see* Aimery de Pierrebourg
Pierre-Quint, Léon, critic, 209

Pirandello, Luigi (1867–   ), Italian dramatist, 204
Pisa, 238
Pisanello, Vittore (Antonio Pisano, ca. 1380–ca. 1456), Italian engraver, 186
Planté, François (1839–1934), pianist and composer, 228 f.
Pliny the Elder, 98
Pliny the Younger, 98
Poe, Edgar Allan (1809–1849), American poet, 289
Poincaré, Henry (1854–1912), mathematician, 87 f.
Poiré, Emmanuel (1858–1909), called Caran d'Ache, cartoonist, 39
Politics, discussion of, 32, 52
Pollaiuolo, Antonio (1429–1498), Italian painter and sculptor, 238
'Polybe,' pseudonym of Joseph Reinach, 245
Polyeucte, 31, 228
Pompadour, Marquise de (1721–1764), 244
Porché, François (1877–   ), poet, 82
Porto-Riche, Georges de (1849–1930), dramatist, 295
Post-War manners, 233, 256
Pozzi, Samuel-Jean (1846–1918), physician, 52
Prado, the, 50
Pragins, 126
Prague, 293
Prejudices and virtues, relation between, 248
Pre-Raphaelites, 295
Prévost d'Exiles, Antoine-François (1697–1763), novelist, 227
Primoli, Count Joseph, Roman patrician, 67–70, 79, 235
Primont, Baronne de, 250
Prix Goncourt, 192, 293
Prizes, literary, 294
Production the enemy of meditation, 290
Proust, Marcel (1871–1922), writer, 35,

316

INDEX

264, 273, 297; personal appearance, 154 f.; voice, 155; like no one else, 155; translator of Ruskin, 156 f.; trip to Rouen Cathedral, 156 f.; meeting with Madame Scheikévitch, 158 ff.; at the Cabourg Casino, 160–164; conversations and misunderstandings, 164–167; *Du Côté de chez Swann,* 167–176; narrative summing up his later work, 176–182; importance of this summary, 182; friendship with Walter Berry, 183; passion for reaching the truth about people, 184 ff.; daily way of life, 186 f.; at the Trianon, 187–190; evening at Ciro's, 190 ff.; last days, 192–203; criticism and letters, 203–216

Proust, Robert, professor of anatomy in the University of Paris, 197, 198, 199, 200, 202 f.

Prouté's, 107

Prud'hon, Pierre-Paul (1758–1823), historical and portrait painter, 101, 102, 110, 140

Publicity, literary, 291–294

Publicity articles, 294

Quatre Sergents de la Rochelle, 116
Queen Victoria, 273
Quotations, game of, 242 f.

Rabaud, Henri (1873–   ), composer, 207

Rachel (Élisa Felix (1821–1858), called), tragedienne, 131

Racine, Jean-Baptiste (1639–1699), tragic poet, 134, 243

Radiguet, Raymond (1903–1923), novelist, 291

Ranc, Arthur (1831–1908), writer and politician, 225, 226

Ravel, Maurice-Joseph (1875–   ), composer, 42

Ravenna, 238

Reading and writing things of the past, 291

Reboux, Madame Caroline, 158

Reboux, Paul (1877–   ), writer, 158

Régnier, Henri de (1864–   ), poet and novelist, 296

Reinach, Adolphe, archeologist, 245

Reinach, Joseph (1856–1921), publicist, 79, 242–246, 273

Rembrandt (1607–1669), Dutch painter and etcher, 29

Renaissance Theatre, the, 147

Renan, Ernest (1823–1892), philologist, 121, 126

Réveillon (Seine-et-Marne), 92

Révoltée, 147

Revue Bleue, the, 120, 121

Revue des Deux Mondes, the, 120, 250

Rheims, 122

Rheims, archbishop of, *see* Gousset

Rheims Cathedral, 240 f.

Riffault, General, 222

Ritz Hotel, 197, 201

Rivarol, Antoine (1753–1801), writer, 220

Rivière, Jacques, 200

Robert, Henri, *see* Henri-Robert

Robert, Louis de (1871–   ), novelist, 182, 209 ff.

Robespierre, Maximilien (1758–1794), revolutionist, 141

Rochecotte, 231

Rodin, Auguste (1840–1917), sculptor, 104 f., 244

Rohan, Duchesse Herminie de, 250

Roi de Lahore, 229

Roi des aulnes, 228

Rolland, Romain (1868–   ), writer, 150, 174

Romano, Colonna, actress, 57

Rome, 49, 68, 102, 293

Ronsard, Pierre de (1524–85), poet, 279

Rostand, Edmond (1868–1918), dramatist, 117 f.

Rostand, Maurice (1891–   ), novelist, 168, 170, 280

Rouen Cathedral, 156 f.

Rouen Museum, 265

INDEX

Roumania, 292
Royon, 136
Rubens, Peter Paul (1577–1640), Flemish painter, 220
Rubinstein, Madame Ida, actress, 238
Ruskin, John (1819–1900), English critic of art, 156 f.
Russia, 1–22
Russian ballets, 159, 167, 265
Russian literature, 159
Russian Revolution, the, 280

Saint-Aubin, Mademoiselle, piano teacher, 229
Saint-Aygulf, 47
Saint-Denis Basilica, 224 f.
Sainte-Beuve, Charles-Augustin (1804–1869), poet and critic, 123, 140 f., 144, 222
Sainte-Foy, convent at Neuilly, 120
Saint-Marceaux, Madame de, 113 ff., 145
Saint-Marceaux, Monsieur de, 113
Saint Mary's Institute, Moscow, 4
Saint Philippe du Roule, church of, 97
Saint-Quentin, 100 f., 102
Saint-Saëns, Charles-Camille (1835–1921), composer, 221, 223
Saint-Sulpice, church, 217, 221, 222
Salle, Louis de la, 207
Samain, Albert (1859–1900), poet, 296
Samson et Dalila, 221
Sand, George (Armandine Dupin, Baronne Dudevant, 1804–1876), 244
Sardou, Victorien (1831–1908), dramatist, 52
Sargent, John Singer (1856–1925), American painter, 274
Satie, Erik (1866–1925), composer, 283
Savannah, 300
Savart, Félix (1791–1841), acoustician, 224 f.
Savoy, 278
Saxony, king of, *see* Albert
Sayama, 45
Scheikévitch, Madame Marie, childhood in Russia, 1–22; journey to Paris, 22 f.; girlhood in Paris, 24–45; enters society, 45; meets and weds Pierre Carolus-Duran, 45–52; divorce, 59; salon, 59–63; acquaintance with Gabriele d'Annunzio, 235–241; with Madame Arman de Caillavet, 69 ff., 79 ff., 91–95; with Lord Balfour, 267–275; with Sarah Bernhardt, 51, 57 f.; with Walter Berry, 183; with René Boylesve, 'friend beyond compare,' 254–257; with Carolus-Duran *père*, 47, 51; with Boni de Castellane, 232 ff.; with Jean Cocteau, 282–285; with Miss Douglas, 272 f.; with Gabriel Fauré, 42; with Jean-Louis Forain, 258–262; with Anatole France, 72–112; with René Gillouin, 150; with Rémy de Gourmont, 103; with Julien Green, 302; with Reynaldo Hahn, 270 f.; with Adrien Hébrard ('Nanny'), 103, 115, 138, 150, 158, 170–174, 251 ff.; with Rudyard Kipling, 272; with Jules Lemaître, 113–153; with Paul Morand, 294–297; with Anna de Noailles, 'marvellous child,' 42 f., 270, 276–282; with Count Joseph Primoli, 69 f.; with Marcel Proust, 154–216; with Joseph Reinach, 242–245; with Geoffrey Scott, 274; with Steinlen, 84 f.; with Paul Valéry, 286–291; with Widor, 217–229

Scheikévitch, Victor (d. 1914), barrister, 1, 176
Schirinsky-Chekmatov, Prince, 16, 18–21
Schirinsky-Chekmatov, Princess, 16, 18
Scholastica, Saint, 50
Schooldays in Paris, 26 ff.
Schubert, Franz Peter (1797–1828), Austrian composer, 228
Schwob, Marcel (1867–1905), writer, 295
Scotland, 274

318

INDEX

Scott, Geoffrey (1885-1929), English writer, 274
Scriabin, Alexander Nicholas (1872-1915), Russian composer, 41
Sea, the, 35 ff.
Sée, Germain (1818-1896), physician, 91
Ségur, Pierre, Marquis de (1853-1916), historian, 254
Seine, the, 97 f., 218
Sem, Georges Goursat (1863-), called, 247
Serenius, 121
Serge, Grand Duchess, *see* Elizabeth
Sesame and Lilies, 214 f.
Shelley, Percy Bysshe (1792-1822), English poet, 296
Sherrington, Madame, singer, 219
Sicard, François (1862-1934), sculptor, 41 f.
Sicily, 98
Siena, 238
Silvestre, Armand (1837-1901), writer, 295
Simon, Jules (1814-1896), philosopher and statesman, 90 f., 225
Simone, Madame, actress, 253
Société des Gens de Lettres, 251
Sokols Festival, the, 293
Sophocles, 116
Sorbonne, the, 121
Sorel, Cécile (1873-), actress, 147
Sorrento, 50
Souchon, François (1787-1857), painter and designer, 48
Souday, Paul (1869-1929), critic, 172
Sourdéac, Alexandre de Rieux, Marquis de (d. 1695), 222
Spain, 50
Sparta, 239
Speculation in books and manuscripts, 294
Spiral, the, in drawing, 259
Steinlen, Théophile-Alexandre (1859-1923), designer and painter, 84 ff.
Stettiner, 102

Strachey, Giles Lytton (1880-1932), English writer, 273
Strauss, Madame, 244
Stravinsky, Igor Fedorovitch (1882-), Russian composer, 283
Style a quality of vision, 206 f.
Subiaco, 49 f.
Sue, Eugène (1810-1857), novelist, 301
Sur-réalistes, 264
Sutherland, Millicent, Duchess of (Lady Millicent Hawes), 267, 269
Swann, 162, 168, 170-182, 183, 204, 208, 209 f., 212
Switzerland, 35
Symbolists, 295

Taine, Hippolyte-Adolphe (1828-1893), historian and critic, 126
Talleyrand-Périgord, Charles-Maurice de (1754-1838), Prince de Benevent, statesman and diplomat, 231
Tannhäuser, 264
Taverne de Paris, the, 84 f.
Taygetus, Mount, 239
Tellier, Jules (1863-1889), poet, 119
Tendres Stocks, 297
Thames, the, 273
Thames Embankment, the, 274
Tharaud, Jean (1877-), writer, 82
Tharaud, Jérôme (1874-), writer, 82
Théâtre Français, the, 31, 57, 121, 295. *See* Comédie Française
Théâtre Libre, the, 137
Thèbes, Madame de, pythoness, 130
Thé de Ceylan tea gardens, 43 ff.
Theism and Humanism, 271
Thiers, Louis-Adolphe (1797-1877), statesman and historian, 40, 222 f., 225
Thiers, Madame, 223
Thompson, Francis (1859-1907), English poet, 296
Tiarini, Alessandro (1577-1668), Italian painter, 106
Tinan, Jeande (1874-1898), writer, 207

INDEX

Tinayre, Marcelle Chasteau, Dame (1872–), novelist, 82
'Tochè,' nickname of Madame Bulteau, 135, 139
Toledo, 50
Tolstoy, Leo (1828–1910), Russian novelist, 14 f., 159, 244
Toulouse, 224, 225
Touraine, 135, 153
Tourbey, Madame de, 123 ff.
Touring Club, the, 82
Tourists, 35
Tout Paris, 39
Trarieux, Gabriel (1870–), writer, 207
Travers, 118, 136, 139, 149, 153
Trocadéro Palace, 227
Tronche, Monsieur, 200
Troubetzkoy, Prince Paul (1863–), Russian sculptor, 244
Tschaikovsky, Peter Ilitch (1840–1893), Russian composer, 14
Turgeniev, Ivan Sergeyevich (1818–1883), Russian novelist, 29, 159
Tyrol, the, 35
Tyrrell of Avon, William George Tyrrell, first Baron (1866–), 268 f.

Vaevara, cook, 7
Valentino, Rudolph (1895–1926), cinema star, 40
Valéry, Paul (1871–), poet, 286–291, 292
Vandal, Albert (1853–1910), historian, 126
Vandérem (Vanderheym), Fernand (1864–), dramatist, 253
Vandervelde, Émile (1866–), Belgian minister, 269
Vardar, the, 246
Variétés, 290
Varnishing Day, 47
Vaucouleurs, 229
Vaudoyer, Jean-Louis, 286
Vaudoyer, Madame, 244

Velasquez, Diego Rodriguez de Silva (1599–1660), Spanish painter, 50
Venice, 50, 136
Venizelos, Eleutherios (1864–), Greek minister, 270
Verdun, 301
Verlaine, Paul (1844–1896), poet, 41, 44, 103
Verne, Jules (1828–1905), novelist, 40
Versailles, 91, 92, 204, 223
Vesuvius, Mount, 98
Viaud, Louis-Marie-Julien (1850–1923), called Pierre Loti, 52
Vient de Paraître, 294
Villa Saïd, the, 87, 95, 103, 104, 138, 139
Villiers de l'Isle-Adam, Auguste, Comte de (1840–1889), symbolist, 295
Vincennes, 93
Vinci, Leonardo da (1452–1519), Italian painter and architect, 289
Viollet-le-Duc, Eugène-Emmanuel (1814–1879), archeologist, 289
Virginia, 300
Virginia, University of, 300, 301
Visconti-Venosta, Marquis, Italian diplomat, 269
Visitandines, chapel of the, 126
Vistula, the, 246
Vivonne, the, 206
Voltaire, François-Marie Arouet (1694–1778), called, 84, 243, 244
Vox humana, 285

Waldeck-Rousseau, Madame, 244
Wallace Collection, the, 106
Walpole, Hugh (1884–), novelist, 302
War and Peace, 159
Weimar, 221
Weiss, Jean-Jacques (1827–1891), critic, 121
Wells, Herbert George (1866–), English writer, 40
Whistler, James Abbott McNeill (1834–), American-English painter and etcher, 273

INDEX

White House in Chelsea, 272, 273, 274
Wicar Foundation, the, 49
Widor, Charles-Marie (1845–   ), organist and composer, 51, 217–229
Wiener, Jean, 284
Wiesbaden, 35
Wilde, Oscar (1856–1900), aesthete, 44 f., 296
Will, imposition of, 219 f.
World War, the, 55, 111, 116, 153, 174, 176, 245 f., 256, 261 f., 286, 292, 294, 297, 301
Worms-Barretta, Madame, 145
Worth, dressmaker, 123

X., Professor, 94

Yablonowska, Princess Terka, 43 ff.
Yeatman, Léon, 156, 157
Yeatman, Madeleine (Adam), 156, 157
Yser, the, 246
Yung, Eugène (1827–1887), editor of the *Revue Bleue*, 121

Z., Professor, 55, 56
Zamacoïs, Miguel (1866–   ), dramatist, 52
Zankévitch, General, commander of Russian troops in France, 187 ff.
'Zélide' (Madame de Charrière, 1740–1805), 274
Zola, Émile (1840–1902), novelist, 296